LARGE PRINT EDITION

My Daily Devotion

Stephen J. Carter

My Daily Devotion

God's Promises for Joyful Living

CONCORDIA PUBLISHING HOUSE · SAINT LOUIS

Library of Congress Cataloging-in-Publication Data

Carter, Stephen J., 1941
    My daily devotion: God's promises for joyful living /
Stephen J. Carter.—Large print ed.
    p. cm.
    ISBN 0-570-05816-3 (large print)
    1. God—Promises—Mediations. 2. Devotional calendars—
Lutheran Church. 3. Lutheran Church—Prayer-books and devotions—
English. 4. Large type books. I. Title.
BT180.P7 C37 2000
242'.2—dc 21   00-052381

2 3 4 5 6 7 8 9 10 11   11 10 09 07 07 06 05 04 03 02

Preface

In this devotional book, I offer to you God's promises for joyful living. He has strengthened my faith through His Word. In Scripture verse after Scripture verse, God has exposed my sin and pointed me to the cross of His Son, Jesus Christ for forgiveness. The writing has challenged me to open my heart and mind to His powerful, life-changing Gospel and to see His presence in the world of robins, mountains, family quarrels, church windows, baseball games, and prison cells.

As you read the devotions privately or in the family circle, read the Scripture section suggested because the devotional thoughts flow from the chosen verses. Before reading each devotion, take time to focus your thoughts and heart on the living God. Pray that He will use His words to point you to His Son. Pray that you will be receptive in your inner being to be shaped by His Word—convicted of sin, comforted with forgiveness, laid bare before Him, covered with the blood of Christ.

Hymn stanzas are used frequently as prayer thoughts. I rejoiced to discover how the hymns of God's people echo the words of Scripture and speak to the problems and joys of daily living. The hymns also remind us that personal and family devotions belong in the context of God's people gathering together around Word and Sacrament. In that spirit, the rhythm of the church year guides the devotional selections, though the church year doesn't match with the calendar year.

Modern life presents many difficulties, discouragements, and temptations. You and I struggle to live with faithfulness and compassion. I pray that these daily devotions will help to strengthen you in the Word as you receive God's promises for joyful living!

A Fearless New Year

Israel is afraid as they camp on the eastern banks of the Jordan River. Within eyesight, the Promised Land flows with milk and honey. But strong, hostile tribes rule Canaan. Israel must defeat these alleged giants. Moses has just dropped the bombshell that he will not enter the new land with them. They feel desperate without his leadership. They fail to seek God for courage and strength.

On the threshold of a new year, with the parties over, the noisemakers silent, and the business of daily living ahead, we need the words of Moses as greatly as Israel did. The events of the new year lie hidden from our gaze. Perhaps the international situation will worsen or nature will unleash its fury to destroy buildings and people. Perhaps your family will experience major troubles. Like Israel, we often face the future anxiously and fearfully. We too frequently fail to look to God for strength and courage.

But Moses reassures Israel. And we know that the God of Moses will likewise enter the new year with us. We have the even greater assurance that God's Son, born in Bethlehem's stable, permitted Himself to be forsaken by the Father so we might never be forsaken by God. Jesus experienced the fear and despair of being alone as He shouldered our burdens on Calvary. We can say with the confidence of Moses: "The LORD YOUR God ... will never leave you nor forsake you." (Deuteronomy 31:6). So bring on the new year, unknown, fraught with trials, filled with challenges, but marked by God's presence and promise. A fearless new year to all of you!

Prayer: Dear Lord, help me to face the new year trusting Your sure promises. Amen.

Trust the Lord for Help

What a struggle American farmers have endured in recent years, many losing their land or facing staggering debt and decreasing land values. Israel in David's day faced similar problems. Many righteous people saw the wicked prospering at their expense. They were filled with anger and worry. But the anger and worry only led them deeper into trouble.

We survey the past year and see many difficult and discouraging events. We cry out for help. All the while we notice that the wicked seem to be prospering. Anger fills our heart. "It's not fair. Why should they prosper while I struggle as I try to do what is right? Why, God, do You permit these things to happen?" Worry consumes us. "What will I do now? How can I make ends meet?" Anger and worry only lead us deeper into trouble. We feel helpless.

But the psalmist suggests that we trust the Lord for help. He knows that God alone gives the victory. True happiness comes from the Lord, not the desires of our hearts. Ultimately the wicked will destroy themselves while the Lord upholds the righteous. We wait patiently for the Lord to act.

God, our help in ages past and our hope for years to come, sent His Son, Jesus Christ, to live on this earth and die for the world's sins. He gives us an inheritance that will not fade. He freely gives us trust in His promises. Anger and worry aside, we trust the Lord for help now and eternally.

Prayer: We gather up in this brief hour The mem'ry of your mercies: Your wondrous goodness, love, and pow'r Our grateful song rehearses; For you have been our strength and stay In many a dark and dreary day Of sorrow and reverses.

Trust the Lord for Guidance!

We look to the new year with all sorts of plans and intentions. Relying on God's help, the psalmist wants us to trust the Lord for guidance.

The wicked scheme, plot, and manipulate. They know how to steal from others, amass land, and accumulate wealth. They seek and gain power over others and laugh at the helpless. They go their own way.

We deplore such conduct on the part of others and agree with the psalmist that the wicked should be punished. But do we not often chart our own course and resort to scheming and manipulating to get our own way for what we believe to be a good cause?

How beautiful the person who trusts the Lord for guidance. "Though he stumble, he will not fall, for the LORD upholds him with His hand." (Psalm 37:24). Admitting our waywardness, we place ourselves in the strong hands of the God who sent His only Son to go the way of the cross. Resting in Him, we seek God's guidance for the new year.

God supplies the direction in His Word. He leads us to glorify Him by serving others. We live the love of Jesus Christ on the job, in our homes and neighborhoods, in our community, and in our church. We will stumble because of our sin and weakness, but we will not fall because the Lord upholds us with His hand.

Prayer: Then, gracious God, in years to come, We pray your hand may guide us, And, onward through our journey home, Your mercy walk beside us Until at last our ransomed life Is safe from peril, toil, and strife When heav'n itself shall hide us.

Sleepless Nights?

Sleepless nights lately? Worried about work or school or family? Fretting about providing food for the table, meeting high mortgage payments, paying for college, setting aside enough savings for retirement? Stewing about people who unfairly criticize you and seem to prosper despite their disregard of God's commands?

The psalmist suggests: "Lie down and sleep in peace," because God alone makes us "dwell in safety" (Psalm 4:8). Aware of unfair treatment by others, prone to anger and resentment, sometimes depressed by worry, the psalmist discovers a peaceful rest in the sure protection and promises of God.

Sleepless nights may call for confession of sins—doubts, self-pity, resentment, bitterness, misguided reliance on self. Confession leads to God's peace and God's rest because the Obedient One, who slept in a boat amidst a storm, also went to the sleep of death to win the victory and bring lasting peace.

As Jesus woke from death, victorious over His enemies, so we wake, refreshed each day, from peaceful sleep in His protection, ready for a life of service until we awake in heaven to serve Him forevermore.

Problems remain. Worries abound. Evil appears to triumph. Long nights and tired eyes remain. Counting sheep gets old. But sleep beckons for the child of God—safe, forgiven, sustained, refreshed, quiet, and at rest, trusting in Christ Jesus.

Prayer: Oh, may my soul in thee repose, And may sweet sleep mine eyelids close, Sleep that shall me more vig'rous make To serve my God when I awake!

Troubled or Joyful about His Birth?

Herod was troubled at the news of a king's birth. He could not afford a pretender to his throne. So he sweet-talked the Wise Men, then prepared to slaughter the innocent children in Bethlehem.

Horrible, brutal—yet are we troubled at the Christ Child's birth? Since Eden and the raised fist of rebellion against God, we have an obsession for power and a desire to be king—king of the snow hill, king or queen of the family, top of the ladder at work. Sometimes we sweet-talk others to get our own way, and sometimes we resort to ruthless techniques. So we may well be uncomfortable at the birth of a Child who is King of kings and Lord of lords.

Herod was troubled, but the Wise Men were overjoyed. They saw the star at Bethlehem and rejoiced "with exceeding great joy." Their joy at finding the infant King led them to kneel in worship and to bring Him costly gifts. They claimed no kingship but honored Christ as King of their lives. God's good news filled them with joy.

Are you troubled like Herod or joyful like the Wise Men at Christ's birth? Confessing our desire to be kings, we look to God's revelation as He speaks to us in His Word, the water, the wafer and wine. He points us to a King who became a servant for us—born in a manger, nailed to a tree for our sins. God fills us with exceeding great joy. Our kingship discarded, we kneel to worship and bring the costly gifts of our very lives to Him.

Prayer: As with joyful steps they sped, Savior, to thy lowly bed, There to bend the knee before Thee, whom heav'n and earth adore; So may we with willing feet Ever seek thy mercy seat.

Arise, Shine!

I'll never forget the closing candle ceremony in the Cotton Bowl during Explo '72 in Dallas. Following a stirring message to take the evangelism zeal back home, each of the 85,000 youth and adult counselors in the audience lit a candle. The flames grew until the Texas night was aglow with the light. It was certainly symbolic of the Epiphany message of God to Zion through the prophet Isaiah: "Arise, shine!"

In Matthew's Gospel, the Wise Men saw the light of a special star and journeyed to Bethlehem to see the infant King. And the words speak to our hearts as well: "Arise, shine!" Hold up Jesus as the Light of the world for everyone to see.

Why are we to arise and shine? The world lies in darkness. Isaiah writes: "See, darkness covers the earth and thick darkness is over the peoples" (Isaiah 60:2). Israel had lived in the darkness of rebellion and ended up in the darkness of heathen Babylon. Today our world suffers from an energy crisis called sin, which extinguishes all lights.

How can we arise and shine? God has shined in our dark world with the light of His Son, Jesus Christ. He brought Israel home to Jerusalem and sent the Messiah in the fullness of time. In the darkness of Good Friday, Jesus, the Light of the world, could not be extinguished. Victorious and risen, He shines brightly as Savior and Lord. His Word illumines us. Drawing on that unfailing light each day, God shines through us with the light of His Son.

Prayer: Arise and shine in splendor, Let night to day surrender; Your light is drawing near. Above, the day is beaming, In matchless beauty gleaming; The glory of the Lord is here.

Jesus as the True Israel

The well-known story of the holy family's flight to Egypt tells us about much more than God's protection of the Christ Child. Matthew clearly presents Jesus as the true Israel. The original Israel (Jacob, son of Isaac, grandson of Abraham) fathered a great nation intended to be a blessing. But Israel failed miserably in rebellion and sin. Now God sends us His own Son to be the true Israel and hope of the world.

Note the comparisons. Pharaoh ordered the slaughter of all Hebrew male children. King Herod orders the slaughter of male infants under two years old in Bethlehem. God preserved Moses and Jesus. Matthew quotes Hosea 11:1: "Out of Egypt I called My Son." God led Israel out of Egypt through the mighty Exodus. He led Jesus out of Egypt and back to the Promised Land. God provided the Israelites manna and quail in the wilderness. Jesus fed 5,000 in the wilderness. God gave the Law on Mt. Sinai. Jesus preached a sermon on the mount. The parallels mount. Yes, Jesus is the true Israel.

Despite our frequent rebellion, God chooses us as His people. He frees us from our slavery in Egypt by the exodus of His suffering, death, and resurrection. He leads us through the waters of Baptism into the wilderness of temptation and the Promised Land of eternal life. He calls us out of darkness into His marvelous light and helps us shine for the world as part of the new Israel. In this Epiphany season, we praise and proclaim Jesus, called out of Egypt into Galilee, as the true Israel!

Prayer: Dear Father, thank You for the fulfillment of the Old Testament prophecies in the life, death, and resurrection of Jesus Christ, the true Israel. Amen.

Misguided Trust?

We live in a day of powerful weapons, nuclear submarines, laser beams, sophisticated computer technology, and deadly missiles. Raw force is pitted against raw force with boasts of superiority. We struggle to understand the meaning of modern military arsenals and pray that the world will not be reduced to ruins. We feel personally powerless.

The psalmist recognizes the importance of chariots and horses, the dreaded war machines of that day. Both Israel and her enemies possess armies and weapons. However, he lauds Israel for trusting not in chariots and horses but "in the name of the LORD our God" (Psalm 20:7). Conscious of the great Red Sea victory of Yahweh over Pharaoh's chariots and horses, aware of the stunning victories of Joshua and Gideon over seemingly superior forces, thankful for God's grace in his own life as commander and king, David relies on the powerful name of God, who will bring ultimate victory through the death and resurrection of His Son, Jesus Christ, the Suffering Servant. Nothing can stop the kingdom of God from bringing grace and salvation to a world in desperate need.

Empowered by God's forgiving love in Jesus Christ, we dare to speak His name to others in a world of mighty superpowers, knowing the Gospel will penetrate hungering hearts and the kingdom of God will continue to come with salvation.

Prayer: With might of ours can naught be done, Soon were our loss effected; But for us fights the valiant One, Whom God himself elected. Ask ye, Who is this? Jesus Christ it is, Of sabaoth Lord, And there's none other God; He holds the field forever.

The Taste Test

Several years ago, a major soft drink company changed the formula of its most popular cola. Immediately, strong reaction erupted from lovers of the old taste and from consumers of rival colas. The bottom line was not expensive advertising or colorful packaging but the taste test.

In today's Scripture verse, David suggests the taste test for experiencing the true God. He writes: "Taste and see that the LORD is good; blessed is the man who takes refuge in Him" (Psalm 34:8). David has experienced personally the mercies of God in his life—protected as a shepherd boy from wild animals, able to slay mighty Goliath, preserved from the jealous wrath of Saul. Now David looks for deliverance in the promised Messiah and asks others to taste the sure promises of the living God and find refuge in Him.

From the seed of David came the Messiah to experience life in our stead. He tasted rejection, ridicule, suffering, and death on a cross for the sins of a rebellious world. David's challenge rings out to us too. We admit that selfishness, materialism, and thrill-seeking leave a flat taste in our mouth. We turn quietly to the living Word of God, where we taste and see that the Lord is good.

We taste the body and blood of Jesus Christ in the bread and wine. And we know that for time and for eternity we have refuge in Him. The ultimate taste test never fails—for David or for us.

Prayer: I come, O Savior, to your table, For weak and weary is my soul; You, Bread of Life, alone are able To satisfy and make me whole. Lord, may your body and your blood Be for my soul the highest good!

A Path to the Future

In our world of rapid change, people spend great sums of money trying to discern the future. Futurism is a big business. Trends, forecasts, economic predictions abound. Fortune-tellers, astrologers, and palm readers market their shadowy views of the future. We feel we must find the right path for our lives. Who will guide us?

The psalmist knows where to turn. He recognizes that the Word of God is a lamp to his feet and a light to his path. Obedience to the Law of God marks the right path. But the psalmist also confesses the sins of his youth and his rebellious ways (Psalm 25:7). Going his own way leads only to confusion, fear, and uncertainty about the future.

God makes known His ways to us just as clearly today as He did to Israel of old. His Word reveals the Law, which is good and just and true. But the psalmist also remembers the Lord's great mercy, as he writes, "For You are God my Savior, and my hope is in You all day long" (Psalm 25:5). He clings to the forgiveness of a Covenant God who not only shows the way but sends His Son to be "the way, the truth, and the life" (John 14:6). Jesus walked the path of the Father all the way to Calvary, where He fully paid for the sins of the world.

We turn to God's Word, where we are reminded of what Christ has done for us. Trusting Him for salvation, we daily seek His ways and His paths. The future holds no fear because our journey will lead to the heavenly mansions.

Bring on rapid change. Bring on the future. Jesus Christ is our way.

Prayer: *You are the way; to you alone From sin and death we flee; And he who would the Father seek Your follower must be.*

A View from Alcatraz

I remember visiting Alcatraz, the former island prison in the San Francisco Bay. As part of the prison tour, we were invited to step into the solitary confinement vault and have the door briefly closed. I experienced total darkness and isolation. What would it be like to spend days or weeks alone in that darkness?

The psalmist knows the darkness of sin and rebellion, and the darkness of hiding in a cave from dangerous pursuers. But rather than succumb to paralyzing fear, he boldly proclaims, "The LORD is my light and my salvation" (Psalm 27:1). He remembers the Creator God who spoke the word that first brought light. He believes that God will ultimately shine in the world's darkness with the light of the Messiah.

From a human standpoint we have much to fear—the darkness of terrorism, violent crime, war, and perplexing personal problems. At times the darkness closes in on us.

Then the reassuring words of the psalmist flood our consciousness. We remember that the God who caused the light to shine out of darkness has shined in our hearts with the light of His Son, Jesus Christ. In the darkness of Good Friday, when it seemed that evil had triumphed, the Son of God died to pay for our sins so the light of salvation would continue to shine in an Easter world. Jesus, our Light, can penetrate every corner of darkness in our life, exposing and forgiving our sin, restoring hope and joy. Rekindled by the light of God's Word, we go forth to shine as lights in a dark world.

After that brief stay in solitary darkness, the Alcatraz door swung open, and eventually we walked out into a sunswept view of the bay. Similarly, the Lord has not left us in darkness.

Prayer: Dear Lord, lead me to Your eternal light! Amen.

Tunnel Vision Transformed

Some people suffer from an eye problem called tunnel vision. The eyes can only see straight ahead with no peripheral vision at all. So much of God's creation goes unseen. One cannot drive a car safely or participate successfully in athletics. With a world to see, reality lies only straight ahead.

Unfortunately, Christians often view God's church and the Christian life through tunnel vision. Reality is limited to my home, my work, and my church. I see no one else. I fail to see other Christians, other countries, other people in need of the Gospel. I insist that God operate only within my field of vision.

The psalmist widens our vision tremendously by speaking of "the ends of the earth." Israel often suffered from tunnel vision. Jonah suffered God's wrath by refusing to preach to Nineveh and trying to run in the opposite direction. But God's name and His praise reach "to the ends of the earth." He made the world. He sent His Son to die for the world. And He spreads His Gospel Word over all nations.

My tunnel vision broadens considerably when I hear about a wonderful Savior from the Japanese Lutheran Hour speaker or work with fellow Lutherans from South Africa and Tanzania or talk to enthusiastic Haitian students or learn of exciting Christian fellowship groups in Communist China. Indeed, God has made me a world Christian and transformed my tunnel vision into eyes that see a universe alive with His name and His praise.

Prayer: Can we whose souls are lighted With wisdom from on high, Can we to those benighted The lamp of life deny? Salvation! Oh, salvation! The joyful sound proclaim Till those of ev'ry nation Have learned Messiah's name.

Ready to Explain the Hope Inside

Outside: hopelessness. Inside: hope. I sit in a warm, comfortable family room looking out at a snow-covered lawn with barren trees and a wind-chill factor below zero. Outside are evils like homelessness (made all the worse by the cold), hunger, violence, abortion, homosexuality, immorality, opposition to Christianity, and a host of others. Outside: hopelessness.

But we also know God's hope. A fallen world redeemed by the blood of the Lamb without blemish; new birth into a living hope through the resurrection of Jesus Christ from the dead, an inheritance that can never perish, spoil, or fade; an incorruptible Word that stands forever; status as a chosen people. St. Peter's words are meant for our heart. Inside: hope.

So Peter writes to us the words of our text. We Christians live differently from the world. We, too, suffer, sometimes struggle, and live in the midst of hopelessness. But we have a living hope that generates a smile, a caring touch, a vitality and energy that shows. We know Christ as our Savior. We rejoice in Word and Sacrament. We treasure the fellowship of God's people. We eagerly anticipate eternal life in heaven.

All Peter asks: Be ready to explain the hope inside. Know how to talk about your faith, your God, your hope. Tell the story of God's faithfulness in your life. No fancy words needed. Use the Apostles' Creed. Use John 3:16. Use your favorite hymn. Use your own words. Practice on your family and Christian friends at the supper table, in the coffee hour, at church. Outside: hopelessness. Inside: hope. Let God help you bring that hope from inside to outside.

Prayer: *If you cannot speak like angels, If you cannot preach like Paul, You can tell the love of Jesus; You can say he died for all.*

Mr. Inside and Mr. Outside

Back in the 1940s, Army had an outstanding football team under Coach Red Blaik. Anchoring their undefeated team in 1946 were the "touchdown twins," Doc Blanchard and Glen Davis. Known as Mr. Inside and Mr. Outside, they combined powerful inside running with fleet, shifty, outside running.

Evangelism necessarily combines Mr. Inside and Mr. Outside. The target for evangelism is "first for the Jew" (Mr. Inside) and "then for the Gentile" (Mr. Outside). The powerful Gospel of salvation aimed first at the Jew, self-satisfied by birth into God's people, often self-righteous, sometimes entrenched in tradition. Church members today often fall into a similar category. The Gospel also aims at the Gentile, often nonreligious or idolatrous and immoral. The unchurched person today often displays similar characteristics.

Evangelism provides impressive power. The Greek word for *power* is related to our word "dynamite." Dynamite for the Jew. Look how God transformed the apostles into dynamic witnesses. Look how Saul was dramatically changed to Paul. Church members today are likewise transformed as they live in their Baptism and listen to God's Word.

Dynamite for the Gentile. The church grew by leaps and bounds as the Gospel changed people like the jailer at Philippi and his household. The same change occurs with the unchurched today as sin is exposed and needs are met in the death of Jesus Christ.

Whom does God tap as the messengers of evangelism? You and I minister to one another with the good news of Jesus Christ. God equips us to share the Gospel of Christ.

Prayer: Dear Lord, use me to reach those inside and outside the church with Your power unto salvation through Jesus Christ. Amen.

Encounters with Jesus: Andrew

Andrew—the story of his encounter with Jesus is a simple, powerful one that can help us as we seek to share the faith.

Andrews are needed to hear about Jesus. A little-known disciple of John the Baptizer sees the man from Nazareth and hears Him identified as the Lamb of God. He believes and rejoices. Before going out to witness, we see Jesus as the Lamb of God. By His grace we believe and rejoice.

Andrews are needed to follow Jesus. Andrew, having seen Jesus, asked where He was staying and followed Him to learn more. He obeyed and became one of Jesus' disciples. We also need to follow Jesus. Believing, we want to hear Him again and again. He makes us His disciples. We regularly grow through Word and Sacrament. We study the Word personally and in groups. We serve as Jesus leads.

Andrews are needed to bring others to Jesus. The minute Andrew left Jesus, he hurried to tell his brother, "We have found the Messiah." Then he brought Simon to Jesus. And Simon Peter became a powerful spokesman for the early church. Andrew: a quiet witness, a relatively unknown follower of Jesus, an important instrument of God's love.

God needs us also to bring a brother or sister to Jesus. He brought us to faith in our Baptism. We see Jesus, crucified and risen for us. We follow Him by hearing and obeying.

He provides us with power to witness. Very simply and quietly we go to the family member, the neighbor, the coworker, the friend and say, "We have found the Messiah." And we bring that person to Jesus through His church. Yes, Andrews are needed today. That means you and me.

Prayer: Lord Jesus, use me like Andrew to bring someone to You. Amen.

Encounters with Jesus: Philip

During the Epiphany season our eyes focus on Jesus as the Light of the world. In John's Gospel many people had encounters with Jesus. How did they respond?

Jesus finds Philip and simply says, "Follow Me." No other introductions. So far only Peter and Andrew have been called as disciples. An absolute call. No strings attached. No explanations given. Simply, "Follow Me."

Philip obeyed. Immediately he went to Nathanael and told him that they had found the Messiah. A response of faith in Jesus as Savior and witness to a friend.

Jesus likewise finds us and simply says, "Follow Me." He comes to us in our Baptism, in His Word, and in Holy Communion. "Follow Me." For life. Day-by-day. Without reservation. Although we may insist on knowing more details, on qualifying our answer, He continues calling, "Follow Me."

The motion picture *The Hiding Place* recounts a real call to discipleship. During World War II, the ten Boom family lives in the Nazi-occupied Netherlands, where Jews are being captured and exterminated. They are faced with the decision of whether to hide Jews in their home. They decide they must obey by hiding Jewish refugees in a secret room. Ultimately, when detected, they pay dearly.

God worked in Philip's heart to follow Jesus. He moved Corrie ten Boom and her family to do the same. And He sent His Son to pay for our sins by dying on the cross so we might follow Him as well.

Prayer: Jesus, still lead on Till our rest be won; And although the way be cheerless, We will follow calm and fearless; Guide us by your hand To our fatherland.

Encounters with Jesus: Nathanael

Philip finds Nathanael and tells him about Jesus of Nazareth, the Messiah. Rather than following Jesus immediately, Nathanael questions, "Nazareth! Can anything good come from there?" (John 1:46). Notice that Nathanael is a God-fearing man, "a true Israelite, in whom there is nothing false" (John 1:47). Yet he questions Jesus and His credentials.

In the motion picture *The Hiding Place*, while the ten Boom family decides to follow Jesus at great risk, the local pastor visits them and wrestles with the moral choices involved. He questions. Finally, out of fear he decides not to get involved.

But Jesus reaches out to a questioning Nathanael. Philip answers Nathanael with the simple invitation, "Come and see." As Nathanael approaches, Jesus identifies him as a true Israelite. Still questioning, Nathanael asks, "How do you know me?" Jesus replies, "I saw you while you were still under the fig tree before Philip called you" (John 1:48).

Now Nathanael responds in faith and is ready to follow, "Rabbi, You are the Son of God" (John 1:49). Jesus leads him on to greater understanding and greater service.

In the same way Jesus answers our many questions with the simple invitation, "Come and see." He then lets us know that He has called us by name. We belong to Him. He lived and died for us. He knows our potential for service. And He has a wonderful plan for our future as we follow Him. Our questioning is turned into a simple confession of faith, "Rabbi, You are the Son of God."

Prayer: *Dear heavenly Father, forgive my endless questioning of Your love, Your Word, and Your plan for my life. Help me like Nathanael to confess Jesus as Lord and Savior. Amen.*

Bearing Witness to the Lamb

All of us treasure events we have personally witnessed—a presidential inauguration, a World Series, or a Superbowl game. We freely tell about our experience.

John's Gospel records a dramatic moment in history. John the Baptist watches a man walk among the crowds of Israel. It is the long-awaited moment when the Messiah begins His public ministry. John, aware of this decisive moment, bears joyful witness: "Look, the Lamb of God, who takes away the sin of the world!" (John 1:29). The phrase "Lamb of God" echoes Isaiah 53, where the Messiah is described as a lamb led to the slaughter. Clearly John labels Jesus as the world's Savior.

Each of us has seen the Lamb of God, crucified and risen, in the pages of Holy Scripture. Through our lives of service and our words, we can say to others, "Look, the Lamb of God!" Yet we often fail. Our witness fades when the going gets rough. Or we fall into the trap of witnessing to ourselves—our faithfulness, our commitment—instead of to the Lamb of God.

John could have experienced the same witness problems. But God chose John, empowered him through the Word, and disciplined his life so his witness to the Lamb never faded. He focused steadfastly on the Lamb of God.

The same God who sent the Lamb to be sacrificed on our behalf also makes us His strong, unwavering disciples through a disciplined life of Word and prayer. Refusing honor for ourselves, we steadfastly bear witness to the Lamb of God who takes away the sin of the world!

Prayer: See, the Lamb, so long expected, Comes with pardon down from heav'n. Let us haste, with tears of sorrow, One and all, to be forgiv'n.

Follow Me!

Out of nowhere comes a man, walking beside the Sea of Galilee. Born in obscure Nazareth, baptized 30 years later in the Jordan, just beginning to proclaim the kingdom of God, He approaches four fishermen and asks them to follow Him. Incredibly, they follow. Who is this man? What authority elicits such a total response from these rugged fishermen?

We live in a skeptical age. Many voices call us to follow— endless salespeople, TV evangelists, political leaders, etc. Generally we tune out the voices and follow the line of least resistance. Year after year we keep the same job, live in the same home, observe the same traditions.

When the Man from Galilee visits you and says, "Follow Me," how do you respond? Turn His voice off as one more sales pitch? Listen halfheartedly and respond with a polite affirmative to get rid of Him? Agree to follow Him when it seems convenient? Who is He? With what authority does He speak?

Admitting our lethargy and rebellion, we meet face-to-face Jesus the Savior of the world. We cannot follow on our own. But He has blazed the path of personal self-giving and death on a cross to pay for our sins. His call to follow carries with it the power for us to leave our nets and follow Him.

The adventure begins loving Him, fishing for others to follow Him as well, finding new meaning and sparkle in our daily routines, living and loving with purpose and joy. Troubles and persecution may lie ahead. Temptations will abound. Other voices will try to lead us astray. But the forgiving, loving, empowering Man from Galilee continues to sound the gentle, life-changing call, FOLLOW ME!

Prayer: Lord, help us to follow You. Amen.

The Need for Refreshment

A typical day in the ministry of Jesus! He taught and expelled a demon in the synagogue. He spent the lunch hour healing Peter's mother-in-law of a fever. In the evening He was mobbed by townspeople looking for help.

Exhausted by the day's labors, does He sleep late the next day and eat a leisurely breakfast? On the contrary, Jesus gets up in the predawn darkness and goes to a solitary place for prayer. As true man He needs refreshment and finds it in a devotional communion with the heavenly Father. Immediately the demands of the next day's ministry crowd in on Him. Refreshed, He continues His preaching throughout Galilee.

What kind of typical days do you have? Hectic demands from family and coworkers. Hurried banking and shopping for supper. Endless trips to piano lessons and dental appointments. The telephone ringing off the hook. Evening meetings. Another similar day to dread. Do you need refreshment?

Many say, "With my schedule, I don't have time for a daily devotional period with God." Jesus needed the refreshment of prayer precisely because the demands of His ministry were so great. In obedience He steadily moved to the cross, where He died for our sins, including our devotional failures. He makes available His Word and also other Christians to encourage us in our devotional life.

Picture that quiet time—early morning, midday, or late at night—a few moments alone in the presence of a loving, strengthening God, an oasis for refreshment, a new surge of energy and enthusiasm for the rest of the day, direction and guidance for loving ministry to others.

Prayer: Dear Lord, refresh me with Your Word and support me in my daily devotional time with You. Amen.

Need a Doctor?

How sad when a desperately sick person refuses to admit the need for help! A cancer may be growing inside, but everything seems normal on the outside. The increasingly sharp pains or a suspicious lump are ignored. Doctors stand ready to help, but the fatally diseased person continues pretending health.

Jesus serves as the Great Physician of physical and spiritual diseases. Approaching Levi at a tax collector's booth, He summons him to follow. Recognizing his spiritual alienation, Levi forsakes his questionable occupation and receives spiritual healing from the Savior. Jesus then eats with other tax collectors and notorious sinners to offer them similar healing. Meanwhile the self-righteous Pharisees protest His associating with such people.

Where are you, my friend? Do you pretend health, though desperately sick with sin? Do you feel righteous because of a decent moral life, membership in a church, service to your community—while looking with disdain at alcoholics and drug addicts, divorced couples and unwed mothers, families on welfare, and minority groups? Or do you let the Great Physician probe your innermost heart, diagnose a fatal disobedience and rebellion against God, and offer you Himself as the full payment for sin, the only treatment for your disease?

Jesus came for you. He loves you. He offers you life, now and for eternity. NEED A DOCTOR?

Prayer: We deserve but grief and shame, Yet his words, rich grace revealing, Pardon, peace, and life proclaim. Here our ills have perfect healing; We with humble hearts believe Jesus sinners will receive.

Power Source Unlimited

Today our world knows limits. We need tremendous power every day to drive industrial machines, light cities and homes, fuel cars, and heat buildings. What power sources can we find? Power in great demand. Power sources limited.

How exciting are the words of Paul in the spiritual realm! We need tremendous spiritual power in our world to carry out God's saving plan for humanity. Writing to the Ephesians, Paul describes a power source unlimited, "His incomparably great power for us who believe. That power is like the working of His mighty strength, which He exerted in Christ when He raised Him from the dead and seated Him at His right hand in the heavenly realms" (Ephesians 1:19–20).

We have power for Christian living, God's power. He demonstrated that power by raising Christ from the dead. The resurrection powerfully announces God's acceptance of Christ's sacrifice for our sins. Weak and helpless on our own, inept to help others, we receive God's power when He works faith in our hearts at our Baptism. In short, Christ's resurrection power becomes available "for us who believe." Christ continues to reign in power at the right hand of the Father. Therefore, plugged into Christ by faith, we possess a power source unlimited.

In the next three devotions we explore how that power of God can be unleashed in our lives for the blessing of many. But what a comfort to know that God's spiritual power source will never run low!

Prayer: All hail the pow'r of Jesus' name! Let angels prostrate fall; Bring forth the royal diadem And crown him Lord of all.

Word Power

Dynamite packs terrific power. Atomic and hydrogen bombs contain terrifying power. Modern technology sports an impressive array of powerful machines. But words perhaps convey even greater power. A word triggers the dynamite in the bombs and instructs powerful machines to operate.

We looked yesterday at God's spiritual power source unlimited, focusing on the resurrection of Jesus Christ from the dead. Romans 1:16, part of our text, describes the Word that unlocks that power source.

Gospel—the Word. Good news. God's good news about a Savior who took on Himself our unrighteousness. Righteous, He paid the price on the cross. God declares the world righteous for Christ's sake. That righteousness comes to us by faith in Christ.

And Paul calls that Gospel the power of God for salvation, "dynamite" according to the Greek word for "power." Word power. Gospel power. What sheer joy as a believer to have in our possession such Word power. The church preaches that Word and administers the sacraments as visible words.

We hear the Gospel every day for our own assurance and power. We speak the Gospel every day for the salvation of others. We live the Gospel because we have been instructed to operate with power for others. Word power unlocks God's spiritual power source unlimited.

Prayer: The Gospel shows the Father's grace, Who sent his Son to save our race, Proclaims how Jesus lived and died That man might thus be justified. It is the pow'r of God to save From sin and Satan and the grave; It works the faith, which firmly clings To all the treasures which it brings.

Go Power

America, a nation on the go. We work, travel, exercise, play, and celebrate. We get up early, work through lunch, and stay up late. We live by the clock and the watch and the odometer. And we need "go power" to keep moving—breakfast cereals, fruit juices, vitamins, candy bars, and pep pills. Nevertheless, we frequently run out of gas and lie exhausted in front of the television.

Most of us would agree that some of this "going" makes little sense. There is one going, however, that is of the utmost importance. Jesus speaks of it when He says, "Therefore go and make disciples of all nations, baptizing them in the name of the Father and of the Son and of the Holy Spirit, and teaching them to obey everything I have commanded you" (Matthew 28:19–20). Not a going to get rich or to find thrills, but a going to make disciples of all nations, to share that Gospel Word power with family members, friends, coworkers, church friends, and people in other lands. Good reason for going.

But where do we get the power for such going? "All authority in heaven and on earth has been given to Me," He says (Matthew 28:18). He supplies the go power from His limitless supply. Crucified and risen from the dead, He offers forgiveness and endless refreshment. Through Word power—His Gospel—we receive all the go power we will ever need. He promises to be with us always, to the very end of the age. What comfort!

Prayer: *Send now, O Lord, to ev'ry place Swift messengers before your face, The heralds of your wondrous grace, Where you yourself will come.*

Staying Power

True power needs to last. Many distance runners start with a burst of energy but fade on the stretch. The best athletes sometimes lose to a steadier team that takes better conditioning into the final period. We are describing staying power.

Yes, God provides a power source unlimited in the resurrection of His Son. He also supplies Word power, the Gospel, to unlock that power source. And He intends for us to use His resources to have staying power.

Paul, the great on-the-go missionary, learned the importance of staying power when God sent him a thorn in the flesh, some illness or physical handicap that simply wouldn't go away. Paul prayed and hoped, but the problem remained. Discouraged and frustrated, Paul finally understood that he was being conditioned for the long haul. At that point he learned to accept his weakness and rely totally on God's grace and power. Now he could face any troubles because Christ was always there for him.

Similarly we will experience discouragement and frustration after our initial "going." We will experience God's testing in our personal lives as well as in our witnessing efforts. But God says also to us, "My grace is sufficient for you, for My power is made perfect in weakness" (2 Corinthians 12:9). We look to the weak and helpless Son of God, nailed to a cross for us, then experience His resurrection power flowing to us in our weakness.

Prayer: *Sing, pray, and keep his ways unswerving, Offer your service faithfully, And trust his word; though undeserving, You'll find his promise true to be. God never will forsake in need The soul that trusts in him indeed.*

Snow for Slowing Down

In many parts of America, now is the time for heavy snow-storms. Snow for building snow forts and snowmen—the delight of all red-blooded American children. Snow to be shoveled and reshoveled—the plague of all middle-aged men.

A little four-year-old boy named David recently asked his mother, "Why does God let it keep snowing so much?" She told David, "God is making it snow because He thinks we've been going too fast and should slow down." It's true that snow slows us down. We complain because snow-covered streets prolong our drive to work or force us to cancel plans.

Could such delays be good for us? Are you spending some time with your family? The snow may be a blessing in disguise. Use the time to relax at home. Try relaxing and reflecting a little on your life.

Perhaps God is saying to us: Slow down and think. Through our text, He reminds us how great He is and how much He is in control. When we slow down, God has a chance to enter our thoughts. He can point us to the passing of time and to our many shortcomings. He can remind us that His own Son, Jesus Christ, came into this world to bring us salvation. Jesus did not always hurry. He took time out to go on a mountain alone to pray. He relaxed at the home of His friends Mary, Martha, and Lazarus. Even His suffering and death were basically passive. He remained silent while His captors put Him to death.

Perhaps we need more snow time to think about God and His Son, Jesus Christ, and to make Him a part of our family life.

Prayer: Thank God for the snow and for the opportunity to slow down for time with Him and one another.

Snow for Serving Others

I notice that heavy snow seems to bind people together and moves them to help one another. Sunday morning two men shoveled out their entire court so all of the apartment residents could get their cars out.

Perhaps we have a second answer to David's question: "Why does God let it keep snowing so much?" God is sending snow to encourage us to, as Paul says in Galatians, "Serve one another in love" (Galatians 5:13). The two answers are complementary. We need to slow down and recognize our need for God. He alone can make us His own and forgive our sins through Jesus Christ. Then when we realize that He has done everything for us, we are moved in turn to start helping others.

So often we show indifference to others. Perhaps a snowstorm is needed to wake us up to people obviously in need of assistance. But I suspect that if snow continues, our initial enthusiasm for pushing stalled cars and shoveling whole parking lots might quickly fade.

Nevertheless, helping others can be a real joy. The comradeship and enjoyment you experienced from helping your neighbor in the snowstorm can become a permanent part of your life. Stop thinking only of your own problems. Get involved in the lives of others. That's the meaning of serving one another in love.

Remember why you serve and how you are able to serve—because God sent His Son, Jesus, to be a servant and to humble Himself and become obedient unto death, even death on a cross. He served you and frees you to serve others. Let it snow!

Prayer: Consider ways to serve others in small practical ways. Ask God's strength and guidance for Jesus' sake.

Needed—a Gospel Partnership

Lonely, depressed Christians. Paul writes to the Philippian Christians from prison in Rome. A lonely Christian? Persecuted and suffering for his faith, Paul could be lonely and depressed. But he writes the joyful words of our text.

Paul knows he is not alone because he has the Philippian Christians as partners in the Gospel. They heard and believed the message of Christ crucified when Paul first visited Philippi. No wonder he rejoices and continues his own Gospel ministry with power.

Are you a lonely Christian, wallowing in self-pity and despair, afraid to stand up for the Gospel, helpless before the onslaught of a rebellious world? Or do you see the partnership in the Gospel from the first day until now—the Christian pastor faithfully proclaiming the Gospel and administering the sacraments, the retired factory worker with years of Gospel experience amidst the trials of life, the teenager excited about telling friends about Jesus? Sinful, struggling believers, to be sure, but Gospel partners, washed clean by the blood of the Lamb, sustained by God through suffering, and giving of themselves to others with a quiet joy, rooted in the Gospel promises.

Jesus Christ endured a lonely death on the cross so you might be forgiven and drawn into the fellowship of the Gospel. And you—yes, you—can be a partner in the Gospel every day.

Prayer: Blest be the tie that binds Our hearts in Christian love; The unity of heart and mind Is like to that above.

Promised—Continued Partnership Power

How many partnerships begin with great hopes and dreams only to end in failure and broken promises? A wagon train heads west with the common goal of finding a good location to settle. The train thins out as desert, Indian raiders, and illness take their toll. Finally, a crude settlement develops at journey's end. The future looks bright, but a few years later—bypassed by railroads, battered by severe winters, empty of gold—the original wagon train partnership ends in a ghost town.

Paul knows the temptations threatening the Philippian Christians—persecution, strife and jealous bickering from within, discouragement over his absence and imprisonment. Therefore he adds the precious Gospel promise that God will bring His work in us to completion. By human efforts even the closest fellowship will eventually disintegrate. But the God who sent His Son to the cross will continue nurturing His church through the Gospel.

Your Gospel partnership will be threatened both from without and from within. People move out. Neighborhoods change. Pastors come and go. Buildings age. Sometimes biblical mission is neglected. But Paul's confidence applies to you as well. Centered in the Word and sacraments, you see again that the same God who began the Gospel partnership around His crucified and risen Son will continue that good work until Jesus comes again.

Prayer: The Church's one foundation Is Jesus Christ, her Lord; She is his new creation By water and the Word. From heav'n he came and sought her To be his holy bride; With his own blood he bought her, And for her life he died.

A Backward Desire

We live backward, trying to avoid death at any cost. Anxiously we review the holiday death tolls, shudder at tragic air crashes and natural disasters, and tremble at dreaded terminal diseases. We try to hide death behind nice-sounding words and cosmetic surroundings.

Paul didn't view death or life that way. Imprisoned in Rome, uncertain as to his future, he welcomed the thought of death: "I desire to depart and be with Christ, which is better by far" (Philippians 1:23). Earlier he wrote, "To me ... to die is gain" (Philippians 1:21). Paul knew that Jesus Christ endured death on a cross to pay for the sins of the world. Alive from the dead, Jesus was preparing a place for Paul in heaven, a glorious way to spend eternity. Believing in Christ, confident of a far better eternal life in heaven, Paul had a zest and a purpose for living.

Do you desire to "be with Christ, which is better by far"? Do you kneel penitently at His cross, recognizing the full forgiveness of your sins? Do you joyfully see the empty tomb and anticipate the heavenly celebration around the throne of the Lamb? God supplies a foretaste of the heavenly feast through His Holy Meal. As the desire grows to be with Christ forever, the zest returns for living joyfully today in humble service to others.

A backward desire to the world, but a life-giving approach to life and death for the Christian. Death may be near, but with faith in Christ the future is secure. We are free to live for others backward from death to life.

Prayer: *If death my portion be, It brings great gain to me; It speeds my life's endeavor To live with Christ forever. He gives me joy in sorrow, Come death now or tomorrow.*

Profit or Loss?

How we guard and cultivate our assets in life—degrees, promotions earned, civic honors, financial balance sheets, club memberships! While wanting to appear humble, we secretly savor our accomplishments and expect to profit from our assets, perhaps even in God's heavenly ledger.

Paul understood our drive for profit. He was a Hebrew of Hebrews, a Pharisee, a persecutor of the church, and a faultless observer of legal principles. He honestly sought to please God by his actions—until he found himself in the dust of the Damascus road, at odds with Jesus Christ, whom he persecuted. Blinded, alone, convicted of his many sins before God and men, Saul of Tarsus is baptized and comes to know Jesus as the crucified and risen Savior.

Now Paul sees all his own righteousness, however humanly impressive, as mere rubbish. He gladly lays it aside for the priceless righteousness that comes from God and is by faith in Christ. He now lives with reckless abandon for Christ, his only profit.

A painful review of our assets is in order. Before God we are weighed in the balance and found wanting. Selfish, rebellious, manipulative, we find ourselves with mere rubbish before God and others. But Christ's righteousness, demonstrated by His sinless life and sacrificial death, stands for us as profit before the Father. Trusting in Christ alone for salvation, we live unburdened, using our assets by His grace to proclaim Jesus Christ and the power of His resurrection. What gain when we count our profit as loss and His sacrificial loss as our profit!

Prayer: Dear Lord, help me to count all as loss for Your sake. Amen.

Daily at the Door

Many successful people started out at the doorstep of those they admired. Many children in American history came to the doors of printers, blacksmiths, and bakers to apprentice themselves for a career.

Proverbs 8 personifies wisdom and declares, "Whoever finds me finds life and receives favor from the LORD." (verse 35). Pride and arrogance stand condemned. Evil behavior and perverse speech are hated. But simple, humble willingness to come to God and let Him guide into all truth brings wisdom. Daily at the door of God's wisdom brings life.

Today's world provides many competing doorsteps—scientific knowledge, business acumen, psychological strategies, secular philosophies. Each beckons for a daily visit at the door. Wisdom's door described by Proverbs may appear less appealing.

But that wisdom leads to Christ, the Power of God and the Wisdom of God. Try reading Proverbs 8, substituting Christ for *wisdom* and its pronouns. Wait at the door of Bethlehem, the temple, the Nazareth synagogue, the home of Mary and Martha, the Upper Room. Follow Him on the dusty roads, along the seashore, through the Jerusalem streets to Calvary, to the mountain in Galilee. Read the Word. Worship in His house with bread and wine. Daily at the door—His door—means life, eternal life, for you and those you bring to Him.

Prayer: Wisdom's highest, noblest treasure, Jesus, is revealed in you. Let me find in you my pleasure, Make my will and actions true, Humility there and simplicity reigning, In paths of true wisdom my steps ever training. If I learn from Jesus this knowledge divine, The blessing of heavenly wisdom is mine.

The Saving Boast

We boast. Family pictures quickly available in our wallet for everyone to see. Trophies in our family rooms of past athletic glory. Service awards proudly displayed on the wall behind our desk. Country club luncheons for clients where the head waiter knows us. Fashionable clothing with the right labels displayed. We boast. Sadly, we boast about externals that provide nothing permanent.

They boasted in Paul's day too. The Judaizers came with requirements for the new believers in Jesus Christ. A return to Jewish laws and customs for authentic faith. Circumcision most of all. The external mark that counts. Something to boast about. Sadly, they missed the mark because all the external customs in the world provide nothing permanent.

Paul, one of the circumcised, could have joined the external boasting. Instead, he writes powerfully, "May I never boast except in the cross of our Lord Jesus Christ, through which the world has been crucified to me, and I to the world. Neither circumcision nor uncircumcision means anything; what counts is a new creation" (Galatians 6:14–15). Paul describes the saving boast, the only legitimate boast—clinging to the cross of Jesus Christ for full and free salvation.

We boast. Not of ourselves nor of our accomplishments. We boast that Jesus Christ renounced all boasting and went to the shameful cross to pay for our sins. We have been crucified with Christ. Therefore we live. No, Christ lives in us. We belong to His new creation. Thank God for the saving boast!

Prayer: *Till then—nor is my boasting vain—Till then I boast a Savior slain; And oh, may this my glory be, That Christ is not ashamed of me!*

Skin-Deep Beauty

We place great value on outward beauty. Teenage magazines sponsor dream guy and beauty queen contests with emphasis on looks and personality. Men and women of all ages work, sweat, diet, and exercise to remain trim and avoid wrinkles. As for the inevitable aging process, cosmetic and fashion companies provide expensive ways to make us appear more beautiful. We emphasize skin-deep beauty.

Saul filled the bill as an attractive king for Israel. But Saul's beauty turned out to be only skin-deep. Shortly after becoming king, he revealed his inner character by disobeying God on two successive occasions. To make matters worse, he tried to cover up his sin by lying and blaming others. The Lord came to Samuel and said, "I am grieved that I have made Saul king, because he has turned away from Me and has not carried out My instructions" (1 Samuel 15:10).

Saul's skin-deep beauty and inner ugliness make us look at our own lives. Are we guilty of devoting major attention to our outward appearance while neglecting our relationship to God? Do we cover up physical blemishes so artfully that we also cover up our sins against God and others? In honesty, we need to confess a beauty that is only skin-deep and sinful hearts, deserving the clear label of ugly.

God knows our hearts and sent His Son to die for our sins. He covers our sins with Christ's righteousness. He makes us truly beautiful in Christ. As His children we have no need to concentrate on a beauty that is only skin-deep.

Prayer: Forgive us, dear Father, for pursuing skin-deep beauty. Point us to Your Son, who died on the cross to make us truly beautiful. Amen.

His Ugly Beauty

Yesterday we described the world's fascination with outward beauty. "Dress for success," we are told. By the same token, society shudders at ugliness. We try to hide the sick and handicapped behind the walls of institutions.

But God reverses the process. In Isaiah, God describes the Suffering Servant as physically ugly: "He had no beauty or majesty to attract us to Him, nothing in His appearance that we should desire Him" (Isaiah 53:2b). Jesus Christ, the beautiful and all-powerful Son of God from eternity, became a true human being at Bethlehem. Although a king, He chose to serve by suffering. "He was despised and rejected by men" (Isaiah 53:3a). He was nailed to a cross, the most despised death available. From a human standpoint, His birth, life, suffering, and death were ugly.

Yet God saw beauty in His ugliness. He came for us, for a world trapped in the ugliness of sin. "He took up our infirmities and carried our sorrows. ... But He was pierced for our transgressions, He was crushed for our iniquities; the punishment that brought us peace was upon Him, and by His wounds we are healed" (Isaiah 53:4a, 5). God says, "I will give Him a portion among the great ... because He poured out His life unto death" (Isaiah 53:12). God raised Jesus Christ from the grave to His right hand. Unsurpassed beauty.

We look at Him, amazed. We bow in humble adoration before His nail-pierced hands and crown of thorns. We rejoice in His ugly beauty.

Prayer: Beautiful Savior, Lord of the nations, Son of God and Son of Man! Glory and honor, Praise, adoration Now and forevermore be thine!

Inner Beauty

Full circle. We looked at skin-deep beauty, so appealing to the world but masking the inner ugliness of sin. Then we focused on Jesus Christ, whose humble, suffering life and death appeared ugly to the world but provided a beautiful salvation for us. Today the apostle Peter describes inner beauty as he pens words to husbands and wives.

He writes to wives, "Your beauty should not come from outward adornment, such as braided hair and the wearing of gold jewelry and fine clothes. Instead, it should be that of your inner self, the unfading beauty of a gentle and quiet spirit, which is of great worth in God's sight" (1 Peter 3:3-4). He proceeds to describe beautiful inner qualities for husbands and all believers, including consideration, respect, sympathy, love, compassion, and humility. True beauty lies in the heart.

Do we display inner beauty to others? As husbands or wives, as parents or children, as employers or employees, do we radiate God's love? You see, inner beauty comes only from God. We do not buy it. In fact, our nature will lead us to sin and ugliness.

But God sent His own dear Son to live and die for us. Jesus demonstrated humility, a quiet spirit, compassion, and love as He ministered to the multitudes and went obediently to the cross. He died for our inner ugliness.

Now Christ lives in us through our Baptism. Clothed with Christ's righteousness, we also, by His grace, display the inner beauty that comes from Him. Through our daily example others see Christ, and His beauty becomes theirs as well. Inner beauty—His gift to us for others!

Prayer: Dear Father, give us the inner beauty of a life yielded to You. Amen.

A Mouthful

Picture a delightful, tasty morsel filling your mouth—a juicy filet mignon, a tangy lemon meringue pie with flaky crust, or a superb pasta with zesty meat sauce. What a mouthful to be savored, then swallowed with delight. But before long, the stomach grows full and the appetite wanes.

The psalmist describes a different kind of mouthful that is no less delightful, "My mouth is filled with Your praise, declaring Your splendor all day long" (Psalm 71:8). Struggling with evil around him, needing deliverance from the grasp of wicked and cruel men, he nevertheless remembers the marvelous blessings of God from the moment of his birth. He sees God as his Hope, Refuge, and Rescue. Therefore, his mouth is filled with God's praise, not just for a hungry moment, but all day long. The more he declares the splendor of God, the more he enjoys his mouthful of praise.

Do we fill our mouth with complaining, profaning, slandering words all day? Or can we say with the psalmist, "My mouth is filled with Your praise, declaring Your splendor all day long"? How often our indulgent mouthfuls turn flat and indigestion follows. How often negative words leave our mouth stale and empty, with an emotional hangover remaining.

But God spoke His joyful word at creation, at Bethlehem, at Jordan, and at the empty tomb. He still speaks at the baptismal font, the lectern, and the altar table that our sins are forgiven as we eat Christ's body and drink His blood. Indeed, by His grace—from birth to death and beyond—our mouth is filled with His praise all day long. What a mouthful!

Prayer: *"O Lord, open my lips, and my mouth will declare Your praise" (Psalm 51:15). Amen.*

Who Do You Say I Am?

A pivotal question in the Gospel of Mark: "Who do you say I am?" (Mark 8:29). Jesus stands with His disciples at Caesarea Philippi and raises the question of His Messiahship. They have been listening to Him for some time now and observing His miracles. How will they answer?

Peter answers simply and clearly, "You are the Christ." A beautiful confession, a life-giving answer. Peter has listened, watched, and believed. But shortly thereafter, when Jesus describes who will suffer, die, and rise again, Peter rebukes Him for such foolish talk. Much to learn.

Jesus stands in our midst and raises the same question about His Messiahship. We belong to churches, listen to sermons, study the Bible, talk with one another about our faith, participate in Holy Communion. How will we answer? Some say Jesus was a great teacher, a brilliant philosopher, a bold prophet, a fiery revolutionary, a great martyr, and a wonderful, loving man. We answer simply, "You are the Christ." We know that He is the Son of God, the promised Messiah. But are we prepared for Jesus' description of the kind of Messiah He is—a rejected, suffering, dying Christ? Do we rebuke Him and choose a prosperous life also for ourselves? Much to learn.

Jesus has shown us who He is and why He came. He went to the cross for us to pay for our sins. He has given us new life in Baptism. He gives us a life to lose and a cross to bear for His sake. Peter later preached on Pentecost: "God has made this Jesus, whom you crucified, both Lord and Christ." He learned to answer the pivotal question, and so have we. Thank God!

Prayer: Lord Jesus, confirm in our hearts that You are the Christ, our crucified and risen Savior. Amen.

Mountaintop Experiences

Mountaintop experiences. Easter Sunday morning—Easter lilies, full choir, trumpets, a rousing message. Confirmation—questions and answers, white robes, special flowers, standing before the altar, public confession of faith, special Bible verse, the joy of Holy Communion. "It is good for us to be here."

Mountaintop experience. Near the end of His ministry, Jesus takes three disciples with Him on a high mountain. Suddenly He is transfigured before them with clothes dazzling white. Moses and Elijah appear with Jesus, attesting that He is the beloved Son of the Father, the promised Messiah. Frightened and overwhelmed. Peter says to Jesus, "It is good for us to be here" (Mark 9:5). No doubts about Jesus as Messiah or His power to save. Privileged to bask in the presence of God Himself—why not stay?

But they could not stay on the mountain. Soon they saw only Jesus in His normal state and returned down the mountain to problems with a demon-possessed boy. Soon would come the cross. Nevertheless, the three were strengthened for the coming events.

Rejoice in your mountaintop experiences where you see Jesus clearly as exalted Lord and Savior. Relish those moments. Say without reservation, "It is good for us to be here."

But recognize that the valley awaits. The cross looms ahead even as it provides for us the complete atonement for our sins. We take up our crosses and follow Him by faith, not by sight. But we are confirmed in our faith by the risen Lord Jesus, who promises a heavenly eternal mountaintop experience.

Prayer: How good, Lord, to be here! Yet we may not remain; But since you bid us leave the mount, Come with us to the plain.

The Reason We Misunderstand Jesus

Shortly after His transfiguration, Jesus spoke privately to His disciples, "The Son of Man is going to be betrayed into the hands of men. They will kill Him, and after three days He will rise" (Mark 9:31). Mark records that the disciples didn't understand.

Jesus spoke with simple words and repeated His message. Why did the disciples misunderstand? When the disciples reached Capernaum, Jesus asked what they had been arguing about on the road. They kept quiet because they had been arguing about who was the greatest. In short, the disciples misunderstood because they were selfish. They wanted success and fame. They couldn't understand Jesus' talk about suffering, service, and a cross.

Why do we fail to understand Jesus? We have the benefit of the Holy Scriptures. We know much more about Jesus' life, death, and resurrection than did the disciples at the time of this text. Yet we misunderstand as badly as the disciples because so often we are in effect arguing about who is the greatest. Forgetting about our suffering Savior, we tend to push for success and recognition. When Jesus talks about suffering, service, and a cross, we screen out His words with our selective filters.

What can we do to understand Jesus? In the text Jesus takes a little child in His arms and says that whoever welcomes one of these children welcomes Him. God will give us the humility of a child. Exposing our selfishness and stopped-up ears, He gives us His Son, who humbled Himself unto death, even death on a cross! By God's grace we understand Jesus.

Prayer: Lord, open my heart to understand Your Word. Amen.

Like a Child

Today we often have no time for children or for the child in each of us. We forget what we experienced as children. We bury feelings and spontaneous joys because we have learned not to show our feelings. We wear masks.

Jesus, on His final journey to Jerusalem, could have rejected the children brought to Him. But He says, "Let the little children come to Me, and do not hinder them, for the kingdom of God belongs to such as these" (Mark 10:14). He took the children in His arms and blessed them.

For the moment forget your busy schedule and your self-importance. Picture yourself as a child in your favorite room. As you play, Jesus enters the room and comes to you. You are excited to see Him. He looks at you with a kindly sparkle in His eyes, a smile on His face. He holds out His arms to you. You run to Him with a big hug, then sit in His lap, talking with Him and listening to Him telling you stories. You feel so happy, secure, and relaxed. You know He loves you.

God can make you like a child. He has sent His Son to take the burdens for you. He knows how you hurt inside. Humbly depending on Him like a child, you can face the world's problems with new strength and determination. Jesus, who had time for the children, taught us to call God our Father. Martin Luther commented on this as follows:

Prayer: "God would by these words tenderly invite us to believe that He is our true Father and that we are His true children, so that we may with all boldness and confidence ask Him as dear children ask their dear father." (Small Catechism, "Lord's Prayer," Introduction)

Surprising Greatness

Who is the greatest? How would you answer that question? You could survey the public for their choices—politicians, journalists, religious or business leaders. You could turn to historians for their estimate based on the historical contributions of great individuals.

James and John were working for a prominent place in Jesus' kingdom, one on His right and the other on His left. They were measuring greatness by prestige or status. The other disciples were furious when they heard about that request, probably because they wanted the same status.

Are we any different? Do we not strive for greatness in our own way—degrees, job title, net worth and material possessions, social standing, number of celebrities we know personally, community organizations we join, or even church positions we hold. We struggle, climb ladders, cultivate the right kind of friends, and hope to achieve greatness.

Jesus must have shocked the disciples when He spoke the words of our text. As the greatest man who ever lived, He described His mission in life: "For even the Son of Man did not come to be served, but to serve, and to give His life as a ransom for many" (Mark 10:45). He washed the disciples' feet and "humbled Himself ... to death, even death on a cross!" (Philippians 2:8). Surprising greatness in humble service.

Jolted by Jesus' words, we confess our fond ambitions and manipulative struggles to achieve greatness. Redeemed, restored, forgiven, we pick up the towel and ready the basin of water for a life of service as we reach out to others. Surprising greatness!

Prayer: Lord, make me great in service, as You served on the cross for all. Amen.

To See Again

I'll never forget the first time I put on glasses to correct my near-sightedness. I walked out into the bright sunlight and saw the whole world clearly. Oh, how great to see again!

My experience pales in comparison with that of blind Bartimaeus. Somehow he knew about Jesus and was willing to ask for help. Helplessly blind, he cried out, "Jesus, Son of David, have mercy on me!" (Mark 10:47). Even when others rebuked him, Bartimaeus persevered. With Jesus near, the man threw his cloak aside, jumped to his feet, and came to Jesus, asking for help. Jesus immediately restored his sight, and Bartimaeus followed Jesus along the road.

What an example for us who are blind in sin. Are we willing to ask for help in our deepest need? Are we willing to persevere in asking Jesus? When He calls us, are we willing to go quickly and ask for specific help? And when Jesus supplies our need, do we willingly and immediately follow Him?

When Jesus, the Sight-Giver, was on His way to the cross, no mission or crowd was too important for Him to help an individual in need. When Bartimaeus came forth, Jesus asked, "What do you want Me to do for you?" (Mark 10:51). He let Bartimaeus admit his specific need and ask for help. Then, by His almighty power, Jesus restored his sight.

Jesus, having restored our spiritual eyesight, can use us to help others see again. He can help us to place individual needs first, ahead of crowds of people and goals we pursue. With His help we use God's power through His Word and sacraments to restore people's spiritual sight.

Prayer: Amazing grace! How sweet the sound That saved a wretch like me! I once was lost but now am found, Was blind but now I see!

Reach Out

REACH OUT—and touch the stars in the dark winter sky.

REACH OUT—and feel a snowflake melt in your hand.

REACH OUT—and breathe in the cold heady air of February.

REACH OUT—and let Him touch you—gently, lovingly, firmly, permanently.

REACH OUT—and let the fresh wind of the Spirit sweep the cobwebs from your mind, body, and spirit.

REACH OUT—and come alive in the newness of an exciting life and a brand-new day.

REACH OUT—and let the Word speak to you with words of power, conviction, meaning, truth, love, joy, and life.

REACH OUT—and breathe your new life—His life—into another.

REACH OUT—and place your arm around the one you love.

REACH OUT—and touch the untouchable, the unlovable, the lost, the frightened, the weak, the overbearing, the aging, the dying, the comic, the phony—with His love and care.

REACH OUT—and sing a new song from the bottom of your soul and from the top of your soaring spirit.

REACH OUT—and march side by side with the searchers, the mourners, and the helpers.

REACH OUT—and tell the truth about yourself, your triumphs, your Leader, your Savior, your Power, and your Joy.

REACH OUT—and don't stop reaching out until your arms have become His arms, your love His love, His death your death, His resurrection your resurrection, and until every person has come to know and believe that He is reaching out to them forever.

Prayer: Lord, help me to reach out! Amen.

Jesus' Exodus and Ours

One Greek word in Luke's account of the transfiguration stands out. The word for "departure" is "exodus." Moses talks with Jesus "about His exodus" (Luke 9:31).

Moses had been called to a heavy responsibility. He had to face mighty Pharaoh and ask him to let the people go. Jesus was called to deliver the world from slavery to sin, death, and the devil. Standing on the Mount of Transfiguration, Jesus faces the journey to Jerusalem, where He will suffer and die. With the call of the Father at His Baptism fresh in mind, He willingly shoulders the world's sin and begins His exodus.

We also are called to a new exodus from slavery to freedom. Moses took Israel with him on the journey, grumbling and complaining though they were. Jesus took His disciples with Him on that final journey also, confused and resistant though they were. Called in our Baptism as children of God, we stand free in Christ. We bear a heavy responsibility to bring Gospel freedom to the world. Like Moses and the disciples, we often make excuses, complain, and even long for our former slavery.

But God supplies strength and guidance for our new exodus. He strengthened Jesus on the mount, filled Him with glory, reassured Him through Moses and Elijah, the cloud and the voice. Jesus strengthened the disciples following His resurrection and poured out His Holy Spirit on them. He strengthens us as we worship together, hear His Word, and receive His body and blood. What a joy to follow Jesus on the journey from slavery to freedom!

Prayer: Jesus, still lead on Till our rest be won; Heav'nly leader, still direct us, Still support, console, protect us, Till we safely stand In our fatherland.

Compassion for the Lost

In the abstract we can feel compassion for lost sinners. In the concrete, however, compassion comes with much greater difficulty. We lead our daily lives to meet personal needs, earn a living, and keep family together. On occasion we may respond to a mission sermon and make calls for a new adult class. But normally we don't think much about the lost. If they intrude on our comfortable lives, we may even resent them.

How different the single-minded compassion of Jesus for the lost sheep. By example He also challenged His disciples to a similar compassion. They had just returned from a successful preaching mission in the villages of Galilee. As they are reporting to Jesus, so many people crowd around them that they don't even have a chance to eat. Jesus, recognizing the need for rest, suggests that they go by boat to a quiet place. However, when they arrive they discover that multitudes have gone around the lake on foot to meet them. Does Jesus send them away until a more convenient time? No, He teaches them and later feeds the 5,000.

Compassion for the lost. Only God can fill us with it. Jesus sought us out as a shepherd searches for sheep. He gave His life for us on the cross. He personally binds up our wounds and forgives our lack of compassion. He knows our need for rest with Him. But He also places before us constantly people who need His love and forgiveness. And He wants to use us to teach, feed, and heal them. How we need Jesus' compassion for the lost!

Prayer: Raise up, O Lord the Holy Ghost, From this broad land a mighty host; Their war cry, "We will seek the lost Where you, O Christ, will come."

Preventive Prayer

"An ounce of prevention is worth a pound of cure." So goes the saying. Preventive measures are stressed in many areas today. Fitness gurus promote aerobics, exercise machines, health foods, weight loss programs, and special cookbooks. Some people, however, ignore all preventive efforts.

Jesus sees danger ahead as He visits the Garden of Gethsemane with His disciples. He knows that suffering and death await Him. He realizes that the disciples also will be tested severely. He asks them to pray with Him. Preventive prayer works, not to remove problems and temptations but to tap God's powerful resources for handling them.

Note the outcome. The disciples fall asleep, despite Jesus' efforts to rouse them. They do not pray. Consequently, when the hostile crowd comes, they fall into temptation. They desert Jesus and flee. Peter denies his Lord three times.

Observe the contrast. Jesus practices preventive prayer. His soul overwhelmed with sorrow, He prays three times for the Father's will to be done in His life. The Father equips Him to bear the intense suffering. Jesus steadfastly and silently goes to Annas, Caiaphas, Pilate, Herod, and Calvary. He fully and completely bears the sins of the world and wins the victory.

How many times we fail to pray! Without the regular habit of communing with God, we are in danger of falling into sin when the crisis comes to test our faith. Thank God that Jesus did not fail but won the victory for us. Through His Word and sacraments, He strengthens also our prayer life.

Prayer: Go to dark Gethsemane, All who feel the tempter's pow'r; Your Redeemer's conflict see. Watch with him one bitter hour; Turn not from his griefs away; Learn from Jesus Christ to pray.

Small in Number, Large in His Love

The motion picture *Hoosiers* describes a small-town high school with only 64 students that fielded an amazing basketball team. The team managed to defeat school after school on its way to the state championship game in Indianapolis. Pitted against a large city school with taller players, the embattled team worked together, came from behind, and at the buzzer scored an outside jump shot to win. Small town, tiny high school, outsized team, but a large heart and a great victory.

Moses reminds Israel as they wait on the east bank of the Jordan to enter the Promised Land that they face a major challenge—seven nations larger and stronger. He assures Israel that the Lord has chosen them as a special people, His treasured possession. Israel, small in number but large in God's covenant love, crossed the Jordan and by God's power won the victory.

Often we feel outnumbered as Christians. We see evil gripping our society. Sex outside of marriage. Abortion on demand. Broken homes and child abuse. Crime. Drugs and alcohol. Many scoff at religion and especially Christianity.

God promises us victory. He sent His own Son into a sinful world. Originally popular, Jesus gradually lost His following as opposition mounted, and He ended up alone on a cross, forsaken even by His friends. But against all odds, He won the victory over sin, death, and Satan for us and our salvation. He chose us in Baptism to belong to His special people and sends us out to win the world with His love. Like that tiny Hoosier basketball team and Israel of old, we will win the victory.

Prayer: Lord, thank You for choosing us by Your loving grace. Help us, though small in numbers, to win the victory by sharing Your love with others. Amen.

Living Simply

At the 1964 World's Fair, General Electric featured a Carousel of Progress. As the audience revolved on a carousel, four scenes showed material progress in its own era—turn of the century, the 1920s, the 1940s, and the modern age. Yesterday's luxury becomes today's necessity. Jesus confronts the rich young ruler with the startling call for a simpler life. Faced with giving up his wealth, the man goes away sorrowing.

We find purpose and security in money and possessions. We work hard to attain them, then work harder to protect what we own. These possessions complicate our lives, often failing to make us happy. At the same time we rationalize our need to provide for our family and our old age.

Look at Jesus' simple living. Although not wealthy, He enjoyed life with good friends, with sufficient food and clothing. He furnished the Passover meal for His disciples, visited with Mary and Martha, and fed 5,000 people. Yet He placed all material possessions in service to His Father and other people. And Jesus willingly gave up all possessions in death. He went to the cross, where they divided His garments and gambled for His seamless robe. He died simply for the sins of the world, including greed and the selfish use of possessions.

Only Jesus Christ counts in life. Saved by His death, we receive full forgiveness and rejoice as His followers. Material possessions serve as gifts from Him to be enjoyed and used in His service. The struggle continues, but He makes it possible for us to live simply as we follow Him.

Prayer: Dear Father, reorient my complicated use of possessions into a simpler life of service based on the life, death, and resurrection of Your Son for me. Amen.

Love Your Enemies

You may know the story of Dave Wilkerson, the country preacher from Pennsylvania who came to New York City to start a ministry among street gangs. In one dramatic episode he approached Nicky Cruz to show concern, and the hardened gang fighter drew a knife to attack him. Dave simply said, "I love you and Jesus loves you." Those words haunted Nicky Cruz and eventually led to his conversion. Dave Wilkerson loved his enemy.

Who is your enemy? The closer the enemy, the more difficult the relationship. Love our enemy? Love with a self-giving, long-suffering love?

Our problem: We often live selfish, undisciplined lives, controlled by our feelings. When the other person treats us unfairly, we want to lash back with bitter, vindictive actions. We sin. We hate our enemies.

Enter Jesus Christ. Although He loved everyone, enemies abounded in His life—enemies out to trick Him, badger Him, damage His reputation, and ultimately destroy Him. Yet His death on the cross made all the difference. God changed us from His enemies into His friends through the sin-atoning sacrifice of Jesus.

The Spirit stands ready to help us. By Dave Wilkerson's words, Nicky Cruz was changed from an enemy of God into His friend. Similarly transformed by God's "I love you," we can begin to love our enemies with God's own self-giving love. We can say to them: "I love you and Jesus loves you."

Prayer: Dear Father, as You have loved us "while we were still sinners," help us to love our enemies with the sacrificial love of Your Son, Jesus Christ. Amen.

Fruit-Bearing Required

Jesus tells a harsh parable about required fruit-bearing. He reminds the people of His time that they have a mission to bear fruit with their lives. This particular fig tree had failed to bear fruit for three years, so the owner ordered it cut down. Jesus warns the people that they have failed to live for God.

God has made us beautiful fig trees in our Baptism, nurturing us to a growing faith in Jesus Christ as our Savior. He intends us to bear the fruit of Christ in our lives by His grace. Yet often we, like Jesus' contemporaries, fail to produce fruit. We may conduct ourselves poorly at sporting or social events, use foul language and unkind words, or fail to care for others, to attend church regularly, and to share our faith in Christ. Like the people to whom Jesus spoke, we need to repent.

In the parable the owner gives the fig tree another chance, a year of grace to bear fruit. The gardener plans special nourishing care to give the tree every chance. God's grace and mercy pours forth to us as well. We have no need to despair. Because of Christ's death on the cross, God gives us another chance. He provides maximum nourishment. As we come humbly to Him, He forgives and restores us. His love alone can produce fruit in us. What the church needs most is fig trees receiving nourishment and, by God's grace, continuing to bear fruit in word and deed. Fruit-bearing is required and supplied through Jesus Christ!

Prayer: He like a tree shall thrive, With waters near the root; Fresh as the leaf his name shall live, His works are heav'nly fruit.

Tested by Flood

Normally Fort Wayne, Ind., provides peaceful living, with houses nestled among three rivers that converge in the downtown area. In March 1982 the town was tested by flood. The spring thaw and steady rainfall brought rising rivers. Dikes started to give way. Water poured over the banks and submerged residential areas despite the efforts of sandbaggers. How solidly built were the homes and dikes? The flood of 1982 put them to the test.

Jesus describes the believer's life in terms of wise and foolish builders. The one digs deep and lays the foundation on rock. The other builds on the ground without a foundation. During normal times, both homes appear safe and livable. But when the flood comes, the house built on rock endures the torrent while the house built on the ground collapses.

How securely are you building your life? Have you concentrated on external features such as wealth, popularity, success? Or have you been building on the bedrock of Jesus Christ? As Paul writes, "No one can lay any foundation other than the one already laid, which is Jesus Christ" (1 Corinthians 3:11). Both spiritual houses may appear safe and livable. But when crisis situations come—sickness, family breakdown, death, loss of job—then our lives are tested. We either collapse or stand firm, depending on our foundation. When we hear Jesus' words and put them into practice, we rest on the unshakable foundation of Jesus' blood and righteousness.

Prayer: His oath, his covenant, his blood Sustain me in the raging flood; When all supports are washed away, He then is all my hope and stay. On Christ, the solid rock, I stand; All other ground is sinking sand.

Put Your Hands Together

During the destructive flood of 1982, residents of Fort Wayne, Ind., faced a major crisis. Despite round-the-clock efforts of city workers, the waters continued to rise. Sandbags could not be filled and placed in position fast enough to hold back the waters. An emergency call went out to the citizens of Fort Wayne. And they responded in droves. They put their hands together and worked until their backs were weary and their hands bruised. The battle was finally won as the waters receded. Later city leaders used as a slogan to help economic recovery, "Put your hands together, Fort Wayne."

Paul in our text suggests that Christians need to work together within the fellowship of believers. Faced with persecution and ridicule for confessing Christ, the Philippian believers needed one another. Entrusted with Christ's command to be witnesses to the ends of the earth, they could succeed only by putting their hands together.

Paul urges us to witness to the Savior's love continually. Faced with ridicule, indifference, and anti-Christian values, we desperately need one another within the fellowship of believers.

Paul provides power for this cooperative venture by pointing to the one who put His hands to work for us. He took the nature of a servant, was made in human likeness, humbled Himself, and became obedient to death—even death on a cross. Because Jesus Christ completed His saving work for us, He joins us to the Christian community in our Baptism and enables us to serve one another joyfully as we reach out to the world. Put your hands together!

Prayer: *Stand up, stand up for Jesus; The trumpet call obey; Stand forth in mighty conflict In this his glorious day.*

Lenten Listening Posts: With the Sanhedrin

Preparing again to remember the death and resurrection of Jesus Christ, we station ourselves at various Lenten Listening Posts to see what we can learn.

The chief priests and Pharisees call a meeting of the Sanhedrin to discuss how to deal with Jesus of Nazareth. Their scheming sounds sinister to us. But from their point of view, they were developing a plan, not a plot. They loved the temple and the laws. They loved their nation with its heritage. They wanted to protect that heritage and saw Jesus as a threat. The high priest's suggestion that one man die for the people provided a reasonable, though distasteful, way to solve their problem. Despite their rationalizations, these leaders were plotting, not planning, to get rid of the Son of God.

We develop our plans also. They seem quite reasonable. We love our heritage in home, church, and nation. We assume that what is good and right for us is good and right for everyone else. The Lord must be on our side. Nevertheless, like the Pharisees, our plans can easily turn into plots. Sin, rebellion, selfishness, and disobedience can easily lurk beneath the surface of our righteous-sounding plans. God exposes our plots as we examine ourselves with the searchlight of His Word.

Over our plots stands God's saving plan for the world. God took the plotting of the scribes and Pharisees and used it to make His Son the sacrificial lamb. The high priest's words stand as a prophesy, "You do not realize that it is better for you that one man die for the people" (John 11:50). And God works in us and through us despite our bungling. He forgives our plotting and transforms us into Gospel agents of His saving plan.

Prayer: Father, forgive our plots and use us in Your saving plan. Amen.

Lenten Listening Posts: In the Upper Room

We listen to the disciples in the Upper Room on Thursday of Holy Week. What was their mood? We usually interpret the Upper Room in the light of Good Friday. Therefore, we assume the disciples were somber and reflective. A better case could be made for linking Maundy Thursday with Palm Sunday. Jesus had entered Jerusalem triumphantly. The Messiah was coming into His own. Opposition, yes, but Jesus could win with His popular support. The disciples probably anticipated a great future for themselves. No doubt they relished the thought of a Passover meal with the soon-to-be-crowned Messiah.

They probably felt joyful, confident, and expectant. Internally they swelled with pride because of the good fortune they were experiencing. They disputed as to which of them should be considered the greatest.

How do you feel when everything seems to be going well? Externally you feel joyful, confident, and expectant. Internally you swell with pride and wonder whether you have received sufficient recognition for your accomplishments. At least in our minds, we join the dispute about who is the greatest.

But listening to Jesus produces a completely different result. He has come not to be served, but to serve. He washes the feet of the disciples, an act of lowly service. He tries to prepare them for the coming events. He goes as Suffering Servant to the cross, wearing a crown of thorns for us.

We look to Jesus. Confessing our pride, we rely on His service on our behalf. We cling to Him and rethink our values, placing our confidence not in our abilities or accomplishments, but in His promises.

Prayer: Lord, replace our pride with Your humble service. Amen.

Lenten Listening Posts: In Gethsemane

Jesus' disciples seem incredibly naive about evil. Still expecting Jesus' popular triumph, they don't look at the gathering storm clouds. Although warned repeatedly by Jesus about His imminent suffering and death, they continue hoping. They underestimate the forces of evil and overestimate themselves. They agree with Peter that they will never disown Jesus, even if they have to die with Him. Offered the opportunity to pray with Jesus for strength, they fall asleep. Naive about evil.

How often we live with the same false optimism. We don't look ahead, though forewarned by Scripture about great evil in the end times. We underestimate the forces of evil—while the family unit is breaking down, human lives are snuffed out, and massive attacks are aimed at the church. We believe our faith can withstand any tests, and we promise to remain faithful even unto death. Yet we avoid opportunities to commune with our Father.

By contrast, Jesus faced His darkest hour realistically. Looking ahead with full knowledge of the cross, He accurately counted the cost and His own need for communion with the Father. He prayed and was strengthened. He moved on to the Judgment Hall and Calvary, defeating evil with His sacrificial death. He died for the naive disciples and us.

He stands by us. Turning our naiveté into a realistic look at evil, we embrace Jesus Christ in faith and claim His victory. We come daily to His Word, live in our Baptism, and go to the Holy Supper for strength and forgiveness.

Prayer: Lord, prepare us realistically to fight evil through Your shed blood. Amen.

Lenten Listening Posts: In the Council Room

We listen in the council room where the Sanhedrin is trying Jesus. Do they praise or blaspheme God?

Some of Israel's leaders gather to uphold the honor of God by striking out against the "blasphemous" Jesus. Ostensibly they praise God by their actions. In reality they blaspheme God because they are mockng God's Son. They meet illegally at the high priest's house instead of at the temple, at a forbidden time—night—using false witnesses, without adequate time for the verdict to stand. They mock Jesus, slap Him, and treat Him roughly. Blasphemy on their part, not praise.

But surely we praise Jesus while condemning the Sanhedrin! We believe in regular worship. We strike out against religious enthusiasm. Or is our intended praise really blasphemy? We limit Christ in our midst, restricting Him to our forms of worship. We don't want Jesus to rule our lives. In effect we place Him on trial for exceeding the bounds of religious traditions. Blasphemy on our part, not praise!

Jesus was accused of blasphemy. He dared to forgive the sins of the palsied man. He stated who He was as the Messiah and Son of God. Actually His life was filled with praise. He obeyed the Father at every point. He died for the blasphemers, praying, "Father, forgive them, for they do not know what they are doing" (Luke 23:34). His death and resurrection lifted praises to the Father.

Jesus turns our blasphemy to praise. He forgives our sin. He frees us to live as little Christs. By His grace we are sons and daughters of the living God. That's not blasphemy, but praise.

Prayer: Lord, fill us with Your praise. Amen.

Lenten Listening Posts: In the Courtyard

Peter displays much courage in the garden when he draws his sword to protect Jesus, though hopelessly outnumbered by the temple guard. He follows Jesus to the courtyard at great personal risk. What courage! He loves Jesus and stands up for Him. We could call this self-courage.

We also know the inadequacy of Peter's self-courage. A servant girl challenges him. Another does the same. Then others say, "Surely you are one of them, for your accent gives you away" (Matthew 26:73). Three challenges to his self-courage, three denials, the last one with curses. Then the remembrance and the remorse. Self-courage defeated.

What self-courage we sometimes display. We handle household emergencies, deal with lingering illness, manage a change in job or school, and stand up to be counted for our faith. We love Jesus. But our courage also fails us. We often run and hide. We deny our Lord when pressed at home, on the job, and even in our church. We remember the words of Jesus and weep bitterly. Self-courage defeated.

Thank God for Christ-courage. He depended on the Father in the hour of trial. He moved unflinchingly to His arrest, trial, and crucifixion. He had the necessary courage to endure the taunts and jeers, the lashes and crown of thorns, all the brutal agony. Christ looked at Peter with love. He forgave him and filled him, after the resurrection, with Christ-courage. Peter, repentant for his denial, became a bold spokesman for the Gospel. Christ fills us also with His courage. Forgiven, we can daily receive strength from God's Word to tackle our witness opportunities at home and in the community.

Prayer: Lord, give us Your courage in crisis. Amen.

Lenten Listening Posts: In the Judgment Hall

Jesus' enemies seem to have Jesus on the defensive. They display such dignity! The scribes and Pharisees in their rich garments, Pontius Pilate, resplendent as Roman governor. These leaders possessed status and authority. Dignified, indeed!

In reality they acted defensively. The leaders and the crowd had to cover up and prove their point. They had no clear case for the death penalty. Their trumped-up charges grasped at straws. They protested too much. Pilate, too, was defensive. His wife warned him not to prosecute. He tried to assuage the angry crowd in several ways. Ultimately, afraid of a riot, he washed his hands, hoping that would cover up his actions. Clearly defensive, not dignified!

We like to appear dignified as leaders at home, in the community, at work, and at church. But like Pilate and the Pharisees, we often live defensively. We make up excuses for our actions—why we don't attend church regularly or witness or love our relatives. We protest too much by asserting our innocence and blaming someone else. Inside, like Pilate, we are afraid to stand up against popular opinion. Undignified, which means unworthy, we are clearly defensive.

Only Jesus Christ, the defendant, displayed true dignity. He remained silent before His captors. He looked every inch the king, though suffering with a crown of thorns. He felt no need to defend Himself. "Worthy is the Lamb who was slain!"

And Jesus makes us worthy by His death and resurrection. We need not be defensive as we admit our sins. We can be dignified as we give ourselves for others, affirming their worth.

Prayer: *Lord, give us Your dignity as we praise You. Amen.*

TGIF

How often we use the expression TGIF—Thank God, It's Friday. Teachers sigh with relief as the weekend approaches. Factory workers seek a change of pace from the tiring routines of the assembly line. Wall Street traders leave the hectic noise of the exchange. TGIF—Thank God, It's Friday.

No such relief for the Son of God. Friday brought the greatest intensity of His suffering. Mark simply records, "Then they led Him out to crucify Him" (Mark 15:20). Arrested, tried, flogged, sleepless, He stumbles on to Calvary, where six hours of agonizing pain await His weakened body. He bears our sins, the sins of the world, on His shoulders and fights the combined forces of Satan, sin, and death. Instead of saying, "TGIF," Jesus cries out, "My God, My God, why have You forsaken Me?" (Matthew 27:46).

But in that death He wins the victory by His once-for-all sacrifice. "It is finished!" becomes His triumphant cry. Justified by His blood, we enjoy peace with God. That Friday in Holy Week becomes Good Friday year after year.

How much more pertinent to think of Jesus every Friday. TGIF—not mere relief from the week's work through a weekend of relaxation, but a reminder of Good Friday and eternal life through the death and resurrection of Jesus Christ. Thank God, it's Friday.

Prayer: Dear Lord, thank You for Your willing suffering on that first Good Friday to pay for our sins. Fill our hearts with joy each week as we complete our labors and rest in Your forgiveness. Amen.

Ministry Temptations Waiting

Were Jesus' temptations in the wilderness merely personal temptations? Certainly He was personally attacked. Forty days without eating left Him vulnerable to Satan's appeal to change stones into bread. But Luke seems to indicate that these temptations were ministry temptations. God's plan for the world was at stake in Jesus' ministry. The wilderness temptation stands between Jesus' baptism and the beginning of His public ministry. If He succumbs to temptation, His ministry is destroyed. Luke records the third temptation as occurring at the temple in Jerusalem, where Jesus' ministry will ultimately take Him. Furthermore, Luke indicates that "when the devil had finished all this tempting, he left Him until an opportune time" (Luke 4:13). In other words, Satan will continue threatening Jesus' ministry. How glorious that Jesus overcomes Satan's temptation and carries out His ministry of salvation!

When Satan tempts us, are they merely personal temptations? Certainly we sometimes think of temptations as threatening our salvation. But in a broader view, are not our temptations also ministry temptations? God's plan for the world in Christ works through us. Jesus' ministry is our ministry. When we succumb to Satan's temptation, ministry damage is done.

Weak, often gullible and unsuspecting, we need the strong Son of God in this Lenten season. Victor over the wiles of Satan, crucified in payment for our sins, Jesus stands at our side with His Word to give us victory over temptation and encouragement for caring ministry during this Lenten season.

Prayer: Reflect on your ministry during Lent. Consider specific temptations facing you right now. And claim the forgiveness of Christ for power over Satan's temptation.

The Temptation to Seek Bread

Hungry? Forty days without food creates a gnawing hunger. The devil's temptation struck at this point of need. But more calculatingly, Satan raised the question of Jesus' purpose on earth. "If You are the Son of God ..." (Luke 4:3). Later He would be tempted to act as a wonder-working Messiah, bringing worldly prosperity, rather than a Suffering Servant bringing forgiveness through a cruel cross.

Here as elsewhere, Jesus defeats the devil with the Word of God. "It is written, 'Man does not live on bread alone' " (Luke 4:4). Sustained by the Father's Word, Jesus moves on to a ministry in the shadow of the cross.

Hungry? Indeed, we need daily bread and desire much more. Life in a materialistic society creates a gnawing hunger for bread and cars and clothes. The devil's temptation strikes at this point of need. He suggests that if we truly believe in Jesus, He will surely give us more and more prosperity. Always we are tempted to revere Jesus as a bread king who will provide for our worldly needs. Then our purpose is sabotaged. We seek to gain wealth rather than lose ourselves, to be served rather than to serve, to receive rather than to give.

As with Jesus, our antidote to Satan lies in the Word of God, "It is written, 'Man does not live on bread alone.' " Convicted of our insatiable hunger for more and more things, we turn in repentance to Jesus as Suffering Servant and receive His full forgiveness won on the cross. We feed on that forgiving Word, eat His body, drink His blood, then rise to follow Him on a Lenten ministry in the shadow of the cross.

Prayer: Dear Lord, forgive me for seeking bread more than You. Amen.

The Temptation to Compromise

What an offer! The kingdoms of the world in exchange for simply worshiping the devil. All Jesus has to do is compromise, and He would have the world at His feet. "No one needs to know about the arrangement. Just think how much good You can accomplish—and without the cross!"

A recurring theme throughout history, not just in Luke's account of Jesus' temptation. *Faust, The Devil and Daniel Webster, The Year the Yankees Lost the Pennant* (on which the Broadway musical *Damn Yankees* is based)—all tell the dramatic story of some earthling tempted to sell his soul to the devil in exchange for some greatly desired success. Are we immune to this temptation?

"Sell my soul to the devil? Never. I'm loyal to God." But just a little compromise. Nothing so drastic. Sleep in this Sunday morning. Keep working those extra hours. Your family will understand. "So if you worship me, it will all be yours."

But Jesus sees the devil's temptation for what it is. He replies, "It is written: 'Worship the Lord your God and serve Him only' " (Luke 4:8). No room for compromise. God or Satan. There is no in-between ground.

Our compromises abound. We divide our loyalties and our worship. Satan's offer appeals. Exposed, we repent and look to the one who alone makes our worship worthy. "Worthy is the Lamb who was slain." He forgives, heals, and fortifies us to live and worship without compromise. Victory is in sight because of Jesus' victory in the desert and at Calvary.

Prayer: Confess recent compromises at home, school, and on the job. Thank Jesus for His victory over Satan. Claim His victory for your own life.

The Temptation to Success

The scene, Jerusalem, site of the holy temple, focal point for a nation looking for deliverance from Roman oppression. Jesus with the devil at the pinnacle of the temple, looking down. Satan says, "Jump down," a sure path to spectacular success. If He lands safely in the temple courtyard, all Israel will be astir. The Messiah has come. Let's rally behind Him and win our independence. Jesus becomes hero of the hour. But at what cost? His only business in Jerusalem is a cross rather than a crown. Fully aware of His mission, Jesus answers Satan, "It says, 'Do not put the Lord your God to the test' " (Luke 4:12).

The scene, North America, site of prosperity, focal point for a culture based on spectacular success. The 1984 Olympics in Los Angeles captured our hearts as a glittering array of medals were handed out. For months afterward, Olympic stars were seen on television endorsing everything from cereal to shoes. Spectacular success is a key ingredient of our culture. We teach our children early to succeed with an endless chain of Little League baseball, scouting, and beauty contests. We struggle to advance on the job, move to the right neighborhood, and belong to the proper social clubs.

The glory beckons in America. But our only business as the people of God is humble service to others, not spectacular success. Recognizing our misplaced priorities, we look to the one who willingly permitted Himself to be taken to a skull-shaped hill outside Jerusalem, where He died for our sins. His victory over Satan becomes the only victory we need for a life of service here and a life of praise hereafter.

Prayer: Dear Lord, by Your cross forgive me for my compulsion to succeed. Give me Your eyes to see the joy of serving others. Amen.

The Need for Cleansing

Electric dishwashers painlessly produce sparkling plates. Electric washing machines with the right detergent turn soiled shirts into fresh, garments. And what of sin? A small problem?

Not so! Think of the sin of David. Bathsheba was bathing when he first saw her. And "she had purified herself from her uncleanness," 2 Samuel 11:4 tells us. But ugly sin protruded. Adultery, the clear charge. Another man's wife was made pregnant by David. The need for cleansing was real. No easy solution. No human solution. The harder David tried to erase the stain, the more soiled the garment became. Uriah, home on leave at David's command, too much a loyal soldier to cover up David's foul deed. Front-line battle for Uriah, cold-blooded murder. The stain grows and grows. The need for cleansing is now desperate.

What sin stains your heart right now? Less dramatic, perhaps, than David committing adultery and murder. Human solutions seem workable. Rationalization. Excuses. But the harder you try to erase the stain, the more soiled the garment becomes. Others probably know. Ugly sin protrudes. Certainly you know. And God knows. More than a ritual prayer, you speak with the agonized cry of a terrified sinner, "Wash away all my iniquity and cleanse me from my sin" (Psalm 51:2).

And God alone cleanses us from our sin. "The blood of Jesus, His Son, purifies us from all sin" (1 John 1:7b). "Though your sins are like scarlet, they shall be as white as snow" (Isaiah 1:18). With the need for cleansing so great, thank God for the daily reminder of a cleansing Baptism in the name of the Father and of the Son and of the Holy Spirit.

Prayer: Lord, cleanse me from my sin. Amen.

The Terrible Knowing

David knows the depth of his sin, a terrible knowing. He did not start with that knowledge. He knew that all people were sinners. He knew that adultery and murder were sins in the sight of God. He knew that he had committed both sins. But he does not "know" his transgressions until the Lord sends Nathan to him with a story about a rich man who takes for himself the only ewe lamb of a poor man. Then Nathan says, "You are the man." Now David knows and tells Nathan, "I have sinned against the Lord" (1 Samuel 12:13). He acknowledges his sin, a terrible knowing.

Consider the case of a terminally ill woman, discovering the nature of her illness, a terrible knowing. She knew that everyone will die sometime. She knew that she had not been feeling well lately. But she doesn't "know" her condition until the doctor announces that she has the terminal illness. Even then, she does not acknowledge her condition until she is able to accept the truth, a terrible knowing.

Jesus says, "I know My sheep and My sheep know Me—just as the Father knows Me and I know the Father—and I lay down My life for the sheep" (John 10:14b–15). Paul writes, "I want to know Christ and the power of His resurrection" (Philippians 3:10). He adds in his letter to Timothy, "The Lord knows those who are His" (2 Timothy 2:19b). God's terrible knowing of the world's sin is balanced by His Son's complete payment for that sin on our behalf.

Prayer: Lord, to You I make confession: I have sinned and gone astray, I have multiplied transgression, Chosen for myself the way. Led by you to see my errors, Lord, I tremble at your terrors.

The Naked Confession

Adam and Eve were naked and were not ashamed, according to the creation account in Genesis 2. But soon they were hiding among the trees of the garden and wearing fig leaves. Why the change? They had rebelled against the Lord God by disobeying His command. Adam replies to a questioning God, "I was afraid because I was naked; so I hid" (Genesis 3:10). They now also cover up with excuses and passing the blame.

David sinned in his nakedness with Bathsheba. And he started covering up with lies, deception, and murder. His guilt only grew within. But now, confronted by the prophet Nathan, he makes the naked confession, "I have sinned against the Lord" (2 Samuel 12:13). God has seen David's naked sin all along. But now David makes a naked confession. Through Nathan, God can say to David, "The Lord has taken away your sin. You are not going to die" (2 Samuel 12:13). God accepts David and forgives him. He stands righteous before God because of the Son, the descendant of David, who will someday, stripped of clothing, hang naked on a cross to pay for the world's sin.

Will you make a naked confession of your sin? Fig leaves and trees cannot cover you. Excuses and blaming others cannot screen God's X-ray vision. We may well have sinned against the spouse or the children or the neighbor or the boss. But ultimately we need to make the naked confession to God, "Against You, You only, have I sinned and done what is evil in Your sight" (Psalm 51:4). And God assures us that He has taken away our sins through the Son who died exposed upon the cross. We are clothed in His righteousness alone, faultless to stand before the throne.

Prayer: *Lord, I have sinned against You. Forgive me. Amen.*

Iniquity Blotted Out

Oh, the stains that mar our lives—red beet juice on the favorite tie, grease on the white skirt, coffee stains on the linen tablecloth, household pet stains on the family room carpet, grass stains on the new tennis shoes, mustard on the car upholstery. And the attempts to blot out those stains often meet with utter frustration. Home remedies, expensive solvents, powerful solutions, and elbow grease take their turn, usually making the stain worse. And for every successful stain removal, another stain takes its place.

That's how David must have felt about his sin-stained life. How could he blot out his adultery with Bathsheba and his murder of Uriah? Convicted of his sin by Nathan, David knows he is helpless to remove it. No ritual cleansing will work. Consequently, he cries out to God, "Blot out all my iniquity" (Psalm 51:9). Only God can blot out David's sin. God would later say through the prophet Jeremiah, "I will forgive their wickedness and will remember their sins no more" (Jeremiah 31:34b). Iniquity completely blotted out, stain removed, sin forgotten.

The stain of our sin proves far more troublesome than coffee on a tablecloth. We see the stains and so does God—unkind words, selfish actions, ugly thoughts, simmering resentment, green-eyed envy, bitter complaining, halfhearted worship. All our efforts to blot out these stains only seem to make them more obvious. We cry out to God, "Blot out all my iniquity."

God sent His Son to blot out our iniquities. "He was pierced for our transgressions, He was crushed for our iniquities ... the Lord has laid on Him the iniquity of us all" (Isaiah 53:5a–6b).

Prayer: O Lamb of God who takes away the sin of the world, grant us Thy peace. Amen.

Created and Renewed

Familiar words, part of the Sunday liturgy, prominent also during Lent. What do these words mean for self-sufficient, stylish, outwardly successful people today? We create jobs, ideas, leisure activities, dream homes, get-rich-quick schemes, and friendships. We make things happen and pull ourselves up by our own bootstraps. Or do we?

David used the word "create" to ask: "Create in me a pure heart, O God" (Psalm 51:10). Now on the other side of his tragic affair with Bathsheba, he recognizes his need for cleansing with a terrible knowing that leads to a naked confession. He knows the darkness, chaos, and confusion of his heart. He is nothing and can do nothing to make his heart pure. God needs to create in him that pure heart. God alone can make something out of nothing. He alone can bring renewal. "God, who said, 'Let light shine out of darkness,' made His light shine in our hearts to give us the light of the knowledge of the glory of God in the face of Christ" (2 Corinthians 4:6). The Creator became a creature in the person of Jesus Christ, the second Adam. He lived with a pure heart and willingly died on a cross to bring light out of darkness. With the coming Messiah in view, God created a pure heart in David, granting full forgiveness. David's spirit was renewed for creative service.

"If anyone is in Christ, he is a new creation; the old has gone, the new has come!" (2 Corinthians 5:17). Laying aside our confused darkness and our shabby attempts to create our own world, we turn to the Creator, who points us to Christ and grants us a pure heart. His creative Spirit renews us for service.

Prayer: Create in me a pure heart, O God. Amen.

Joy Restored

Instant happiness. The goal of our age. Live life to the fullest. Grab what you want. Enjoy. Make big money. Above all, be happy. Appealing?

David grabbed for instant happiness, enjoyed a few fleeting moments with another man's wife, then plunged into a nightmare of guilt, sorrow, and despair. He learned the difference between the "happiness" of the moment and God's kind of joy. Repentant, he prays, "Restore to me the joy of Your salvation" (Psalm 51:12). Joy has its source outside of David, in God's salvation. God forgives David and preserves his life, even after his dreadful sin. The joy of God's salvation is restored.

And what of you? Do you seek that moment of exciting happiness, that forbidden pleasure—grabbing for the top job at any cost; golf on Sunday mornings; the occasional fling with someone else's spouse; the constant overindulging in food, alcohol, or drugs—fleeting happiness that can plunge you into a nightmare of guilt, sorrow, and despair?

"Restore to me the joy of your salvation." A fervent prayer to the God who can turn wailing into dancing and replace sackcloth with the clothing of joy. God's salvation makes the difference—the manger, the Upper Room, the cross, the empty tomb, the font, the altar with bread and wine, the circle of God's people, the reunion before the heavenly throne. Joy overflows from the saving acts of God to produce a peaceful mind, a clear conscience, a voice of praise, ready hands. Lasting joy instead of instant happiness for David and for us.

Prayer: Bane and blessing, pain and pleasure By the cross are sanctified; Peace is there that knows no measure, Joys that through all time abide.

Lips Opened for Praise

Are you having trouble praising God? Do you find yourself going through the motions of worship? Perhaps you blame your lack of musical ability or knowledge of the liturgy. You are in for a surprise. The secret of praise lies with God.

Look at David. He was a master musician, often playing the harp to soothe Saul's fits of rage. He is credited with writing many psalms, a major part of the "hymnbook" of the Old Testament church. He obviously was gifted in speech as king and psalm writer. Yet he finds it necessary to ask God to open his lips so he can praise the Lord. Why?

Could it be that David's lips had been sealed from praise because his heart had strayed from God? During the whole Bathsheba incident he had undoubtedly spoken and perhaps sung many words with his lips, but few words of praise to a God who disapproved of his sin. But having used words of confession to God for his sin, David prays for open lips, and God enables him to praise once again.

Forget about musical ability or a facile tongue. Look to your heart. Confess the words that spring from wrong thoughts and attitudes. With David pray, "O Lord, open my lips, and my mouth will declare Your praise" (Psalm 51:15). He will hear. God sent His Son, Jesus, to begin a new song with His birth, life, death, and resurrection. His cries of loneliness, forgiveness, and completion signal victory over all evil. God places the new song in our hearts at Baptism and opens our lips each day to declare His praise in word and song. He accepts our praise because He has accepted Christ's sacrifice for us.

Prayer: "*O Lord, open my lips, and my mouth will declare Your praise.*" *Amen.*

The Sacrifice of Brokenness

Formal sacrifices permeate the pages of the Old Testament, instituted by God with good purpose. But sacrifices sometimes became mere formalities without the worship of the heart.

David, a faithful proponent of formal sacrifices, has learned a lesson from his fall into the sins of adultery and murder. He writes, "The sacrifices of God are a broken spirit; a broken and contrite heart, O God, You will not despise" (Psalm 51:17). God has broken David's spirit by using the prophet Nathan to convince him of his sin. David has fully confessed his sin before God. In his brokenness David claims the mercy and promises of God. His broken spirit presents to God a pleasing sacrifice. Now the external sacrifices on the altar reflect the internal spirit of dependence on God for everything.

Are we not sometimes guilty of religious formalism? We think that our external acts—attending church, contributing financial resources, serving on church boards—count before God as pleasing sacrifices. All the while we may have haughty, hardened spirits that harbor secret sins. God knows our hearts and condemns our willful sin. He leads us to brokenness, where we recognize the inadequacy of our sacrifices.

We look to the once-for-all sacrifice of Jesus Christ as the spotless Lamb of God. God accepts Christ's sacrifice on our behalf. We respond by presenting our bodies as living sacrifices. The external acts remain as a testimony to Christ's sacrifice for us. We worship, give, serve, and love. But we start internally with the sacrifice of a broken spirit. Broken, we remember the one who was broken for us. We let the sweet savor of His sacrifice permeate our lives to the glory of God.

Prayer: Lord, break my heart so I may serve You. Amen.

A Disciple Depends

The next eight devotions will focus on the word *disciple*. Each devotion will highlight one letter to describe a characteristic of discipleship.

The first letter of *disciple* emphasizes that a disciple *depends*. In John 15 Jesus illustrates our relationship to Him with the imagery of the vine and branches. Detached branches can only wither and die. But attached branches, totally dependent on the vine, receive life and bear much fruit.

In the story of Holy Week we can see the contrasts. Simon Peter asserts his independence and falls short. He vows that he is ready to go with Jesus to prison and to death. He depends on himself and gets into trouble. True to Jesus' prediction, he denies his Lord three times. Jesus, on the other hand, depends totally on the heavenly Father. He prays, "Not My will but Yours be done" (Luke 22:42). He receives strength and resolutely moves on to the arrest, trial, and crucifixion for us.

We have much to learn from this biblical contrast. Like Peter we stress our independence. We make big promises but flee into the darkness and deny our Lord when the going gets rough. We need to confess our failure to depend on Him.

But Jesus, who depended on the Father, draws us to Him with His tender love and forgiveness. God attaches us to Christ, the Vine, by grace. His life flows through us and teaches us to depend on Him for everything. Like Jesus we can resolutely stand tall against the world and faithfully carry our crosses. Yes, a disciple *depends*!

Prayer: Faith clings to Jesus' cross alone And rests in him unceasing; And by its fruits true faith is known, With love and hope increasing.

A Disciple Imitates

Around the turn of the century, a novel was written entitled *In His Steps*, which has exerted wide influence. In it a pastor challenges some parishioners to live with the constant question, "What would Jesus do?" As the novel unfolds, the question changes the lives of many people.

The second letter of the word *disciple* emphasizes that a disciple *imitates*. Jesus taught by example. For three years the disciples followed Him everywhere. In the Upper Room Jesus washed their feet and asked them to follow His example. The disciples could not imitate Jesus on their own. They faltered, stumbled, and fell. They needed His saving action on the cross to bring them new life and the Spirit's outpouring at Pentecost to empower them. But by God's grace they later remembered His example and lived as He had taught them, also passing His example on to others.

How well do you imitate Jesus? During Lent you can retrace His steps to Jerusalem and Calvary. You can see His love, courage, obedience, and self-sacrifice. As a student and servant, you can learn to know your Teacher and Master.

Like the disciples, we falter, stumble, and fall. We learn to depend totally on God's grace in the death and resurrection of Jesus Christ. Then we can follow in His steps, living, in Luther's words, as "little Christs." We imitate Jesus in our words and actions. We disciple others to follow Jesus' example as well. Yes, a disciple *imitates*.

Prayer: "Come, follow me," said Christ, the Lord, "All in my way abiding; Your selfishness throw overboard, Obey my call and guiding. Oh, bear your crosses, and confide In my example as your guide."

A Disciple Serves

An upper room in Jerusalem. The night on which Jesus is betrayed. Jesus takes a towel, pours water in a basin, stoops down, and begins to wash the dust-crusted feet of His disciples. Twelve times He stoops and washes feet.

The third letter of the word *disciple* emphasizes that a disciple *serves*. The disciples learned from Jesus to serve in little, distasteful ways. Many times a disciple thinks of service in dramatic terms—going to a foreign mission field. But Jesus starts with dirty feet. The disciples learned to serve without glory or recognition. Belonging to community service organizations and church committees helps build a career. But Jesus washes feet in the privacy of an upper room. The disciples learned to serve simply because of love. Can we serve when there's nothing in it for us and when the act is not appreciated? Jesus loved His disciples and therefore washed their feet. We would rather be served than serve. We often avoid distasteful tasks and seek recognition for our service efforts. We confess our shabby discipleship before Almighty God.

But "the Son of Man did not come to be served, but to serve, and to give His life as a ransom for many" (Matthew 20:28). How else can you explain the bloody sweat, the stripes on His back, the crown of thorns, the weight of the cross on His shoulders, and the prayer, "Father, forgive them for they do not know what they are doing"? (Luke 23:34). He served us by dying and in the process forgave our sins. He fills us with His love and motivates us to *serve*.

Prayer: In sickness, sorrow, want, or care, Each other's burdens help us share; May we, where help is needed, there Give help as though to you.

A Disciple Commits

The fourth letter of the word *disciple* emphasizes that a disciple *commits*. Jesus says, "Follow Me." The disciple does not commit to a philosophy, a program, an organization, or a cause, but to a person, namely, Jesus Christ. What a difference! Jesus committed Himself totally to His disciples. He called them. He trained them. He provided for their needs. He admonished them. He forgave them. He prayed for them. He suffered and died for them. That's commitment.

Commitment means suffering and a cross, as Jesus said in our text. Peter resists the thought that Jesus, the Messiah, should have to suffer and die. By implication he doesn't want suffering and a cross for his own life either.

Suffering and a cross are not popular. We want status, success, wealth. We try to avoid suffering and live the good life. But Christ calls us to suffer for Him. Confessing our soft and easy Christianity, we turn to Jesus for forgiveness. He suffered and bore the cross for us so we might be able to suffer and bear our crosses for Him.

Commitment brings life and joy to the disciple. Jesus says, "Whoever loses his life for My sake will find it" (Matthew 10:39). Strangely, in forgetting ourselves and reaching out to others we find new life and the joy of discipleship. God grants that life. Helpless, exhausted on our own, we discover His life flowing through us to others. Yes, by God's grace, a disciple *commits*!

Prayer: Then let us follow Christ, our Lord, And take the cross appointed And, firmly clinging to his word, In suffering be undaunted. For those who bear the battle's strain The crown of heav'nly life obtain.

A Disciple Instructs

The fifth letter of the word *disciple* emphasizes that a disciple *instructs*. Before ascending into heaven, Jesus asked His disciples to make disciples of all nations by baptizing and teaching.

Disciples are first taught by the Master Teacher. Jesus instructed with words. Can you imagine listening to the Sermon on the Mount or hearing Jesus' parables? Jesus shared intimate moments with His disciples when He prayed to the Father and prepared them for the time after His death and resurrection.

Jesus also instructed with His life. He lived in close relationship with the Father. He acted obediently in every situation. He demonstrated compassion and took children in His arms. He exposed the hypocrisy of the Pharisees. Most of all, Jesus went willingly to His death on the cross and after His resurrection showed the disciples His hands and feet.

A disciple instructs. We speak words about Jesus as the only Savior from sin. We teach the Word of God and continue to study it. We instruct our children and grandchildren in the commandments of God and assure them of His love and forgiveness.

We also instruct with our life. We set the example of regular church attendance, sacrificial firstfruits giving, study of the Word, and Christian witness. We treasure our family relationships and our opportunities for service. We also admit our sins, ask for forgiveness, and live in that forgiveness. We rejoice in God's free gift of eternal life. By word and example, we *instruct* others so they can pass it on.

Prayer: *Lord, teach us Your saving truth so we can disciple others. Amen.*

A Disciple Prays

The sixth letter of the word *disciple* emphasizes that a disciple *prays*. Jesus tells His disciples to pray. He promises them, "You may ask Me for anything in My name, and I will do it" (John 14:14). That same evening in the Upper Room Jesus prays His High Priestly Prayer (John 17) on behalf of the disciples and the world.

Think about Jesus' prayer life. He prayed on mountaintops and in the wilderness, alone and with His disciples, early in the morning and late at night. At the time of His suffering and death He prayed in the Upper Room, in Gethsemane, and on the cross. What an example for the disciples and for us. Certainly prayer strengthened Jesus for His saving mission.

As disciples we are privileged to pray because Jesus has given us access to the heavenly Father. As God's dear children we can come freely into His presence. We praise God, confess our sins, thank Him for His many blessings, and pray for ourselves and others. We come to Him in prayer, admitting our need for help and seeking answers in His Word.

Prayer takes discipline. Trials come to test our faith and make prayer difficult. We often try regular prayer times but fail to sustain our efforts. Often we are distracted by busy schedules, interruptions, or wandering thoughts. But Jesus has paid for all our sins, including failure in prayer. We earn no merit because of our prayers. He forgives us in Word and Sacrament and moves us to respond in prayer and thanksgiving. He promises to answer our prayers. Certainly we may ask Him for a stronger prayer life, and He will supply it. Yes, a disciple *prays*!

Prayer: *Lord, teach us to pray. Amen.*

A Disciple Loves

The seventh letter of the word *disciple* emphasizes that a disciple *loves*. Without love all the other qualities mean nothing. In the Upper Room on Maundy Thursday, Jesus tells His disciples, "My command is this: Love each other as I have loved you" (John 15:12).

Note the source of a disciple's love—the Father and the Son. "As the Father has loved Me, so have I loved you. Now remain in My love" (John 15:9). We don't find our example of love in Hollywood or Valentine's cards or even in the sentiments of Mother's Day, but rather in the Father and the Son. In Pidgin English the word for "love" means "God hurts in His heart for us." That describes God's love beautifully. He hurts for us and sent His Son at great cost to die for us. That sturdy, enduring, self-giving love is the source of our love.

Jesus commands that we love each other as He has loved us. What a challenge! Not love because the other person loves us or meets certain conditions, but love despite others' reactions. "While we were still sinners, Christ died for us" (Romans 5:8).

We fall short. Our love flames up, then sputters and fizzles. Our love reaches out, then, rejected, turns to hatred and disillusionment. We confess that of all the qualities of discipleship, love exposes our sin the most.

But the same Jesus who commands love promises His unending love for us. He comes to us in His Word and in the Holy Meal where we are united together around His table. Yes, forgiven and loved, a disciple *loves*!

Prayer: *Father, help me to love others, based on the sacrificial love of Your Son, Jesus. Amen.*

A Disciple Enjoys

The final letter of the word *disciple* emphasizes that a disciple enjoys. In the Upper Room, on the night when He will be betrayed Jesus tells the disciples, "I have told you this so that My joy may be in you and that your joy may be complete" (John 15:11). In His hour of deepest sorrow Jesus talks about joy.

Jesus is the source of the disciples' joy. He rejoices in His relationship to the Father and with the disciples. The writer to the Hebrews states that "for the joy set before Him [Jesus] endured the cross, scorning its shame" (Hebrews 12:2).

In Jesus' joy we rejoice and, therefore, enjoy our discipleship. The disciples would sorrow, Jesus predicts, as they see Him arrested, tried, and crucified. They would sorrow also because of their sin in deserting Him. But like a woman going through childbirth, their sorrow would be turned to joy. They would see Jesus risen from the dead and ruling the world. They would live as disciples in that Easter joy. Yes, failure and sin. But always the joy of salvation, the joy of His presence in the Holy Supper, and the joy of a promised reunion in heaven.

We can enjoy discipleship in a similar fashion as we confess our sins, look to Jesus, fellowship at His Table, obey His commands, and anticipate the heavenly celebration.

We have considered the eight qualities of a disciple: **Depends, Imitates, Serves, Commits, Instructs, Prays, Loves,** and **Enjoys.** May your Lenten observance focus your attention again on the Master, Jesus Christ, crucified and risen, so by His grace you will joyfully live as a *disciple*!

Prayer: *Lord, make us faithful disciples. Amen.*

Spring and Creation

Spring has officially arrived. In many areas of the country, people are experiencing balmy breezes and soaring temperatures. Everyone wants to get outside and breathe the fresh air, to start thinking about gardening, golf, or fishing. Not only can we say, "Spring is here," but also "God is here." In the return of greenery to the earth, the budding of trees, the warbling of the birds, the warm sun, and the balmy breezes, God is announcing once more that He is alive.

In the words of Isaiah 45, the prophet is telling how God will use Cyrus to bring His people back to their homeland. He uses the language of creation to describe the salvation of His people. In many ways, we have tarnished God's creation by our sins. We have turned against God and tried to use His creation for our own glory rather than His. But God also makes possible a new birth for us so we can live for Him. He sent His only Son to bear our sins by dying on the cross. He conquered death and the devil and rose from the dead one spring Sunday morning to prove His victory. All who believe in Jesus Christ have new life and the promise of eternal life in heaven. "If anyone is in Christ, he is a new creation; the old has gone, the new has come!" (2 Corinthians 5:17).

Think about these things as spring begins. Turn to Christ for new life. Then ask God how you can best use the blessings of creation to serve Him and to help those in need. He will give you the life that is "springtime fresh."

Prayer: You forest leaves so green and tender That dance for joy in summer air, You meadow grasses, bright and slender, You flow'rs so fragrant and so fair, You live to show God's praise alone. Join me to make his glory known.

Needing the Cross

An assorted crowd stood beneath the cross, many of them hiding their need for Christ. Picture the arrogant scribes and Pharisees. Very much under control, they didn't need Jesus at all, except to get rid of Him as a threat to their religious standing. Picture the cocksure and hardened Roman soldiers—accustomed to this gruesome sort of routine work. Picture the cursing, mocking malefactors—guilty of some serious crime, using their dying hours to show their hardness and venom. All three groups, though externally hardened, were hiding their need for the cross.

What is our attitude when we come to the cross? Sometimes we might appear arrogant. We have our life under control and pity all the others who struggle and lack what we have. Sometimes we come across as hardened. We are able to act worldly and even find ourselves cursing and mocking in order to hide our own guilt. Yes, like the Pharisees, Roman soldiers, and malefactors, we often hide our need for the cross.

But one of the malefactors at the cross brings his needs to Jesus. Observing His innocence, His dignity in death, His power, this man asks Jesus for mercy. He admits his own guilt, sin, and fears. Only the cross of Jesus can help him. Lonely, afraid, guilty, and helpless, we also need the cross of Jesus.

And we hear Jesus' answer. To the pleading malefactor He says, "I tell you the truth, today you will be with Me in paradise" (Luke 23:43). All pretense removed, his needs freely confessed, the dying thief receives eternal life, which flows from the cross of Christ. Jesus speaks the same life-giving words to us: I am dying for your sins. You will be with Me in paradise.

Prayer: Lord, I need You and Your cross. Amen.

Drawn to the Cross

Powerful magnets attract metal, an almost irresistible attraction. Jesus talks about a drawing power that comes only from the Father, "No one can come to Me unless the Father who sent Me draws him" (John 6:44). He is talking about how the heavenly Father draws us to His cross for salvation.

Unfortunately, we often follow the wrong attractions. We revere magnetic personalities—professional athletes, entertainers, or political figures. Many times they draw us astray. In Jesus' day many forces drew people's attention and loyalty—the Maccabeans and zealots promoted political and military victory over the enemy, and the Pharisees and Sadducees convinced Judas to betray Jesus for money. These powerful forces which draw people to them will ultimately fail. They lead to slavery and destruction.

The only drawing power that works is the cross of Christ. We see it in the women who watched near the cross and later visited the tomb. We see it in John, the beloved disciple, who stood there with Jesus' mother. And a Roman centurion was transformed by the drawing power of that cross as he said, "Surely He was the Son of God" (Matthew 27:54).

Despairing of the phony magnetic attractions, we are drawn by the Father to the rugged cross where Jesus died to pay in full for the sins of the world. We are drawn to the cross, where we receive forgiveness and eternal life. Jesus gives us pardon, purpose, peace, and power—and our witness is used by God to draw others to that same saving cross.

Prayer: Drawn to the cross, which you have blessed With healing gifts for souls distressed, To find in you my life, my rest, Christ Crucified, I come.

Nailed to the Cross

Hammer blows ring through the morning air as the Son of God is nailed to the cross. Nails through the hands or wrists to hold Him securely. Throbbing pain to an already pain-racked body. Later He would show those nail-pierced hands as proof of His physical resurrection from the grave.

But the nails have even more significance. Paul writes, "I have been crucified with Christ ... Christ lives in me." (Galatians 2:20). In a sense we have been nailed to that cross of Christ. Certainly our sins have been nailed to it. In Romans, Paul writes: "We were therefore buried with Him through baptism into death" (Romans 6:4). We are in effect crucified, dead, and buried with Christ. Paul further writes, "Our old self was crucified with Him so that the body of sin might be done away with" (Romans 6:6). Yes, when we became children of God, we were nailed to the cross.

The cross makes a significant difference in our daily lives. In both Galatians and Romans, Paul tells us that our sins are nailed to the cross, thereby providing power for victorious living. "I no longer live, but Christ lives in me. The life I live in the body, I live by faith in the Son of God" (Galatians 2:20). "Now if we died with Christ, we believe that we will also live with Him" (Romans 6:8).

We live in our Baptism, and Christ lives in us. Nailed to the cross of Christ, we die to sin and live to God. The hammer blows ring out in the morning air. The Son of God dies once for all to pay for the world's sin. Those hammer blows ring for us as well—dead to sin, alive to God through Christ.

Prayer: O Lord, nailed to the cross, thank You for Your daily baptismal power in my life. Amen.

Wearing the Cross

What a common symbol the cross is today! We find crosses of sticks or precious jewels adorning church steeples, altars, homes, wedding cakes, caskets, and cemeteries.

St. Paul recognizes the cross for what it is: foolishness to the Greeks and a stumbling block to the Jews. He knows that the cross does not bring popularity or acceptance or material wealth. Nevertheless, he also knows that, to those who believe, the message of the cross is "Christ the power of God and the wisdom of God" (1 Corinthians 1:24). Therefore Paul proudly "wears" the cross as a symbol of the Gospel. He says, "For I resolved to know nothing while I was with you except Jesus Christ and Him crucified" (1 Corinthians 2:2). He "wears" the cross with his words and his actions.

What does "wearing" the cross mean for you? Certainly you can give witness by wearing a lapel cross or a cross pin or necklace. Some carry pocket crosses which constantly remind us of the one who died for us. But "wearing" the cross also means, declaring "Jesus Christ and Him crucified" not only in church, but at home, in the neighborhood, in school, and on the job. And "wearing" the cross involves actions, a total life lived for Jesus. We care, reach out, counsel, console, challenge, and suffer for Him. The world may scoff or ignore, but we continue "wearing" the cross.

When we conceal the cross or wear it to our shame, God points us again to the simple message that Christ died on the cross for our sins. Bolstered by the power and wisdom of God, we begin anew, wearing the cross for Jesus.

Prayer: *Lord, help me to wear Your cross proudly because of Your death for me. Amen.*

Jesus and Simon of Cyrene

One of the more moving scenes from an Easter pageant sponsored by our church portrays Jesus carrying His cross with great difficulty and falling under its weight. A man is grabbed from the onlookers and forced to shoulder that cross. As Simon stoops to carry the cross, his eyes meet those of Jesus, then the procession moves on to Calvary.

Jesus' journey to Calvary touches Simon of Cyrene. Simon meets Jesus unintentionally. He doesn't volunteer for cross-bearing. Yet Jesus touches Simon. Luke records that he carried the cross behind Jesus. With eyes fixed on Jesus, Simon learns to know Him as Savior. At least his sons, Alexander and Rufus, are later listed as members of the early church.

Jesus' journey to Calvary also touches you. His willing obedience to the Father's plan, His suffering and death, stand as eloquent testimony of His saving love. More than words, His actions and His look of love reach out to us. We may have met Jesus unintentionally. But God draws our eyes to Jesus dying for our sins, and we believe.

Our journey to Calvary also touches others. Simon carried the cross for Jesus and helped Him. As we obey the Father's will, we can touch the lives of others. Our actions, our caring, as well as our words, bear witness to the Christ who died for us. Jesus and Simon of Cyrene met one-on-one. We who know Jesus' personal love for us also can share Him with others one-on-one in the natural settings of daily life.

Prayer: Calv'ry's mournful mountain climb; There, adoring at his feet, Mark that miracle of time, God's own sacrifice complete. "It is finished!" hear him cry; Learn from Jesus Christ to die.

Journey's End

The journey to Calvary started with Jesus' birth, when He was already "a sign that will be spoken against" (Luke 2:34). As the spiritual goes, "Jesus our Savior was born for to die." He began His public ministry with strong strides as He vigorously taught and healed. From the Mount of Transfiguration in the north He "resolutely set out for Jerusalem" (Luke 9:51) on His final journey.

Triumphantly Jesus rode into Jerusalem with shouts of praise. But now He approaches journey's end—each small step agonizing, until He falls and receives help. Yet His greatest hour is at hand. All depends on these last hours. All the rest of the journey, magnificently handled, means nothing without a proper ending. A space shuttle may orbit the earth 36 times, but without a safe landing it will be a disaster.

Jesus no longer has to walk. They lift Him up on the cross. Passively obedient, He continues to suffer. And—even here—He continues to care for others—for the criminal malefactors, for His mother, even for those who have crucified Him. All alone and rejected, He dies. But at journey's end, the victory has been won. "It is finished!" He proclaims. Paid in full. Complete.

We kneel with Jesus at journey's end and leave there our crippling sins and our weary efforts to save ourselves. Dead to sin in Baptism, we rise with Him to a new life and a continuing journey. We press on toward journey's end in heaven with Him.

Prayer: Jesus, still lead on Till our rest be won; Heav'nly leader, still direct us, Still support, console, protect us, Till we safely stand In our fatherland.

Craving Spiritual Milk

People yawn in the pews, waiting for the termination of the sermon. "Do we have to read family devotions again? I've got homework." "I wanted to read my Bible this morning, but I just couldn't get up." How can we persuade one another to read and hear the Word of God?

How much persuasion does a hungry baby need to drink milk? The crying baby grabs hold and eagerly drinks the milk until satisfied. "Craving milk" is St. Peter's expression. He has already explained that we are born again through the living and enduring Word of God. Everything else withers and fades away, "but the word of the Lord stands forever" (1 Peter 1:25). That Word tells of the death and resurrection of Jesus Christ to bring us a living hope and a secure inheritance. Pure spiritual milk indeed!

Craving, you say? Not yawning, enduring, or complaining, but craving? Yes, *craving* pure spiritual milk. Hungry because there is no pure spiritual milk in the world. Malice, deceit, hypocrisy, envy, and slander, but no spiritual milk. We try to make it on our own without drinking God's pure spiritual milk. But we only begin to fret and cry. No one can rock us enough to satisfy that hunger. Close to the pure spiritual milk, we get all excited. We crave it. We grab hold and eagerly drink the Word of Christ's love for us and drink and drink and drink. Contentedly we fall asleep in the quiet confidence that more pure spiritual milk awaits us on the morrow.

Prayer: *Lord, your words are waters living, When my thirsting spirit pleads; Lord, your words are bread life-giving, On your words my spirit feeds.*

Not Ready for Solid Food

Craving the pure spiritual milk. Contented babies nursing. Good imagery for seeking the Word of God, which helps us grow. But infants dare not remain babies if they are to survive. Drinking milk helps them grow, and growing bodies require the nourishment of solid food

Paul writes in a scolding manner to the Corinthian Christians, who seem unable to grow up. Calling them "mere infants in Christ," he writes, "I gave you milk, not solid food, for you were not yet ready for it. Indeed, you are still not ready" (1 Corinthians 3:2). He exposes the evidence of their spiritual immaturity. They live with jealousy and quarreling within their church family. Therefore, they continue to receive nourishment only in the form of milk. They need repentance for their worldly wisdom and sinful conduct. They need Jesus Christ crucified for their sins.

Content to be "mere infants in Christ"? We like to think of ourselves as worldly and sophisticated. But Paul scolds us also for our immaturity. Too often we are not yet ready for the solid food that would give us spiritual growth. We still receive milk and even have difficulty digesting that!

Paul writes this letter to move those Corinthians toward maturity. He has confidence in God's Spirit to do His work, building on the foundation, Jesus Christ. And he humbles us in our Christian walk so we will confess our infantile behavior, turn again to the saving cross of Jesus Christ, and let the Holy Spirit move us from milk to solid food as we grow in His grace.

Prayer: Abide with us, our Helper, Sustain us by your Word; Let us and all your people To living faith be stirred.

A Steady Diet of Solid Food

Craving the pure spiritual milk like newborn babies—a satisfying beginning to our spiritual growth. Not yet ready for solid food—the result of our worldly wisdom and selfish living. But God wants us to eat a steady diet of solid food with the same craving as babies have for milk.

The writer to the Hebrews admonishes believers to seek solid food. He writes, "Anyone who lives on milk, being still an infant, is not acquainted with the teaching about righteousness. But solid food is for the mature, who by constant use have trained themselves to distinguish good from evil" (Hebrews 5:13–14). God wants to communicate the wonderful truth about Christ, who once and for all sacrificed Himself for the world. He wants to explain the implications of repentance, Baptism, and the resurrection of the dead for daily Christian life in a wicked world. But spiritual immaturity stands in the way.

Do we fail to live boldly for God with a clear testimony to the saving act of Jesus because we refuse to grow up spiritually? We ignore our foundation of baptismal faith in Jesus Christ. Can we ever move beyond milk to solid food?

Hebrews suggests constant use of the solid food of God's Word as we train ourselves to distinguish good from evil. God sent His Son to die for our immaturities. He opens up the Word for us with its fresh forgiveness and nurturing power. As we attend to that Word, we receive the nourishment necessary for growth.

Prayer: *Abiding, steadfast, firm, and sure The teachings of the Word endure. Blest he who trusts this steadfast Word; His anchor holds in Christ, the Lord.*

Why His Death?

A young seminary student was killed in a tragic accident. We wondered, "Why his death?" He showed great promise for pastoral ministry, warmly related to others, and demonstrated good ability as a theological student.

I'm certain you can relate to similar deaths. The question pounds: Why his death? Why her death? No easy answer emerges, though we often try to rationalize. Gripped by grief and puzzled, we continue to search for God's answer.

Why His death? The right question when we refer to Jesus Christ. After all, He was and is God's only Son, who came into the flesh because He loved us so much. He lived a perfect life. He healed, helped, and served those around Him. Yet they arrested, tried, and convicted Him on trumped-up charges. And they killed Him by nailing Him to a cross with common criminals. Why His death?

St. Paul answers that question clearly: "But God demonstrates His own love for us in this: While we were still sinners, Christ died for us. Since we have now been justified by His blood, how much more shall we be saved from God's wrath through Him!" (Romans 5:8–9). He died for us so that we might live forever with Him.

I know that the young seminary student stands before God, washed clean in the blood of Christ. Though I don't understand God's timing, I know that this death gives witness to the resurrection of Christ and the sure hope of eternal life for all who believe in Christ crucified and risen from the dead.

Prayer: The sinless Son of God must die in sadness; The sinful child of man may live in gladness; We forfeited our lives yet are acquitted; God is committed!

The Ability to Be Wrong

A few years ago the editor-in-chief of *Time* magazine gave a commencement address at New York University on a subject not taught at any American university: "The Ability to Be Wrong." How many domestic quarrels start and continue because neither husband nor wife has the ability to be wrong? The barrier between teenagers and parents often is caused by the same inability to be wrong.

In the business world the ability to be wrong is also needed. The young junior executive, fresh out of college, offers a fistful of progressive ideas, challenging the traditional operation. The experienced senior executive disdains the cocky, know-it-all newcomer. They hold each other at arm's length, each convinced of the other's wrong position. Political viewpoints harden in a similar fashion, giving rise to bitter controversy and a reluctance to back down.

John clearly addresses this issue. "If we claim to be without sin, we deceive ourselves and the truth is not in us" (1 John 1:8). Not one of us has the right to say that we are always right. The husband and wife, the teenager, the young or older executive, and the politician suffer from the same malady—sin. We can get down on our knees daily and confess our wrongs, asking for God's forgiveness. Then, as John reminds us, "He will forgive and purify us" (1 John 1:9). God sent His Son to suffer and die for our wrongs. God declares us righteous for Jesus' sake. Forgiven, we are free to admit our wrongs to our neighbor at home, at work, and in the community. Only God gives us the ability to be wrong. Think what a difference a good dose of that ability could make in our world today.

Prayer: Lord, help me to admit to others when I am wrong. Amen.

Lessons from a Storm

I remember a Sunday evening storm that came without warning. Fear gripped us as the sky grew livid with flashes of lightning, the rain beat against the window of our apartment, and sirens screamed in the distance. Suddenly, a loud knock at the door urged us to join our neighbors in the basement apartment because tornadoes had been sighted nearby. Hastily gathering our sleeping 1-year-old from his crib, we rushed down the back stairs, and we saw the back door torn off its hinges. Entering the basement apartment, we spotted our other neighbors sitting by candlelight, holding their small children. We felt cut off from the rest of the city, wondering if others had suffered great damage or even loss of life. We prayed. Soon the worst was over, and we returned to our beds.

How suddenly our sense of values can change. Normal events fade into the background when an emergency threatens. With the storm outside, we were concentrating on the essentials of life—surviving, protecting our children. We felt very close to one another and to others in our community in similar danger.

The Bible tells us that the day of the Lord will come like a thief in the night—without time for special preparation. Who knows when we will stand before God? But we can be ready for the Lord at all times. God sent His only Son, Jesus Christ, to die on the cross for our sins and to rise from the grave. God works faith in our hearts and makes us His own people in Holy Baptism. Trusting Christ alone for salvation, we are moved to love others and reach out to them while praising God for His mercy. May God ever bring us closer to His Son, Jesus Christ!

Prayer: Lord, thank You for lessons from a storm. Amen.

Gossip or Gospel?

Gossip—what an ugly word! The dictionary defines it as "idle, often malicious talk, especially about others." The writer of Proverbs bluntly calls a gossip one who "betrays a confidence" (Proverbs 11:13). The word has a disgusting ring.

Rarely do we think of ourselves as gossips. Others talk on the phone at length with the latest news about the new minister. Others enjoy scandalous celebrity newspapers in grocery checkout lines. Others regularly break confidences. But we join in the conversation only when we have the facts.

Could it be that we too are guilty of gossip? We permit others to talk in our presence. We find our own tongue slipping. We damage reputations. We strain friendships. That ugly word *gossip* comes home to roost, and we need to confess our sin.

The word "gossip" comes from the Old English word "God-sibb," meaning "baptismal sponsor" or "relative." To me *God-sibb* suggests the word "Gospel," the good news that God sent His only Son, Jesus Christ, to die on the cross for our sins. In Baptism that Gospel changes us into God's own special people. He gives us confidence and faith in Him as Savior and urges us to share that Gospel freely, no secrets reserved. That Gospel announces full forgiveness for our sins of gossip and gives us the power to hold our tongues when we should and to speak the Good News when we can. You see, Jesus Christ "was oppressed and afflicted, yet He did not open His mouth" (Isaiah 53:7), and when He spoke, many of His words were Gospel.

By God's grace the ugly word *gossip* can be transformed into the beautiful word *Gospel*. Which will it be for you?

Prayer: *Father, forgive us for idle, malicious words. Fill our mouths with the Good News of Your Son, Jesus Christ. Amen.*

Daily Burdens Transformed

Daily burdens mount. Strife in the family. Clutter left behind—dirty dishes, towels. Traffic heavy. Late arrival. Headache begins. Pressures increase. Unfinished work. Decisions to be made. Rushed lunch. Complaints. Traffic heavy. Home for rest. More demands. Children's arguments. Telephone ringing during supper. Late to bed. Daily burdens.

Do you experience daily burdens? Our hectic, modern society is not the only one to claim daily burdens. Israel of old experienced similar problems, the result of sin and selfishness. Nations threatened destruction. Rulers made demands. Each family struggled for survival.

But the psalmist brings a message of joyful praise. God, who brought Israel out of Egypt and into the Promised Land, would also lead Israel in triumphal procession back from captivity to Jerusalem. He who would send a Messiah also daily cared for the needs of His people.

Replay the daily burdens from breakfast to bed. Picture the Lord present to bear them. See Him empowering us to praise Him in the midst of problems. See Him using us to bear the daily burdens of others. Begin the day with the sign of the cross. Remember your Baptism. Fall asleep at day's end with the confidence that all your sins have been fully forgiven in His blood. Look forward with eagerness to the new day. Daily burdens become daily blessings.

Prayer: Let each day begin with prayer, Praise and adoration. On the Lord cast ev'ry care; He is your salvation. Morning, evening, and at night Jesus will be near you, Save you from the tempter's might, With his presence cheer you.

God's Spacious Place

Americans traditionally love wide-open spaces. The move from crowded cities to suburban living reveals this desire for space. Yet we still feel crowded. Cars jam the freeways. We often work among hundreds or thousands of people in a confined space. In short, we often live in narrow, confined prisons of human making.

David in Psalm 18 describes God's spacious place. He reviews his life and the many harrowing escapes from his enemies. He knows the meaning of being hemmed in on every side. He was forced to hide from Saul in caves and behind rocks. How confined and bottled up he had felt!

But David rejoices that God "brought me out into a spacious place; He rescued me because He delighted in me" (Psalm 18:19). Yes, God gave David and Israel the Promised Land and its largest borders. But more important, David learned that God always provides a spacious place for us in the freedom of His promises. He rescues us in His Son, the promised Messiah.

No matter where we live or work, God brings us out into the spacious place of His love in Jesus Christ. Jesus narrowed His road to an appointment in Jerusalem. He was hemmed in by His accusers, confined to a cross between two thieves, and laid in a cave-like tomb behind a huge stone. But God rolled away the stone, and Jesus came out into a spacious place, where He rules the universe. We are free now to praise God and joyfully anticipate the spacious heavenly places forever.

Prayer: Dear Father, free me from the cramped quarters of my sin and bring me out into the spacious place of Your love in Jesus Christ, my Lord. Amen.

A Firm Place to Stand

How shaky our world today! The dollar slips and slides on the world money market. Political leaders rise and fall. Solid jobs disappear with the rapid change from an industrial to an information society. Long-term marriages break up, with shattering consequences. Longtime church members fall away from the faith. Ministers drop out of their calling. Is there no rock, no security, no firm place to stand?

David in Psalm 40 faces the same uncertainties. He describes himself as being in a slimy pit. His situation is desperate. No strength to fight free from the mud and mire. Aware of his sin and the power of his enemies, he cries out to the Lord for help. Joyfully David proclaims the words of our text. God is his Rock, Redeemer, and Fortress. God lifts him out of the mud and mire. Now David has security. Problems and troubles remain. Sin still afflicts him. But God brings deliverance.

As we cry out to God from the mud and mire of our sinful lives, God rescues us as well. He has sent His Son, Jesus Christ, as the Rock of our salvation, the Rock on which He builds the church. Jesus by virtue of His life, death, and resurrection stands firm and unshakable. When we build our house on this Rock, we have a firm foundation.

Problems and troubles remain. The world continues to wobble and totter. Sin still afflicts us. We may fall into other slimy pits. But God stands ready to set us again on the rock of Christ and His unfailing Word. Rejoice. Cling to the Rock. Bring others to the same sure footing.

Prayer: *Rock of Ages, cleft for me, Let me hide myself in thee; Let the water and the blood, From thy riven side which flowed, Be of sin the double cure: Cleanse me from its guilt and pow'r.*

Unrestrained Joy

Joy is not always associated with Christianity. In fact, the stereotype of the New England Puritan gives quite the opposite impression. Cartoonists often picture the Puritan as an austere, gaunt, solemn-faced person dressed in black. The pleasures of this world are rejected in favor of a disciplined, serious, frugal life with plenty of Bible reading and Sunday meetings for worship. In reality Puritans don't deserve the stereotype. They actually wore colorful clothes on occasion. But many people identify Christianity with the caricature of the Puritan.

Nevertheless, joy constitutes a basic ingredient of the Christian life. God created the earth with its fields and streams, crops and animals. And He placed human beings on earth to enjoy these blessings with praise to Him. True, we turned against God and brought ugliness, hatred, and sorrow into the world through our sin. But God still bestows the gift of joy on His people. He continues to shower His blessings on us. He enables us to laugh, sometimes in the face of life's disappointments.

The Christian rejoices for two reasons. First, we know that a loving God has reclaimed us by sending Jesus Christ to die on the cross, and He offers us forgiveness of sins for Jesus' sake. Second, because of this special relationship with God, we also see God's loving hand at work in creation. We rejoice at the goodness of God wherever we see it. The all-conquering power of God marches on to bring joy.

Prayer: Rejoice, the Lord is King! Your Lord and King adore; Rejoice, give thanks and sing, And triumph evermore: Lift up your heart, lift up your voice; Rejoice; again I say, Rejoice!

Is Your House Divided?

Abraham Lincoln once gave a famous "house divided" speech. Although his actual biblical quote comes from a statement of Jesus that Satan cannot drive out Satan (therefore, Jesus could not be possessed by Satan), it nevertheless raises the question: Is your house divided?

Is your life divided against itself? Are you sometimes Dr. Jekyll and sometimes Mr. Hyde? You want to live for Jesus but often live for yourself.

Is your family divided against itself? Jacob and Esau fought, though they were brothers. Absalom rebelled against his own father, David. How does your family scrap, undermine, and shatter the unity that God intends?

Is your church divided against itself? Jews and Gentiles, with differing cultural backgrounds and traditions, clashed in the early church. The congregation in ancient Corinth was plagued by factions. Similar conflicts exist today.

The ultimate division pits Christ against Satan. Satan unites with the world and our sinful flesh to war against God. The battle rages fiercely and reveals itself in our divided lives. See the house divided for what it is—Satan versus God.

Who can unite our lives? Jesus Christ is united with the Father and the Holy Spirit. His life, death, and resurrection, united with the Father's will, works salvation and restores unity between God and humanity. The Spirit rules the flesh. We have power to fight Satan. Christ unites our families through His cross, giving us love to share and forgiveness to heal our divisions. He unites our churches through His pure, inspired Word and the unifying sacraments.

Prayer: Dear Lord, bring us together in Your love. Amen.

A Prophet without Honor

People love to honor heroes and celebrities. Astronauts. Presidents. Olympic athletes. We roll out the red carpet and strike up the brass bands.

Why then did Jesus, the Son of God and Savior of the world, receive such a cool reception in His hometown of Nazareth? He came fresh from several triumphs. He taught powerfully in the synagogue. But the crowd raised serious questions about His authority. "Isn't this the carpenter? Isn't this Mary's son?" they asked. No red carpet. No brass bands. Despite all He had done, Jesus appeared commonplace to them.

We say: "How terrible! We would have given Him a hero's welcome." Would we? Sometimes Jesus becomes commonplace to us. We may fail to honor Him as we use the familiar liturgy, practice the traditional customs, and repeat the doctrinal formulations. We often live our lives as though He didn't exist. Sometimes our familiarity breeds skepticism and unbelief.

But God raised up people who honored Jesus. John the Baptizer honored Him even to the death. The disciples, after His resurrection, obeyed and proclaimed His salvation. Paul asserted, "I resolved to know nothing while I was with you except Jesus Christ and Him crucified" (1 Corinthians 2:2). Why the difference? God changed their attitudes from dishonor to honor. He sent His Son to die and rise, worked faith in their hearts through the Word, and filled their hearts with praise.

In the same way Jesus reveals Himself to us as Savior. Sins of dishonoring Him forgiven, we honor Jesus with our lives. Sometimes we will be treated as prophets without honor, but Jesus moves us to keep on honoring Him every day.

Prayer: Lord, help us to honor You each day. Amen.

Is God's Kingdom Your Treasure?

Buried treasure sparks intense interest—Spanish gold hidden in the Rockies or pirate loot buried on a deserted island. People have invested great quantities of time and money and sacrificed their lives in pursuit of such treasure.

Matthew 13 contains a series of parables on the kingdom of heaven. One brief parable describes a man finding a treasure hidden in a field. You almost can picture his excitement as he uncovers the treasure. He reburies the treasure, rushes away to sell everything he owns, then buys the field.

The parable identifies the treasure as God's kingdom. God rules the universe. He chooses a special people for His own. He redeems them through His Son's death. He calls them to serve in His kingdom. Belonging to that kingdom of God by grace represents a priceless treasure.

Is God's kingdom your treasure? Unfortunately, many glittering treasures beckon that detract from God's kingdom—success on the job, material wealth, family happiness. The root problem: We try to build our own selfish kingdoms. All kingdoms of this world crumble. Glittering treasures turn out to be fool's gold.

But God creates in our heart a burning desire for the treasure of His kingdom. Jesus ushered in the kingdom with His message, His sinless life, and His sacrificial death on the cross. The cost to God was tremendous. God's Spirit has freely given us the treasure of His Son so we might join Him in joyful kingdom service. Valuing God's kingdom, we give our all to the challenge of extending it to the ends of the earth.

Prayer: Hence, all earthly treasure! Jesus is my pleasure, Jesus is my choice.

Hungry for the Bread of Life?

How we hunger for meaning and purpose in life—not just going through the motions and collecting the paychecks! How we hunger for love at a deep level—not just casual friendship or superficial romance, but love! How we hunger for security—a job, a home, a lasting relationship, money in the bank! How we hunger for power—counting for something, having a voice, making choices! How we hunger for peace—quiet privacy, no anxiety! How we hunger for joy—not just happiness, not just laughs, but deep, lasting joy! These hungers cause a craving for something more and better.

Like the crowds following Jesus, we seek to satisfy our hunger with all sorts of food. We seek physical and material goods: bread, cake, roast beef, and gourmet vegetables; high-paying jobs, luxurious houses, sleek cars, and recreational vehicles; exercise and physical fitness. But the hunger remains. We pursue the food of education and science. Books, courses, degrees and advanced degrees, technical training, psychological counseling and group therapy. But our hunger remains.

Jesus describes for the crowds and for us the only food that satisfies our deepest hunger: "I am the bread of life" (John 24:35). He came for us. Hungry in the wilderness, Jesus fed on God's Word. He gave His body on the cross. His flesh is the life of the world. He comes to us in the bread and wine with His body and blood. He provides all that we will ever need. He gives us meaning and purpose, love, security, power, peace, and joy. He creates, then fills, our hunger for Him.

Prayer: I come, O Savior, to your table, For weak and weary is my soul; You, Bread of Life, alone are able To satisfy and make me whole. Lord, may your body and your blood Be for my soul the highest good!

Polite Welcome or Demonstrative Love?

If Jesus came to town for a visit, how would you receive Him? A certain Pharisee gave Him a polite welcome. He provided a meal and conversation. Perhaps the man was a collector of celebrities or a curiosity seeker. He played a good host, but at best he gave Jesus a halfhearted welcome.

We might want Jesus in our home too. He might be good for business or contribute to our status in the community. Might we restrict ourselves to a polite welcome, not really listening to His Word except with a critical or patronizing air? Would we remain untouched by Him or His message, except when He approves of what we are already doing?

A notorious woman enters the house. She wets His feet with her tears and wipes them with her hair. She kisses His feet and pours perfume on them. Jesus praises her act of love. He announces that her sins have been forgiven. Her faith has saved her.

Do you love Jesus with a reckless abandon, sparing nothing in expense or open loyalty? Demonstrative love means a deep caring and total commitment. The critical coldness of self-sufficiency permits at best a polite welcome. Unwilling to admit sin, the Pharisee thinks he needs no help—therefore, he gives no love.

But the woman recognizes a tremendous need for help as a fallen sinner. She accepts Jesus in faith as her Savior from sin. She knows His full forgiveness. She responds joyfully with actions of love. Admitting our need for a Savior—because of our cold, selfish hearts and many other sins—we turn to the Man who poured out unrestrained love on the cross. He forgives fully. Joyful beyond words for His forgiveness, we demonstrate a living, active love.

Prayer: Lord, move my heart to love You. Amen.

Through a Glass Window at Church

Sunday morning our family arrived late for the worship service. We found ourselves sitting on chairs in the overflow area looking through a glass window. We longed to participate and find nourishment in the Word of God, but only snatches of the readings and the sermon drifted through.

Frustration welled up within me. I needed God's peace and assurance, His guidance and direction. I needed to confess my animosity toward my family for making me late and to explain to them why Sunday worship meant so much to me. I felt cut off from the congregation.

Perhaps the psalmist experienced similar feelings when he wrote, "My soul faints with longing for Your salvation" (Psalm 119:18). He felt cut off from God's presence as others persecuted him. But he added, "I have put my hope in Your Word" (Psalm 119:18). He knew that God had promised salvation through the coming Messiah.

Our family learned a lesson that Sunday morning. We discovered how easily we can take hearing God's Word for granted. Distraught in our late arrival and frustrated by our straining to hear, we fainted with longing for God's salvation. But in the car on the way home and at the Sunday dinner table, we put our hope in God's Word. We confessed to one another our wrong words and actions. We shared our need for regular growth in God's Word. And, we looked to Jesus Christ, our Savior, who graced our dinner and even our discouraging hour in the overflow area. We always can see and hear Him, even through a glass window at church.

Prayer: *Lord, give me a longing for Your salvation. Open my ears to hear and my eyes to see You in Your Word. Amen.*

Hearts Burning Within?

What impact does Easter have on your life? Is it a once-a-year celebration with bright-colored clothing and Easter lilies or a life-changing reality that motivates you all year long?

The declaration of the Emmaus disciples describes a lasting Easter effect: "Were not our hearts burning within us?" (Luke 24:32). But on Easter Sunday afternoon they were walking toward Emmaus with heavy hearts. No fire burned within. They were sad because they thought Jesus was still dead. A stranger joined them, whom they did not recognize as the risen Christ. They told the stranger about the women and the message of the angels that Jesus was alive. They even knew about the disciples who had found an empty tomb. Still they hadn't seen Jesus personally and thus doubted His resurrection.

We know the story of Easter and may even accept Jesus' resurrection as an historical fact. But we don't always believe that He is alive today in our lives and for our problems. Like the Emmaus disciples, our hearts are cold.

Jesus makes the difference. He opens the Old Testament Scriptures about the Messiah's saving mission to the disciples. While breaking bread with them in their home, Jesus reveals Himself. Now they joyfully speak the words of our text. They believe in the risen Christ and hurry to the city to bear witness.

Jesus kindles a flame also in our hearts. Sins exposed and confessed, we see Jesus as Savior, alive from the dead. The Scriptures come alive for us. Our hearts burn within, and we hurry to bear witness. It's Easter all year long, burning hearts aglow with the risen Christ present in Word and sacraments!

Prayer: Risen Lord, kindle the fire of Your Word in our hearts. Amen.

Who Will Roll the Stone Away?

The women journeyed sadly to the tomb on a mission of mercy to anoint Jesus' dead body. Then they remembered a problem—the stone. They were thinking of the literal stone, of course, but the "stone" could symbolize obstacles to faith.

As we recall the Easter story, do we come to the tomb with burdens or obstacles standing in the way of our relationship to God? Who will roll the stone away? Financial burdens—paying for the home, having enough money for the college education of our children. Personal burdens—guilt over past sins, loneliness, insecurity, no purpose in life. Family pressures—fights, disobedient children. Who will roll the stone away?

We often try to devise our own solutions. We play politics on the job. We juggle our financial books. We try to make up for our guilt by attending church more regularly. But we can't roll the stone away.

The text tells us, "When they looked up, they saw that the stone, which was very large, had been rolled away" (Mark 16:4). God had already taken care of their problem and more. The angel told them that Jesus of Nazareth was risen from the dead. The women rejoiced and spread the good news: The risen Savior had lifted their burdens.

The stone has been rolled. Jesus, who died for our sins, has risen from the grave. He brings peace and power. He forgives all our sins. He quells our fears. He stands beside us in our loneliness. Helpless on our own, we receive His undeserved love and power. We are free to serve Him.

Prayer: Vain the stone, the watch, the seal; Christ has burst the gates of hell. Death in vain forbids his rise; Christ has opened paradise.

Is Your Christ Dead?

You may be familiar with an interesting anecdote about Martin Luther. He preached again and again that Christ is alive and at our side every day. But he was also subject to periods of depression and discouragement. On one such occasion his wife, Katie, dressed herself in mourning apparel and fixed a sorrowful expression on her face. When Luther saw Katie apparently overwhelmed with sorrow, he was anxious.

"What has happened?" he asked.

"Alas, the dear Lord is dead," she replied.

"What nonsense," he said. "You know that God lives and cannot die."

"Is that possible?" she exclaimed. "I thought surely He must be dead since you seem so distressed."

Then Luther smiled and said, "You are right. I should not be so sad because God—who has been, is, and will be—is always the same, loving God."

We may believe that Jesus Christ rose from the grave, but often we don't act that way. We moan about all the problems in the world. Selfishness dominates our thoughts and actions. How can we be alive in Christ when we act as though He were dead?

Katie Luther was wiser than many of us. In a comical way she reminded her husband that Christ does live, no matter how sad we may feel. He did rise from the grave, just as surely as He mounted the ugly cross to take away our sins. He is with us always as He promised. That never changes.

Prayer: O risen Christ, live in my heart each day according to Your baptismal promise. Amen.

After Weeping, Rejoicing

The sights and sounds of weeping: family members clinging to one another at a funeral; husband and wife at the doctor's office after learning of serious illness; teenage daughter telling parents about lost love; employees learning about a plant closing; tears after ending a marriage.

David weeps also, initially for some physical ailment (Psalm 30:1–5), then for some spiritual problem that led to sackcloth (Psalm 30:6–10). In both cases the weeping seems to endure for an endless night. But David completes the picture: "Weeping may remain for a night, but rejoicing comes in the morning" (Psalm 30:5b). God delivers David from the grave through physical healing and from sin through full forgiveness. Now David rejoices in the God of his salvation (Psalm 30:11–12). After weeping, rejoicing!

Jesus describes a similar situation to His disciples in the Upper Room. They will weep while the world rejoices. Jesus was to be arrested, convicted, beaten, and crucified. But their weeping would be turned to joy as they would see Him risen from the dead. Then they could live joyfully.

Because of our sin and a cruel world, we weep. We cry out to God for healing and forgiveness. We talk about leaving this "vale of tears." We don sackcloth and confess our sins. Like David and the disciples, our weeping remains for a night.

But Jesus, who wept for Lazarus, has gone to the cross for us and risen again. He has clothed us with joy in our Baptism so we rejoice in forgiveness and eagerly await that heavenly morning where there will be no more death or mourning or crying or pain.

Prayer: He lives to silence all my fears; He lives to wipe away my tears; He lives to calm my troubled heart; He lives all blessings to impart.

The Victory that Overcomes

We prize victory highly. Olympic competition stirs national pride. Children grow up in a world of highly competitive sports. That spirit translates into a lifelong pursuit of winning. We often hear that the self-made person wins the victory. If we try hard enough, overcome hardships, and build on achievements, we are told that we will gain victory. This philosophy sounds so American that we are tempted to follow it. But the unholy trinity of the devil, the world, and our sinful flesh cannot be defeated by our puny efforts.

John, instead, points outside ourselves to faith in Jesus, the Son of God, who died to save the world from sin. He grasps Him, clings to Him alone, for salvation.

Victory for the individual comes only through believing in this same Jesus Christ. By the waters of Baptism the Christian is born anew into this victory. By receiving the body and blood of Jesus in Holy Communion, the victory is reinforced and celebrated. By feeding on the Word of the Savior, the Christian not only receives assurance of eternal life in heaven, but also gains power for daily victorious living.

Yes, we need determination, discipline, and confidence for the daily struggle against the world, but our God-given faith in Jesus, the Son of God, supplies us with the power to win the victory. The Easter glow reminds us of Jesus' magnificent victory over death and assures us that the victory is ours for each day and for eternity.

Prayer: Jesus lives! For me he died, Hence will I, to Jesus living, Pure in heart and act abide, Praise to him and glory giving. All I need God will dispense; This shall be my confidence.

For the Flock: An Example of Suffering

When we think of the Good Shepherd, we often picture a peaceful pastoral scene with sheep contentedly grazing in green pastures by a gently flowing brook. In this section of 1 Peter, we are described as sheep gone astray, now returning to the Shepherd of our souls (1 Peter 2:25). How wonderful to be sheep under the loving care of Jesus, our Good Shepherd!

But Peter jars us to attention when he speaks about suffering. The persecuted Christians of Asia Minor needed to hear these words because they wondered why they were enduring such persecution for the sake of the Gospel. Peter describes suffering as part of the Christian life.

How we need to hear the same message! Aware of suffering for Christ in the world, we often perceive the church as an escape from suffering. Peter tells us that God calls us to suffer as Jesus suffered. Jesus, the Good Shepherd, suffered for us regardless of the consequences. He silently went to the slaughter as the spotless Lamb of God. God wants us to follow that example.

But the same Good Shepherd who calls us to follow His example also provides His power for suffering. "He Himself bore our sins in His body on the tree, so that we might die to sins and live for righteousness; by His wounds you have been healed" (1 Peter 2:24). He gathers us scattered sheep from the thickets, takes us in His arms, binds our wounds, and returns us to the flock. Christ's suffering helps us conquer fear and selfishness so we can, if necessary, suffer for the Gospel. Belonging to Christ's flock doesn't mean grazing contentedly but rather following our Good Shepherd on a path that may include suffering.

Prayer: Dear Jesus, help us to suffer for You, if You so will. Amen.

A Giver You Can Trust

We suspect people who give away free gifts. Who is the giver? What are the motives behind the offer? Experience tells us that you don't get something for nothing.

James tells us about a giver you can trust. God the Father created the world, including the heavenly lights. He loves us. You can count on Him. He does not have an angle or a pitch. He gives freely and generously.

Receive His gift. He made us in His image as the crown of creation. He gave us a world to manage and enjoy. We rebelled and shattered the harmony of creation, but He never stopped giving. He sent His Son in the fullness of time as His greatest gift. Jesus lived for us, died a cruel death for us, and rose from the dead. As Paul says, "The gift of God is eternal life in Christ Jesus our Lord" (Romans 6:23). God gave us birth through the Word of truth so we might live with Him forever.

Give His gift away. The Father gives to us by His grace. Now He wants us to give the gift to others. We give the gift by being "quick to listen, slow to speak and slow to become angry" (James 1:9). He wants us to "get rid of all moral filth and the evil that is so prevalent" (James 1:21). By our life we point others to the Giver and to the free gift of eternal life.

All too often we hoard the gift and refuse to live it. But still He gives. He provides the Word planted in us, which can save. He exposes our sin. Humbly we come back to Him. We meet the Giver, our heavenly Father, and praise Him. We receive His many gifts, especially eternal life through His Son. And we eagerly give His gift away to others.

Prayer: Dear Father, thank You for Your faithful giving through Jesus Christ. Amen.

Mirror, Mirror on the Wall

You know the familiar story of Snow White, in which the vain queen looks at the talking mirror for confirmation that she is the fairest one of all. James uses the analogy of a mirror. He says that a person who looks into the mirror of God's Word with its description of the Christian life and then leaves the mirror to live otherwise has a worthless religion. Note several dishonest ways we look into the mirror of God's Word.

We sometimes use the self-righteous look. Like the queen in Snow White we puff ourselves up with pride, consider ourselves perfect, and use makeup to cover our moral blemishes.

At times we employ the judgmental look. We hold the mirror up to other people and let it expose all their sins. By comparison we decide that we live relatively decent lives.

On other occasions we give the mirror a religious look. We admit certain church sins, such as poor attendance, inadequate volunteer service, or delinquent financial giving, but refuse to let the mirror show us any faults in the areas of our job and family life.

But James insists on an honest look into the mirror of God's Word. Confessing all the dishonest looks, we see ourselves in the light of God's Law. The mirror exposes our sin and rebellion. Then we look again into the mirror and see Jesus Christ, who led a perfect life and died on the cross to pay for our sins. We look at the mirror a final time and see ourselves with Jesus Christ inside. God looks at us and sees Jesus; therefore, He declares us righteous.

Prayer: Dear Jesus, help me to look honestly into the mirror of Your Word so, repentant, I may see Your forgiveness and live obediently for You each day. Amen.

A Sunrise Encounter with the Risen Christ

Recently we celebrated an Easter sunrise visit at the empty tomb. But what happens after Easter on a regular day? John presents a dramatic story that occurred at the Sea of Galilee. The disciples have returned to business as usual—fishing. When we return to business as usual, Easter often recedes into the background. The routine often discourages us. We may feel cut off from a close relationship with the risen Christ.

John describes a sunrise visitor who asks the disciples to throw their net on the right side of the boat. Amazingly, the net fills with large fish, 153 to be exact. The risen Christ appears at sunrise unrecognized, on a routine day, to help with a routine problem. Note the response of two disciples. John has the spiritual insight to say, "It is the Lord!" Peter takes spiritual action by jumping into the water and heading for shore.

When the risen Christ appears to us on our ordinary days, God first gives us spiritual insight to see Him as our loving, powerful Lord and Savior. He also moves us to spiritual action by making us eager to respond to His call. Jesus helps us with our daily problems. Through regular worship, prayer, and study of the Word, we recognize Him. Through attention to the needs of others we serve Him.

The risen Christ and the disciples then experienced a breakfast reunion, with a meal prepared by Jesus. How strengthened the disciples felt! Our sunrise encounter with the risen Christ helps us remember our fellowship at the altar and anticipate the heavenly feast. Jesus fills our routine with the joy of Easter morning.

Prayer: Awake, my soul, and with the sun Your daily stage of duty run.

Twin Enemy of Easter: Fear

On Easter Sunday morning Christians boldly proclaim, "Christ is risen indeed!" They stand ready to confess the risen Christ and live for Him. But once the Easter glow fades, the twin enemies of Easter—fear and doubt—creep in to weaken that Easter faith.

At the time of our text, Christ has risen. Mary of Magdala has seen Him alive and tells the disciples. Nevertheless, fear grips them in the Upper Room. They lock the doors for fear. No Easter for them. No joy. No hope. Only fear.

Does fear stand between you and the risen Christ—fear of death, fear of loneliness, fear of failure, fear of the unknown? How do you lock the doors to protect yourself? Are you trying to hide, pretend, keep busy, or build false security to handle your fear? Nothing will work. At its root, fear exposes our unbelief, which is sin. No Easter. No joy. No hope. Only fear.

In John's account, however, Jesus conquers fear. He comes right through the locked doors and says, "Peace be with you!" He shows the disciples His hands and side. Christ crucified lives and has forgiven their sins. The disciples, no longer afraid, rejoice and go on Christ's mission to forgive sins.

The same crucified and risen Christ comes to us through His Word. He breaks down our locked doors and conquers our fears with the words, "Peace be with you!" He assures us in the water and Word of our Baptism. He brings forgiveness in the bread and wine of Holy Communion. No longer afraid, we rejoice and go on Christ's mission to forgive sins.

Prayer: Dear Lord, I confess my unbelief when fear takes over as the enemy of Easter. Thank You for Your resurrection presence in my life through Word and Sacrament. Amen.

Twin Enemy of Easter: Doubt

Easter has twin enemies: doubt and fear. Thomas misses the Easter appearance of Jesus. He hears from the disciples that Jesus has risen from the dead and appeared to them. But he declares, "Unless I see the nail marks in His hands and put my finger where the nails were, and put my hand into His side, I will not believe it" (John 20:25). No Easter for him.

Doubt can destroy Easter for us. Satan raised doubts already in the Garden of Eden. Our modern age questions God, the Bible, the resurrection, and Christian values. We doubt God, ourselves, others, and our future. The twin enemies of Easter show their common birth. Fear traces to the root sin of unbelief, and so does doubt. "Unless ... I will not believe it." We want concrete proof or we will not believe.

Jesus conquers doubt as easily as fear. A week later He appears again in the Upper Room and says to Thomas, "Put your finger here; see My hands. Reach out your hand and put it into My side. Stop doubting and believe." All doubts melted, Thomas joyfully confesses, "My Lord and my God!" (John 20:27–28).

To us Jesus says, "Blessed are those who have not seen and yet have believed" (John 20:29). Jesus comes to us in our doubt with His peace. He shows us His hands and side as we read His Word. He gives us His real presence in the bread and wine of the Sacrament. He forgives our fear, doubt, and unbelief. He bestows faith in His death and resurrection as a free gift. With Thomas we confess, "My Lord and my God!" as we move into a bold new Easter world, the twin enemies of Easter defeated.

Prayer: Dear Lord, transform my doubt into sure confidence in You as my Savior so I may live boldly for You. Amen.

The Risen Christ for Your Trials of Faith

The test of Easter. How well can you apply the power of Christ's resurrection to your daily life? St. Peter directs us to the trials of our faith.

Peter writes to Christians who face growing rejection and the prospect of more severe persecution on the way. Their faith is threatened. Peter understands their problem because he painfully remembers promising to defend his Lord, then denying Him when under pressure.

We face trials of various kinds. Our Christian lifestyle faces the ridicule of a secular world bent on selfish living. We are pressed to abandon faithful marriages, concerned parenting, active church participation, and clean living. We also face the trial of faith in our failures. When we fall short in our Christian living, we often, like Peter, feel defeated. A third trial of faith comes to us by external circumstances such as the death of a loved one, illness, or financial reverses.

But Peter redirects his audience to the resurrection of Jesus Christ. "In His great mercy He has given us new birth into a living hope through the resurrection of Jesus Christ from the dead" (1 Peter 1:3). Jesus reached out to Peter in the Upper Room and at the Sea of Galilee. Assured of forgiveness, Peter was able to live boldly amidst trials and feed the lambs and sheep of God.

Christ lives. Christ lives in us. He stands with us in our trials, forgiving, strengthening, and comforting us. Through Word and Sacrament, He fills us with a living hope.

Prayer: Should thy mercy send me Sorrow, toil, and woe, Or should pain attend me On my path below, Grant that I may never Fail thy hand to see; Grant that I may ever Cast my care on thee.

The Easter Aftermath

On Easter Sunday people flock to church in droves. Easter lilies grace the sanctuaries. Special music fills the air. Voices join in praise to the risen Christ. When ushers take down the extra chairs, the organ postlude ends, and worshipers have filed out of church with a "Happy Easter" greeting to all, life returns to normal. Empty pews greet the pastor on succeeding Sundays, and enthusiasm seems lacking in worship.

The words of Isaiah aimed at a self-satisfied, hypocritical Israel seem appropriate: "These people come near to Me with their mouth and honor Me with their lips, but their hearts are far from Me" (Isaiah 29:13). How easy for us to worship only with our lips, halfheartedly. In the post-Easter season we do well to reflect on our relationship to God. Admitting that our hearts at times are far away from the risen Savior, we turn to Him for mercy. He offers us His nail-pierced hands of love and forgiveness.

Isaiah offers great hope for our ongoing worship from the heart: "Once more the humble will rejoice in the LORD;... Those who are wayward in spirit will gain understanding" (Isaiah 29:19a, 24a). Praise-filled worship awaits as we gather with God's people every Sunday. Moved by the crucified and risen Savior, our mouths and lips reflect the joy of our hearts.

Prayer: Alleluia! Now we cry To our King immortal, Who, triumphant, burst the bars Of the tomb's dark portal. Come, you faithful, raise the strain Of triumphant gladness! God has brought his Israel Into joy from sadness!

Guile or Guilt?

How do you deal with sin in your life—with guile or with guilt? We would much rather explain sin away. Like the serpent in the garden, we use guile in our relationships. In our marriages we often use our spouse to get what we want. Guile. On the job we backbite against our employers and coworkers, slow down deliberately, and take company materials for our own use. Guile. Children sneak a cookie when no one is looking, take something belonging to a brother or sister, and lie to Mom or Dad. Guile. In church we sometimes pretend piety toward God while blaming others for our wrong attitudes and bad example. Guile.

David tried to deal with sin by using guile or deceit—with miserable results. "When I kept silent, my bones wasted away through my groaning all day long. For day and night Your hand was heavy upon me; my strength was sapped as in the heat of summer" (Psalm 32:3–4). When he honestly admitted guilt, David experienced the beautiful forgiveness of God. "Then I acknowledged my sin to You and did not cover up my iniquity. I said, 'I will confess my transgressions to the LORD'— and You forgave the guilt of my sin" (Psalm 32:5).

We confess our guilt to God and to one another, "and the blood of Jesus, His Son, purifies us from all sin" (1 John 1:7). Jesus, who lived a sinless life, fully paid for the sins of the world on the cross. Children of God in Baptism, we regularly receive forgiveness in the Word and at the altar. Ultimately, neither guile nor guilt avail, but grace and Gospel.

Prayer: I lay my sins on Jesus, The spotless Lamb of God; He bears them all and frees us From the accursed load. I bring my guilt to Jesus To wash my crimson stains Clean in his blood most precious Till not a spot remains.

The One and Only You

Are you just a computer listing, a social security number, a face in a crowd? Images of conformity, anonymity—how easy to feel insignificant and unimportant!

But the psalmist describes you the way God views you—as fearfully and wonderfully made. God created you just right in every detail. He formed you in your mother's womb. That's why abortion represents such a heinous crime against God. No two people are exactly alike, not even identical twins.

In false humility we often deny that we are God's unique creation: "I could never do that." "I'm just average." Such denial, however, displays sin against the Creator, in effect accusing Him of doing a poor job when He made us.

God also has a special plan for our lives. The psalmist writes, "All the days ordained for me were written in Your book before one of them came to be" (Psalm 139:16). God knows our sin and rebellion against Him. That's why He sent His Son, Jesus Christ, to save the world from sin. He went to the cross for us and rose from the dead so we could be new creations. Forgiven and restored, we can now live for God uniquely, under His guidance, using the gifts and talents He has given us. Unique creation, special plan, personal attention. God alone by His grace makes you not a number or a carbon copy, but the one and only you.

Prayer: All that for my soul is needful He with loving care provides, Nor is he of that unheedful Which my body needs besides. When my strength cannot avail me When my pow'rs can do no more, Then will God his strength outpour; In my need he will not fail me. All things else have but their hour, God's great love retains its pow'r.

Numbering Our Days

We live by clocks and calendars. Time to get up. Time for lunch. Time for a favorite television show. Time for bed. Marking off the days until school's out.

But the psalmist thinks in broader perspective about God's time, where a thousand years is like a day. We may live for 70 or 80 years, but they quickly pass and we fly away. In that context the psalmist prays, "Teach us to number our days aright, that we may gain a heart of wisdom" (Psalm 90:12). Often we don't number our days. We let them drift along. We tell ourselves that there is always tomorrow. Then we realize that time is slipping by. We have failed to number our days.

Often we try to control our days. We make rigid plans. We try to control our future through disciplined diet and exercise and the careful accumulation of wealth. Then we learn that many things are beyond our control. Sickness comes. Business problems intrude. Death comes to close family members and threatens us. Uneasy, we are afraid.

But God cares. The psalmist writes, "Satisfy us in the morning with Your unfailing love, that we may sing for joy and be glad all our days" (Psalm 90:14). God numbers our days out of love. He sent His Son to live for us. Jesus carefully numbered His days in obedience to the Father. He died for us and rose again. He forgives our slipshod living and our feeble efforts at controlling time. He teaches us to look to His mercy. Each day, then, offers a fresh opportunity to live for Him, making the most of the time until eternity beckons. Clocks and calendars remain so we may number our days by God's gracious time.

Prayer: Lord, give us wisdom to live our days in Your forgiving love. Amen.

Loneliness Lifted

Loneliness is one of the pervasive problems of modern life. People live and work together in large cities. Thousands work side by side in factories. Malls are jammed with shoppers coming from acres of cars in parking lots. Yet we belong to the "lonely crowd." We feel isolated, dehumanized, and computerized. We develop a hard shell of indifference and apathy. We fill our lives with whirlwind activities and material possessions. We bury our heads in television and loud blaring music. But when the music dies down, we experience a wave of loneliness. "Does anyone care? Will anyone reach out to me? If I were to die, would it make any difference?"

Loneliness is as old as the psalmist, who in near despair cried out the words of our text. Tormented by his enemies, reduced to skin and bones, he fell desperately alone and even rejected by God. Can such intense loneliness be lifted?

Loneliness affected the Son of God, who was born in a barn, rejected by His hometown, deserted by His disciples, and even forsaken by God on the cross when He cried, "My God, My God, why have You forsaken Me?" (Mark 15:34).

By His loneliness, Jesus made certain that nothing could ever separate us from His love. He shouldered our sins and defeated our enemies on the cross. Before He ascended into heaven, Jesus promised that He would be with us always. God incorporates us into the fellowship of His church, where we continually meet Him in Word and Sacrament and also meet loving, caring brothers and sisters. Loneliness is lifted.

Prayer: *Dear Lord, thank You for enduring the loneliness of Calvary so I might belong to You and to Your people. Amen.*

An Every-Sunday Glad

How do you feel about going to church every Sunday? The psalmist indicates an enthusiasm for worship. Also the early Christians gladly met daily in homes and at least weekly to worship. An every-Sunday glad!

Unfortunately, we sometimes lack the joy of worship. Why? First, we may subconsciously say, "I was afraid when they said to me, 'Let us go into the house of the Lord.' " We may be afraid to come. We feel unworthy. We come because we feel duty-bound. We want to avoid hell or excommunication from the church. No gladness in worship when we are afraid.

Second, we may say, "I was stubborn when they said to me, 'Let us go into the house of the Lord.' No one can tell me what to do. I'm not coming to church until I feel like it!" No gladness in worship when we are stubborn.

Third, we may say, "I was bored when they said to me, 'Let us go into the house of the Lord.' Other things excite me more, like golf, camping, or even sleeping. I'm bored at church—the same old service and same kind of sermons." No gladness in worship when we are bored.

Only God can give us an every-Sunday glad. He sent His Son for us with a life of glad worship. The temple of His body, though destroyed, was raised up on the third day. He stands at the center of His people with His blood-bought forgiveness. God transforms our hearts through faith in His promises. His Word and sacraments cleanse us of fear, stubbornness, and boredom. We come together into His presence with high expectations. Silent before Him, we hear again of His love. He fills our hearts with gladness that endures.

Prayer: *Lord, fill my heart with gladness as I worship You. Amen.*

Tarrying the Good News

I was driving down Main Street one day and noticed the following sermon title on the bulletin board of a local church: TARRYING THE GOOD NEWS. I thought it rather unusual.

Turning to Luke 24 in the King James Version, I began to get the message. Jesus had personally made possible the Good News by coming to earth, living the Gospel life, dying on the cross in full payment of sins, and rising from the dead. Yes, Jesus wanted the disciples to carry the Good News of His death and resurrection to the ends of the world.

But first He wanted them to "tarry" the Good News. He asked them to wait with prayer and the Scriptures until the Holy Spirit empowered them. During the 10 days of waiting, they reflected on all that Jesus had done. Now "tarrying" the Good News for 10 days, they see that the Old Testament Scriptures explain Jesus as the crucified and risen Messiah. The Holy Spirit enables them to speak what they are learning and carry the Good News boldly to a world in need.

Have you been "tarrying" the Good News? Sometimes we fall short in carrying the Good News through our daily witness because we fail to spend adequate time in the Scriptures. Rather, through worship and Bible study we can reflect on all that Christ has done for us.

As His followers we tarry over that Good News, relish and savor it, discuss it with one another, and prayerfully praise God for it. Then, empowered by the Holy Spirit, we faithfully carry the Good News to a world hungering and thirsting for it. We develop an ongoing rhythm of tarrying and carrying the Good News.

Prayer: Father, help us to tarry for the Good News of Jesus Christ so we may carry it to others. Amen.

"I Shall Return"

In 1942 the Japanese were winning stunning victories in the Pacific. The Americans in the Philippines were forced to leave. At that dark moment, General Douglas MacArthur firmly made a promise to the Philippine people, "I shall return."

Two years later, in October 1944, MacArthur's voice came via radio to the people of the Philippines with the electrifying news, "We have returned." A beachhead had been established in the Gulf of Leyte, and the Philippines would soon be liberated. MacArthur made good on his promise.

Forty days after His resurrection, Jesus gathers together His disciples for some final words about waiting for the Holy Spirit and witnessing to the world. Suddenly He is taken up before their very eyes, and a cloud hides Him from their sight. Then comes a word of promise. Two men dressed in white tell them the words of our text. In effect, Jesus is saying to them, "I shall return."

We live in the period between the ascension of Jesus and His return at the Last Day. Even as the disciples received the Holy Spirit on Pentecost, we, too, through the Word of God, know that the Holy Spirit has brought us to faith. Jesus has already won the victory over sin, death, and Satan. He is with us through Word and sacraments.

We do struggle under occupation forces of evil as Satan directs a continual attack against the church. But we live with the promise that Jesus, who won the victory, will return at Judgment Day to liberate us forever. He will not fail us. One day Jesus will announce, "I have returned!"

Prayer: On Christ's ascension I now build The hope of my ascension.

Elijah: Bold Spokesman of God

No backbone. Always compromising. Blending in with the world. Valid criticisms of modern Christianity. We often refuse to speak for God, to declare His unfailing Word no matter what the cost. We fail to confront abortion, sexual immorality, injustice, and abuse of the Word of God.

Elijah was not like that. Called by God in a wicked period of Israel's history, he accepted the challenge of being God's spokesman. Ahab and his evil wife, Jezebel, ruled Israel and set up altars to Baal. But Elijah obeyed God and predicted a punishing drought. Then, at the Lord's command, Elijah went to Ahab and dared to tell him the words of our text.

In a dramatic confrontation with the prophets of Baal on Mt. Carmel, Elijah said to Israel, "How long will you waver between two opinions? If the LORD is God, follow Him; but if Baal is God, follow him" (1 Kings 18:21). Then he called on God to light a fire on water-drenched wood. God, who had called Elijah, stood by him and brought the victory over the frantic prophets of Baal. The people cried out, "The LORD—He is God! The LORD—He is God!" (1 Kings 18:39).

Despite our weakness and compromise, God calls us to speak for Him. In the midst of a wicked world He sent His own dear Son as the Word made flesh. Jesus both spoke and acted on our behalf. His sacrifice on the cross won the Father's full approval. Forgiven, we speak His Word—His Word of judgment against sin and evil, His Word of love and mercy for that same world. Elijah's example points us to God's victory and fortifies us as bold spokespeople of God.

Prayer: We have a sure prophetic Word By inspiration of the Lord; And though assailed on ev'ry hand, Jehovah's Word shall ever stand.

Elijah: Self-Pitying Fugitive

Today we see another side of Elijah. Although a bold spokesman of God on Mt. Carmel, we find him running for his life. Threatened by Ahab and Jezebel, he reaches Beersheba, sits down under a broom tree, and wants to die. "I have been very zealous for the LORD God Almighty. The Israelites have rejected Your covenant, broken down Your altars, and put Your prophets to death with the sword. I am the only one left, and now they are trying to kill me too" (1 Kings 19:10).

Can you relate to Elijah? We, too, have times of victory when God seems so real and so powerful. Then come the discouraging moments when we feel surrounded by skeptics, cut off from believers, and scorned for our Christian commitment. Like Elijah we run away and wallow in self-pity. Lonely, afraid, discouraged, and depressed, we desperately need help.

God helped Elijah, but not in the way he expected. Instead of reinforcing his self-pity, God takes him to the holy mount and speaks to him with "a gentle whisper." God's Word restores Elijah. He receives instructions and refreshment for his ministry and is assured that he is not alone. There are still 7,000 who have not gone over to Baal, and Elisha, his successor, will work with him.

God also helps us. He speaks also to us with the gentle whisper of His Word. He reminds us that the Savior already has come and endured the loneliness and rejection of death on a cross for us. He assures us that we are not alone but belong to the fellowship of His people gathered around Word and Sacrament. Then He sends us back to serve Him each day.

Prayer: Father, free us from our self-pity to serve You joyfully. Amen.

Answers from Romans 5—No. 1

Many people are asking, "How can I survive with all the turmoil around me?" Rapid change forces us to adjust when we can find no firm ground on which to stand. Jobs change. Lifestyles change. Values change. How can I survive? Conflicts arise both externally and internally. We feel dissatisfied with life and are troubled by inner guilt. How can I survive with all the turmoil around me?

Paul answers with the words of Romans 5:1. Peace provides the answer to turmoil, God's peace. Not a subjective feeling of peace, but an objective peace established between God and humanity. He explains the basis for this peace.

"We have been justified through faith" (Romans 5:1). The peace comes "through our Lord Jesus Christ." God's Son came to earth to restore peace. We had rebelled against God. Satan joined forces with the world to lead us astray. We were helpless to bring peace. But Jesus Christ lived a perfect life for us and died on the cross to atone for our sins. God declares the world righteous because of Christ. Through faith, God's gift, we receive God's peace that lasts forever.

Right with God, at peace with Him through Jesus Christ, we now face a world in turmoil. His peace frees us to experience inner peace and to establish peace with others. We will not always feel peaceful, but God's peace remains. Looking to Him again and again in His Word and sacraments, we discover a growing peace.

Prayer: Through Jesus' blood and merit I am at peace with God; What, then, can daunt my spirit, However dark my road? My courage shall not fail me, For God is on my side; Though hell itself assail me, Its rage I may deride.

Answers from Romans 5—No. 2

Many people ask, "Why does God seem so far away? I pray, but He doesn't seem to hear me. It's the same everywhere. Government seems so big and bureaucracy so tangled that I can't get anyone to listen to me or help me. I have the same problem in the large company where I work. Everyone seems so inaccessible. Even God seems to fall into the same pattern."

Paul writes of Christ in Romans 5:2, "Through [Him] we have gained access." God is not far away. Jesus Christ came into this world and bridged the gap by His death on the cross. We have been brought near by the blood of Christ.

Through Christ we have immediate access to God. The biblical word "access" describes a priest cleansed by sacrifice so he can go into God's presence or a defendant brought before a judge and acquitted or a subject brought directly into the presence of the king for a private audience. We have direct access to the Father. No red tape. No appointments necessary. No obstacles or delays. We have access by faith into this grace in which we now stand. Robed in Christ's righteousness, we stand before God every day with full and free access to His mercy and grace.

God may seem far away. Our prayers may seem to go unanswered. But Paul assures us that we have access and that God speaks to us through His Word and sacraments. Share God's gracious answer with those who are asking, "Why does God seem so far away?"

Prayer: With you, Lord, I have cast my lot; O faithful God, forsake me not, To you my soul commending. Lord, be my stay And lead the way Now and when life is ending.

Answers from Romans 5—No. 3

People commonly ask, "Does a person live after death?" Shakespeare describes life as a poor player who struts and frets his hour on the stage, then is heard no more. Thomas Gray writes pessimistically in his *Elegy Written in a Country Churchyard*: "The paths of glory lead but to the grave." How depressing. The daily struggles and the future planning have little meaning if no life exists after death. Paul writes, "If only for this life we have hope in Christ, we are to be pitied more than all men" (1 Corinthians 15:19). No wonder many people desperately ask, "Does a person live after death?"

Paul gives a ringing answer in Romans 5:2, "And we rejoice in the hope of the glory of God." Not only does he affirm life after death, but he rejoices in the sure hope of eternal life with Christ in heaven. In Romans 8 Paul further explains the hope of the glory of God: "We wait eagerly for our adoption as sons, the redemption of our bodies. For in this hope we were saved" (Romans 8:23b–24a). Because Jesus Christ died for us and rose again, we are justified through faith. Therefore, we rejoice in the hope of the glory of God. Our bodies will be raised at the Last Day to live with God forever. A solid foundation for hope.

Share God's answer. No need for despair, gloom, and futility. True, the paths of human glory lead to the grave. But those of us who believe in Christ as Savior can rejoice in the hope of the glory of God. Daily life is worth living in praise to God because eternal life beckons.

Prayer: I am flesh and must return To the dust, whence I am taken; But by faith I now discern That from death I will awaken With my Savior to abide In his glory, at his side.

Answers from Romans 5—No. 4

A final question asked by many people is, "Why does God permit suffering?" We observe suffering all around us. Innocent people perish in terrorist attacks. Hurricanes and tornadoes claim lives. Diving accidents result in permanent paralysis. The list goes on. On a more personal level, we watch troubles come into our lives and ask, "Why is this happening to me? Doesn't God care? Why does He permit it?" Painful questions.

Paul answers stoutly. Rather than explain away suffering, he meets it head on: "We also rejoice in our sufferings..." (Romans 5:3). The Greek word for "rejoice" literally means "boast." Paul doesn't imply a boasting in self, but rather a boasting about God's work in our lives. Suffering causes us to despair of ourselves and look to God. We are then reminded that we have peace with God through our Lord Jesus Christ, an objective reality. God's peace in the midst of continued suffering produces perseverance in us, which in turn builds character. Ultimately suffering leads to the hope of God's glory. From start to finish, suffering immerses us in the loving God who sent His Suffering Servant Son to pay the price for us.

The suffering may continue. We may feel deserted by God. But He is ready with His unfailing hope for today, tomorrow, and eternity. Refined as gold and silver in the furnace, our faith continues to grasp the Savior. Share God's answers from Romans 5 about the joy of hope through suffering.

Prayer: *In patient trust await his leisure In cheerful hope, with heart content To take whate'er your Father's pleasure And all discerning love have sent; Doubt not your inmost wants are known To him who chose you for his own.*

The Real Issue: Love

What makes a truly alive church—sound doctrine? exciting programs? attractive facilities? meaningful worship services? a faithful pastor and capable lay leaders? When questioned by the Pharisees shortly before His passion, Jesus responds from the Old Testament that the real issue is love.

For the Pharisees the main issue was law. They prided themselves on knowing rabbinic law. They considered themselves experts on legal exceptions. They fastidiously kept the rules. They tithed, observed Sabbath regulations, and performed ritual washings. But how far they were from God!

When asked which is the greatest commandment, Jesus replies, "Love the Lord your God. ... Love your neighbor as yourself" (Matthew 22:37–39). For Jesus the real issue is love. Love God totally. As Luther writes, "We should fear, love, and trust God above all things." We are to love God, His name, His worship. With love flowing out of love for God, love your neighbor. The Law is kept only when love prevails.

We stand exposed. We don't always love God or what pertains to His worship and His house. Often we rebel or only comply dutifully. We fail to love our neighbor at home, in church, and elsewhere. We confess our lovelessness.

Jesus not only talked love but lived love. He kept the law perfectly toward His Father and His neighbor. He demonstrated His love by going to the cross for us. The real issue: His love for us, which frees us from the curse of the Law. He fills us with His love and forgiveness so we can live for Him and others. Then they will know we are Christians by our love—His love.

Prayer: Dear Lord, thank You for making Your love the real issue for my salvation. Love others through me. Amen.

Will You Honor Jesus Today?

Jesus comes to His hometown to be honored as the Messiah. He reads the Word of God. He uses the reference from Isaiah about the coming Messiah to point to Himself as the fulfillment of this prophecy. What an exciting event!

Jesus stands in your midst waiting to be honored. He offers His life-changing Word in personal meditation, and public worship. He comes in the waters of Baptism. He comes in the Holy Meal of His body and blood. He points to Himself crucified and risen for you. What an exciting event!

Yet the townspeople of Nazareth dishonored Jesus. He seemed too familiar. They even drove Him out of town and tried to kill Him. How rude and cold their welcome!

We often dishonor Jesus also. Often He seems all too familiar. We take Him for granted and even become antagonistic toward Him when He calls for our witness, service, and sacrificial giving. How rude and cold our welcome!

But Jesus also provides the power to honor Him in our lives. He preached good news in Nazareth. He came to release the captives and forgive those who dishonor Him. He acted on their behalf by living a perfect life of honor to the Father and going willingly to a dishonorable death for us.

Jesus preaches Good News to us as well, so we can honor Him. We confess our dishonoring and receive forgiveness. We worship, commune, and live in our Baptism so our hearts overflow with praise and we bear joyful witness to Him. By God's grace, we honor Jesus today and always.

Prayer: Savior, again to your dear name we raise With one accord our parting hymn of praise; Once more we bless you ere our worship cease, Then, lowly bending, wait your word of peace.

The Family Crisis in America

During the month of May, Americans celebrate Mother's Day. We can't afford to be too sentimental because families in our society are under attack. The family of "Little House on the Prairie" has changed into the family of "Roseanne." Marriages disintegrate, sexually transmitted diseases run rampant, school violence makes the headlines regularly, and all society suffers.

Joshua speaks to Israel, poised to enter the Promised Land. He recognizes the temptations that will face families in Canaan, clearly labeling the problem as other gods. Our family crisis in America also traces to other gods: the gods of materialism, pleasure-seeking, and secularism. The world appeals to our desires. The true God and His Word fade into the background. As a result, family sins multiply.

Joshua also presents a solution; "But as for me and my household, we will serve the LORD." (Joshua 24:15b). Trusting in God's promise of salvation through the Messiah, Joshua pledges obedience to God's commands. Aware of his own sin and the people's likely failure, he continues to trust God.

We face the family crisis by relying on God's mercy. He sent His Son, born in a family, to live and die for us in full payment for our family sins. We regularly feed on God's Word and sacraments so He can build our trust in Him. Trusting His promises, we then recognize the family crisis for what it is, restore biblical authority at home, and live in daily forgiveness with all of God's family. With Joshua we boldly assert: "We will serve the LORD."

Prayer: Gracious Father, as You have bound us to Your family through the death and resurrection of Your Son, so bind us to our family in faithful service and obedience. Amen.

Spirit-Filled Families Communicating

Which would be more difficult—hearing speakers from different nations talking in their own language or sitting around the supper table with your family in the midst of an argument, each person on a totally different wavelength? Certainly good communication holds a key to Christian family living, and our sin disrupts communication.

The Pentecost story addresses this. After all, communication was a key to the Spirit's outpouring on that day. After Adam and Eve sinned, poor communication caused serious problems. The confusion of tongues at the Tower of Babel disrupted communication. The Pentecost account describes a restoration of good communication. Many believed in Jesus as Savior and formed a loving Christian fellowship.

Poor communication between family members often contributes to our problems. Husbands and wives often talk past each other. One accuses, while the other clams up and sulks. Parents and children struggle with communication. Parents promote high standards and want obedience. Children feel misunderstood and unfairly judged.

The Spirit gently shows us our family communication problems. He points us to the crucified and risen Savior. He offers us a regular feeding on the Word and Sacrament so we listen caringly and speak honestly and lovingly to one another. What a testimony to Pentecost when we see Spirit-filled families communicating.

Prayer: Oh, blest that house where faith is found And all in charity abound To trust their God and serve him still And do in all his holy will!

Tell Your Family

A great miracle has occurred. A demon-possessed man has been healed by Jesus.

Now the grateful man pleads to go with Jesus and tell the world about God's great miracle. He wants to be an itinerant evangelist. But Jesus has other plans for him: "Go home to your family and tell them ..." (Mark 5:19). What a challenge, probably more difficult than going with Jesus. His family must have felt totally estranged by his madness. Would they now accept him as a new person in Christ? Would they forget his past behavior? Would his new peace and sanity continue? The man obeyed Jesus and returned home. Apparently the miracle of readjustment to family and friends also worked, because we are told that the whole region was amazed at what Jesus had done.

Jesus Christ also has worked a great miracle within you. By nature estranged from God and controlled by selfish lusts, you have been cleansed by the blood of Jesus Christ, shed on the cross. In Baptism you have become a special child of God. Clothed in His righteousness, you are in your right mind, a mind new in Christ Jesus.

Grateful, you want to tell the world about Christ, but He has other plans for you: "Go home to your family and tell them." What a challenge! Your family knows your shortcomings, your bad habits. Will they accept your witness? Will they see Christ in you and rejoice at God's mercy? Jesus gives you the power to obey and return home. Just think how great a miracle would occur if families everywhere would experience the healing of God and join in telling other families about His mercy to them in Jesus Christ!

Prayer: Lord, make me a witness of Your love at home. Amen.

Are You Bearing Fruit?

Last winter, from our freezer, we enjoyed homegrown peaches, blueberries, apples, and cherries for home-baked pies. Applied to the Christian life, the gardening question comes from John 15: Are you bearing fruit?

Scripture suggests the following possibilities: (1) Bad fruit. Jesus says, "A bad tree bears bad fruit" (Matthew. 7:17b). Backbiting, badmouthing, and gossip are all evidence of bad fruit in a life. (2) No fruit. Jesus says, "He cuts off every branch in Me that bears no fruit" (John 15:2a). If bad fruit represents sins of commission, no fruit describes sins of omission—a lack of love, joy, peace, and the other fruit of the Spirit. (3) Little fruit. "Every branch that does bear fruit He prunes so that it will be even more fruitful" (John 15:2b). Sometimes unnecessary leaves and shoots drain off nourishment needed to produce fruit. The result—little fruit in both quantity and quality. We are bogged down by the world and its cares. (4) Good fruit. "If a man remains in Me and I in him, he will bear much fruit" (John 15:5b). The Godly person is like a tree "which yields its fruit in season" (Psalm 1:3). The fruit of the Spirit are evident, and a life of witnessing brings many into the kingdom of God.

How can we bear much good fruit? Simply Jesus says, "I am the vine; you are the branches. If a man remains in Me and I in him, he will bear much fruit; apart from Me you can do nothing" (John 15:5). Jesus chose us. He died on the cross for us. He grafted us to Himself. His life flows through us as we feed on His Word so we bear much fruit.

Prayer: Dear Father, thank You for attaching me to Jesus Christ, the life-giving Vine. Help me to abide in the Vine through Your Word so I may bear much fruit. Amen.

Pentecost Power for Our Witness

Yearly we observe Pentecost 50 days after Easter. The story seems strange, with the crowded room, the rushing wind, the tongues of fire, people from many nations hearing the disciples speak in their native languages. What does it mean for us?

Jesus' words give meaning to the event: "You will be My witnesses" (Acts 1:8). Since Jesus will soon ascend into heaven, He intends for the apostles to proclaim the Good News in word and deed. They are to bear witness to the ends of the earth. What a tremendous challenge! And the disciples stand there confused, weak, afraid—wavering in their witness.

The purpose of Pentecost remains for us. We are His witnesses in our own homes, next door, at work, in our community, and throughout the world. What a task! And we hesitate, rationalize, stumble, fear—wavering in our witness.

For that reason God makes available to us the power of Pentecost. The disciples were emboldened to bear witness. Uneducated, sinful, afraid, the Holy Spirit transforms them into unashamed witnesses who cannot but speak the things that they have heard and seen—in the temple, before the council, in the synagogues. Pentecost power in the Word of God.

Wavering in our witness, we also receive God's Pentecost power. Peter points us to the crucified and risen one, Jesus Christ. Convicted of our witnessing sins, we repent and believe the Gospel—Jesus Christ fully paying for our sins on the cross. We cannot help but speak and live the things that we have heard and seen through God's Word.

Prayer: Thank You, Father, for the outpouring of Your Holy Spirit in that first Pentecost. Pour out Your Spirit through the Word so we may witness to Your Son, Jesus Christ. Amen.

Your Body: A Temple

The human body receives major attention today. Scientists study it microscopically. Health magazines prescribe diet and exercise. Magazines glorify fresh, young, appealing bodies. Pop philosophers urge physical love between consenting adults and a "do whatever feels good" approach to the body.

But this attention actually devalues the human body. We look at people externally in terms of physical beauty and treat them as objects to be used, then discarded. Many dislike their bodies because they fail to measure up to a self-imposed standard of attractiveness. People corrupt their bodies with adultery, homosexuality, and other forms of sexual sin. The tragic number of abortions betrays a devaluing of human life.

Paul writes to Christians living in the sexually permissive city of Corinth. He condemns cohabiting with prostitutes, then raises the question asked in our text. Our bodies have great value to God. He created us in His image with a plan for our lives as sexual beings. He sent His Son to be born in human form. Jesus went to the cross to pay for our sins, including the wrong use of our bodies. Paul writes, "You were bought at a price" (1 Corinthians 6:20a). The Holy Spirit lives in our bodies because of our baptismal faith.

Therefore our bodies are temples of the Holy Spirit—sanctified by God's grace. Paul concludes, "Therefore honor God with your body" (1 Corinthians 6:20b). Your body—not a self-serving object to be used for sinful pleasure, but a temple of God to show the saving love of Jesus Christ.

Prayer: Remove the pow'r of sin from me And cleanse all my impurity That I may have the strength and will Temptations of the flesh to still.

Hope Beyond

People often live only for this life. They deny any life beyond the grave. They hope and dream, make plans and carry them out, but only for this life. They may secure an outstanding education, succeed in business, gain great wealth, receive national honors, and help other people. But the hopes fade and the sand falls to the bottom of the hourglass.

Apparently some in Corinth were questioning whether there is such a thing as a resurrection from the dead. Paul points out that our very faith hangs in the balance on this question. With ringing certainty he declares, "But Christ has indeed been raised from the dead, the firstfruits of those who have fallen asleep" (1 Corinthians 15:20). "Firstfruits" implies that more is to come. Because Christ, "the firstfruits," died for us and rose physically from the dead on the third day, we who believe in Him will also rise physically from the dead on Judgment Day—and thus complete the harvest, so to speak. We have hope not only here, but also beyond this life.

Hope beyond the grave through Christ's resurrection leads us to live hopefully here. We seek God's purpose for our lives, tell others about His resurrection, and live daily with the quiet assurance that He will take us to heaven. Easter lives on all year long. Eternity beckons with the open, inviting arms of our risen and ascended Lord. Thank God for the hope beyond!

Prayer: This is a sight that gladdens—What peace it does impart! Now nothing ever saddens The joy within my heart. No gloom shall ever shake, No foe shall ever take The hope which God's own Son In love for me has won.

Dinner Talk

What do you talk about around the dinner table? Do you just sit there in silence surrounded only by the sounds of tinkling glass and fork hitting plate? "Pass the butter, please." "I'll take a little more gravy." Is your evening meal a race to see who finishes first? "May I be excused?" "I have to leave for bowling." "I'm going to George's to do homework."

What do you talk about around the dinner table? Do you take out your frustrations from the day? "Mother, why did you have to make this same old hamburger dish again? I'm tired of it." "I had a terrible day at the office. No one cooperated. I've got a splitting headache." "How was school today, Sue?" No answer. "How was school today, Sue?" No answer. "How was school today, Sue? Are you deaf?" "You wouldn't be interested anyway. What's the matter? Are you afraid I got in trouble or something?"

How different that meal in the Upper Room when Jesus celebrated the Passover for the last time with His disciples. Yes, the disciples argued among themselves and accused each other. But Jesus focused their thoughts on the new covenant of His blood, to be sealed by His death.

The Lord Jesus hosts us in the Upper Room as He gives us His own body and blood. By grace He prepares for us the Heavenly Feast where we will dine with Him forever. And He is present with His forgiving love at every meal we eat, whether hamburger or T-bone steak. He makes it possible for us to care for each other and speak helpful, encouraging words and to gather around His Word together.

Prayer: Come, Lord Jesus, be our guest and let Thy gifts to us be blessed. Amen.

More Dinner Talk

Jesus' last meal in the Upper Room with His disciples certainly stands in sharp contrast to our typical dinners together in the family. You could argue that the Upper Room hardly provided a typical setting for a family. However, looking at the regular gathering of the early Christians for meals gives us reason to reflect further on our dinner talk.

What do you talk about around the dinner table? Sports, the weather, newspaper headlines, parking problems downtown, your grocery list? Perhaps what you say is less important than how and why you say it. The evening meal may provide the only opportunity all day for your whole family to gather together. You can share with each other and show that you really care about one another.

The meal can either draw you closer together or split you into warring factions. If you eat in silence, you may build a barrier of distrust and disinterest. If you make supper a gripe session, you gradually fray nerves and create tension. If you talk only about senseless, superficial things, you may never really get to know the members of your own family.

The early Christian community capitalized on meals together. They took the opportunity to build each other up. They could laugh and talk about common problems. They could talk freely about their faith in Jesus Christ, the crucified and risen One who had changed their lives. As Paul suggests, "Do not let any unwholesome talk come out of your mouths, but only what is helpful for building others up according to their needs, that it may benefit those who listen" (Ephesians 4:29).

What will you talk about around the dinner table?

Prayer: *Dear Lord, grace our table with Your holy presence. Amen.*

Joy Is Like the Rain

After a rainy day in May, I've been thinking about a song entitled "Joy Is Like the Rain." These reflections give new meaning to Jesus' words regarding joy coming forth out of sorrow: "No one will take away your joy" (John 16:22).

Just think about it. Joy is like the rain. Look at the raindrops on your window. Fresh, beautiful raindrops, bringing life to the soil, turning grass to a healthy green. Watch those drops streaking your window, then disappearing. Isn't joy like that? A moment of wonder and happiness in your loved one's arms or at a candle-lit dinner table, on a picnic with the delightful squeals of your laughing children, at peace with God. Then the moment fades; the laughter ceases; the bitterness comes; the loneliness, the envy, the anger. But the joy comes again with the touch of the heavenly Father; a new burst of His love; the beauty of a sunset; the caring of a loved one; the understanding of a friend; the simplicity of a child's faith; the reassuring hand of the Master, Jesus, the Savior, the crucified, the risen One.

Just think about it. Joy is like a cloud. Sometimes silver, sometimes gray, always sun not far away. Are there clouds on the horizon of your life? Do you fret over financial problems, marital problems, medical needs, automobile insurance? Can you see the silver lining in your clouds? Are you looking for the Father's hand? Are you listening for His voice? Will you let the clouds deepen your life? Won't the sun seem all the brighter and more glorious when the clouds pass? Is Christ your Sun of righteousness? Yes, joy is like a cloud.

Prayer: Dear Lord, thank You for shining through the clouds with the sunshine of Your love. Help me to rejoice daily in the middle of rain and clouds. Amen.

More Thoughts on Rainy Joy

Yesterday we looked at the song "Joy Is Like the Rain. " Jesus really meant it when He said, "Your joy will be complete" (John 16:24c). My reflections continue.

Just think about it. Joy is tried by storm. Picture yourself on the troubled Sea of Galilee. The thunder rolls and wind whips the waves to a frightening intensity. Your life's boat is almost torn apart and your heart is full of fear. All seems lost.

There is no joy. But then you remember. Christ is asleep in your boat—your Christ, your powerful, loving, living Christ. And your joyful, victorious shout cannot be silenced by the storms of life. You are whipped by wind, yet still afloat. And you live to see the calm. Yes, joy is tried by storm.

Just think about it. Joy is like the rain. The waters pound the earth, and the rivers, growing from tiny rivulets to mighty, roaring streams, rush through the valleys and plains to the vast oceans of the world. Joy in Christ starts small, but it grows and grows as you experience the love of God. On and on it grows, bit by bit—the still, small voice of God within your soul; the daily yet timeless riches of His precious Word; the love of your brothers and sisters in Christ, understanding, accepting, forgiving, strengthening; the endless meetings with God, in a cloud, in a flower, in church, in a helpful stranger, in a friend, in a deep conversation which is honest and loving. Yes, joy is like the rain.

All this, and more, from a rainy day and a song about joy. God is alive. He speaks. He gives. He loves. He brings joy, complete joy, like the rain.

Prayer Thoughts: Describe specific examples of joy in your life and family. Thank God for filling you with joy even when tried by storm.

Our Nation's Peril

Every May Americans observe Memorial Day, and reflect on the great blessings preserved for us by those who served in war. But the words of Proverbs suggest that our nation faces great peril: "Sin is a disgrace to any people" (Proverbs 14:34).

We often forget those who fought for freedom. We forget the principles on which our nation was founded. Most of all, we forget what God has done for us in the death of His Son. We disobey authority, ignoring the Fourth Commandment, fostering rebellion in our homes, our church, our place of employment, and our government. We often commit the sin of noninvolvement and irresponsibility. We stand by while wholesale abortion continues. We let crime increase. We ignore the poor, the homeless, the handicapped, and the foreigners in our midst. Yes, our nation's peril stems from rebellion against God.

The writer of Proverbs says, "Righteousness exalts a nation." (Proverbs 14:34). God provides a hope through His Son. We have been declared righteous by the life, death, and resurrection of Jesus Christ. Through faith we receive full forgiveness for all our sins. We receive God's power to live righteously as citizens of two kingdoms: as citizens of heaven, we live joyfully and productively as citizens of our country! Remembering God's mercy in Christ and His blessings on our land, we strive to obey authority and to involve ourselves in society. By God's grace we face our nation's peril—sin—and point to our nation's hope—salvation through Jesus Christ.

Prayer: Earth, hear your Maker's voice; Your great Redeemer own; Believe, obey, rejoice, And worship him alone. Cast down your pride, Your sin deplore, And bow before The Crucified. Amen.

Does America Have a Reason to Boast?

Every year near the end of May, Americans pause to remember those who died to keep us free. Jeremiah challenges us to ask whether America has a reason to boast.

Can we boast of our wisdom? Certainly the founding fathers expressed great wisdom in writing the Constitution. But since then we have made our share of foolish choices. Jeremiah, aware of unwise decisions made by kings, declares: "Let not the wise man boast of his wisdom" (Jeremiah 9:23).

Can we boast of our strength? We recall with pride how America rebounded from Pearl Harbor ignominy to build a mighty war machine in World War II. But today we are no longer unique in our military power. Jeremiah, aware of Judah's hollow military boasts, asserts, "Let not... the strong man boast of his strength" (Jeremiah 9:23).

Can we boast of our riches? We have indeed been blessed with abundant wealth. But today we find ourselves struggling. And our wealth doesn't bring happiness. Jeremiah, knowing the vanity of riches, cries out, "Let not ... the rich man boast of his riches" (Jeremiah 9:23).

Jeremiah gives only one reason to boast, "that he understands and knows Me, that I am the LORD, who exercises kindness, justice, and righteousness on earth" (Jeremiah 9:24). America needs to confess sins of vain boasting and look to the Lord who came to die as a humble servant, paying fully for the world's sin. The Christians of America have only one reason to boast—that by God's grace they know the Lord!

Prayer: Till then—nor is my boasting vain—Till then I boast a Savior slain; And oh, may this my glory be, That Christ is not ashamed of me!

From Downcast to Upraised

Have you ever felt downcast? Head bowed. Eyes on the ground. Shoulders slumped. Sighs of heaviness. Everything wrong. The world against you. Circumstances hopeless. Trouble near. God so far away. Thoughts race through your mind without focus and clarity. Gloom overwhelms you.

The psalmist feels cut off from God, longs to worship in the temple, and experiences the depression of emptiness. He cries out, "Why are you downcast, O my soul? Why so disturbed within me?" (Psalm 43:5). He answers his own question with a glance upward, "Put your hope in God." (Psalm 43:5). The human predicament provides no hope. Sin grips our hearts and makes us downcast. But God provides hope of forgiveness and salvation through the promised Messiah, Jesus Christ.

We need hope in God. He comes to us in our discouragement. Jesus' shoulders were slumped with the weight of our sins. His head bowed in death. But by His death Jesus won the victory and brings hope through His resurrection. No longer do we need to be downcast.

Now the psalmist lifts upraised hands to God: "I will yet praise Him, my Savior and my God" (Psalm 43:5). He longs for the temple worship and begins to praise with his lips. God lifts him up and empowers him for praise.

God takes us where we are—downcast, hopeless, discouraged—and lifts our hands to praise Him, our Savior and our God. Filled with the hope of Christ's resurrection, we long to worship in God's house and praise Him day by day. We have moved from downcast hearts to hands upraised in praise!

Prayer: In you is gladness Amid all sadness, Jesus, sunshine of my heart.

The Ever-Present Mountains

Recently I taught a graduate course for pastors in the Denver area. My motel provided a breathtaking view of the mountains and the clear blue sky. Always the mountains. I breathed in the clear air and gazed at the springtime Rockies— snowcapped, with patches of green in the foothills. Driving to class, the mountains were present. In some indefinable way I drew strength from the ever-present mountains.

The psalmist describes God that way. He even suggests that mountains might "fall into the heart of the sea" (Psalm 46:2), and still we need not fear. Life often brings problems and troubles. Threats of danger, destruction, and upheavals surround us constantly. Dr. Martin Luther had this psalm in mind when he wrote, "A Mighty Fortress Is Our God." He was troubled by popes and rulers, attacked on every side. Yet he clung to God. In Jesus Christ he saw the Valiant One who holds the field forever.

In the midst of tumults and uncertainties we can look to an ever-present God. He sent His Son to do battle on a "mountain" called Calvary. His willing obedience unto death, "even death on a cross" (Philippians 2:8), won the victory over the old evil foe.

We may not be in a position to see the ever-present mountains and draw strength from them as evidence of God's matchless creation. But we can draw daily strength—morning, noon, and evening—from God, our ever-present help in trouble. As we fix our eyes constantly on His strength, we receive power for victorious living and lead others to see Him too.

Prayer: May ev'ry mountain height, Each vale and forest green, Shine in your Word's pure light, And its rich fruits be seen! May ev'ry tongue Be tuned to praise And join to raise A grateful song.

The Lord Is My Song!

What kind of song do you sing with your life—dull, flat, off-key, halfhearted or enthusiastic, vibrant, melodious? Isaiah gives us a glimpse of the songs we sing.

We often sing a song of the world. In Isaiah's day the world sang a very discordant song. Greed, vanity, immorality and drunkenness, and exploitation of others blared loud and strident notes in the song of life. Our society, too, produces music which often jars the senses, splits the eardrums, and describes the very worst of life. We worship television, strive to keep up with the Joneses, drink excessively, take drugs, exploit others, and wallow in immorality.

We also sing a song of self. I want. I need. I think. I feel. Going far beyond a healthy self-image, we insist on our rights, satisfy our desires, and live for the moment. We work hard for the "good life" and ignore God, country, and others. How enthusiastically we sing the song of the world and the song of self!

We need to sing a song of confession. Israel ultimately repented. In the Babylonian exile God's people sang a song of confession and looked to God for help with a humble desire to return home. We admit that worldly, selfish songs lead only to fear, defeat, guilt, and unhappiness. We sing a song of confession to God, admitting our sin and our need for Him.

Isaiah tells us that the Lord is our Song. God's people in their repentance looked to Him and His promised Messiah. He became their Strength and their Song. He gave them hope and filled them with joy, so they could sing a different kind of song—a song of praise! Jesus, the crucified and risen Savior, is our Song!

Prayer: *Dear Lord, thank You for being my Song. Amen.*

Singing His Song

Musical references fill the Bible. They speak of praise to God. In the next several devotions we look at the Christian life in terms of musical imagery. Yesterday we saw how we often sing a song of the world and a song of ourselves. Confessing our sin, we learn that the Lord is our Song.

God's song began with creation. He sang it from the mountains and valleys. Despite the discord and disharmony of sin God kept singing His song with His merciful promises. He chose a people, preserved a remnant, and sent His Son to sing a song of love, peace, and victory on the cross. Risen and ascended, Jesus sings on in our world and into our hearts.

Because the Lord is our Song, He fills our life with singing. We respond joyfully to the words of Paul in our text. We join with God's people in regular worship and sing from our hearts in praise to the triune God. We continue singing in our hearts as we sit at the family dining table, drive in hectic rush hour traffic, and walk into our sometimes stressful place of employment. We join the psalmist, "Come, let us sing for joy to the LORD; let us shout aloud to the Rock of our salvation" (Psalm 95:1)—singing His song!

Prayer: Alleluia! Let praises ring! Unto our triune God we sing; Blest be his name forever! With angel hosts let us adore And sing his praises more and more For all his grace and favor! Singing, Ringing: Holy holy, God is holy; Spread the story Of our God, the Lord of glory!

Sounding the Trumpets

Brass instruments always thrill me. Easter victory services with trumpets sounding fill my heart with praise that Jesus Christ is risen indeed. Purcell's "Trumpet Tune" and "Trumpet Voluntary" add celebration to wedding services. Bach and Handel also make such joyful use of trumpets!

The psalmist overflows with joyful praise to God: "Make music to the LORD ... with trumpets and the blast of the ram's horn" (Psalm 98:5–6). Primitive rams' horns sounded the call to battle, the cry of warning, and the summons to worship. Along with the other instruments in the temple, the horns announced the presence of God in the midst of His people. The people were filled with both holy awe and great joy before the God who created them and brought them salvation.

Scripture tells of another use for trumpets, however. The trumpet sounds in Exodus 19, in 1 Corinthians 15, and in the Book of Revelation remind us of our sinfulness and of the end of the world with its final judgment. The Day of the Lord is coming. We need to be prepared. Amidst the alluring and confusing sounds of our world, we need to hear the warning trumpet so we can turn from our sins to God's love and mercy.

And then we hear the trumpet announcing that the Messiah has come. The heralds of good tidings summon us to see Jesus coming as crucified and risen Savior. Bowing down on adoring knees, we thrill to hear the joyful trumpet sounds before the throne of God. Sound the trumpets now! Make music in the congregation of God's people! Alleluia!

Prayer: *Praise him who reigns on high, The Lord whom we adore: The Father, Son, and Holy Ghost, One God forevermore. Rejoice! Rejoice! Rejoice, give thanks, and sing!*

Clashing the Cymbals

The music goes on. Singers sing a song of praise to the Lord. Trumpets sound forth God's glory. The psalmist pulls out all the stops and shouts, "Praise Him with the clash of cymbals, praise him with resounding cymbals" (Psalm 150:5). Yes, loud clashing cymbals. Unrestrained praise to the God of our salvation.

But cymbals can also be loudly out of place. They are used in a negative way by Paul in 1 Corinthians 13:1 to describe a loveless Christian, "If I speak in the tongues of men and of angels, but have not love, I am only a resounding gong or a clanging cymbal." In other words, we may present ourselves to others in a showy fashion and worship in a form of high praise, but if we lack love we are no better than a loud cymbal. So often, instead of praising God we make a discordant sound as people see our selfishness and lack of concern for others. We call attention negatively to ourselves and dishonor God.

God came into a discordant world in the person of His Son. Good Friday resounded with the clanging cymbals of injustice, hatred, and prejudice. But Jesus endured the shame, and His cry of "My God, My God, why have You forsaken Me?" (Matthew 27:46) was followed by the triumphant cry, "It is finished!" (John 19:30). Clashing with evil, His love won the day.

His love frees us to love others. We are attuned to praise Him, and therefore we can joyfully worship Him with the clash of cymbals forever.

Prayer: Creator, humbly I implore you To listen to my earthly song Until that day when I adore you, When I have joined the angel throng And learned with choirs of heav'n to sing Eternal anthems to my king.

Playing the Harps

Harps make beautiful music. We often associate them with angels making music in heaven. Certainly they make appropriate instruments of praise. But in Psalm 137 we find Israel's harps hung on trees, not being used. Why? God's people grieve in Babylonian exile. Gone is the temple in Jerusalem. Far away is their homeland. They don't want to accept the taunts of their captors to make music for them. They remain loyal to God. Repentant now, they long to return home and play their harps again in temple praise.

By contrast, Isaiah criticizes Israel for playing their harps at banquets with "no regard for the deeds of the LORD" (Isaiah 5:12). How easily we can be guilty of joining the world in loose living and disobedience against God. All the while we sing our songs and play our harps.

God wants us to repent and look to the Messiah for our deliverance. He came to make beautiful music in a dissonant world. He restored the harmony of creation by His death and resurrection. He brings us back home to Himself in our Baptism. We dwell in the midst of His temple of living stones. Therefore we can take our harps off the poplars and play them beautifully in praise of Him. And someday we will join "the four living creatures and the twenty-four elders ... before the Lamb" (Revelation 5:8) and use our harps to swell the new song eternally.

Prayer: Unnumbered choirs before the shining throne Their joyful anthems raise Till heaven's arches echo with the tone Of that great hymn of praise. And all its host rejoices, And all its blessed throng Unite their myriad voices In one eternal song.

Praising with Full Orchestra

The last few days we have been looking at musical imagery in the Scriptures. Because the Lord is our Song, we sing a new song to the Lord with our lives. As God's people we sound the trumpets, clash the cymbals, and pluck our harps in praise to the triune God—Father, Son, and Holy Ghost.

The text from 2 Chronicles describes praising God with full orchestra: "So the Levites stood ready with David's instruments, and the priests with their trumpets" (2 Chronicles 29:26). Judah had lived wickedly under Ahaz, neglecting the temple and following false gods. When Hezekiah becomes king, he grieves over Judah's sin and orders temple repair. Now all is ready in the restored temple. Cymbals, harps, lyres, and trumpets stand ready for use. A burnt offering is presented to the Lord, followed by singing and praising God with full orchestra. God's people rededicate themselves to His service.

We recognize our neglect of worship and following after the false gods of secularism, materialism, and self-idolatry. Convicted of our sin, we work to restore true worship. Aware of God's Son going to Calvary for us and earning full forgiveness, we stand ready to praise Him. Singing and accompanied by a full orchestra, we worship Him as our Savior. We join with the psalmist in unfettered praise: "Praise Him with the sounding of the trumpet, praise Him with the harp and lyre, praise Him with tambourine and dancing, praise Him with the strings and flute, praise Him with the clash of cymbals, praise Him with resounding cymbals. Let everything that has breath praise the LORD. Praise the LORD" (Psalm 150:3–6).

Prayer: Now let all the heav'ns adore you, Let saints and angels sing before you With harp and cymbals' clearest tone.

The Side-by-Side Planting

Jesus tells a parable about a man who sows wheat in his field. His enemy sows weeds among the wheat. Not until the wheat sprouts do the servants realize that weeds stand side by side with the wheat. The bearded darner weed or tare is deceptive. In the early stages it resembles wheat exactly. Its roots become intertwined with the wheat. When headed out, the darner weed causes dizziness and sickness.

Satan, the enemy, still plants weeds today among the believers. He sows an evil influence in society. Side by side with believers live people who strive to undermine God's law. We often react naively in an undiscriminating fashion. We see people as "nice, beautiful, friendly." We intermarry and choose close friends from among them. Before we recognize them as weeds, we discover intertwined roots and a tremendous weakening of our faith. Destruction threatens.

While we should oppose Satan's evil planting in society, we should not judge the individual plants or, as unfortunately happened in past centuries, urge the government to root them out. We must realize that only faith in Christ makes the difference. Some whom we consider our kind of people may in fact be weeds. Some make mistakes and repent. Others begin in the faith and fall away. Only God can judge the heart.

Jesus cautions us to await God's judgment at harvest time. Then the weeds will be separated and receive eternal punishment. The wheat will be gathered to eternal life. God alone makes us wheat by His grace in our Baptism. He sent His Son to die for us. He keeps us growing to maturity.

Prayer: Lord of harvest, grant that we Wholesome grain and pure may be.

Pierced Hands

You can learn a great deal about a person by the hands—soft hands, callused hands, firm handshake, flabby handshake, smooth hands, wrinkled hands with brown spots. Today we begin a series of devotions on the biblical significance of hands for our lives as Christians.

A good place to start is with a focus on the risen Christ appearing to His disciples on Easter Sunday evening with the exclamation, "Look at my hands and my feet. It is I myself! Touch Me and see; a ghost does not have flesh and bones, as you see I have" (Luke 24:39). Certainly He was calming their doubts and fears by showing that He was physically alive, not a ghost. But His hands! What kind of hands would the disciples see and touch?

Thomas frames the answer to that question when he sets his conditions for believing that Christ is risen: "Unless I see nail marks in His hands and put my finger where the nails were, and put my hand into His side, I will not believe it" (John 20:25b). Pierced hands! Pierced hands best characterize our Lord. We use our hands to grab things for ourselves, or to push people away. But Jesus permitted His hands to be pierced for us. They nailed Him to a cross and lifted Him off the ground. There, suspended between earth and heaven, He died for us in full payment for our sins. Laid in a tomb, He rose triumphantly in physical form. Alive, He still bears the marks of the nails for Thomas and us to see and touch.

We look to His pierced hands every day. In them lie our salvation, our hope, and our power to use our hands in His service!

Prayer: Point us, Lord, to Your pierced hands so that we may see, touch, and believe! Amen.

Clean Hands

"Come in, Johnny. Supper is on the table. Wash those dirty hands before you eat." From little on, we learn the importance of clean hands from the dinner table to the hospital operating room. But the difficulty of washing off the dirt accounts for the proliferation of soaps, cleansers, and even sterilization equipment for a germ-free environment.

The psalmist talks about clean hands in a spiritual sense: "Who may stand in His holy place? He who has clean hands and a pure heart ..." (Psalm 24:3b–4a). The holy Lord owns the earth and everything in it. The King of glory comes in. Who stands worthy in His presence? The one with clean hands, who does not worship idols or swear falsely. Who qualifies for that kind of cleanliness and purity? No one. "All of us have become like one who is unclean, and all our righteous acts are like filthy rags" (Isaiah 64:6).

Clean hands. How we need them to stand in God's presence. But how stained with sin our hands appear; and we can't find a cleanser of our own making to cover up the stains. That's precisely why the King of glory came in at Bethlehem, at the Jordan, and at Calvary. With clean hands of obedience He lived for us. With nail-pierced and bleeding hands He died for us, paying the price for our uncleanness. "And the blood of Jesus ... purifies us from all sin" (1 John 1:7).

Clean hands. Washed clean in Baptism, we approach the throne with Jesus' clean hands. He welcomes us and sends us out with clean hands to love, witness, and serve.

Prayer: Thank You, Lord, for giving me clean hands through Your death on the cross! Help me to participate in the daily cleansing of confession and absolution. Amen.

Strong Hands

We admire strong hands gripping a railroad tie, sculpting with hammer and chisel, lifting a child from danger, or defending helpless people from an attacker. Strong hands symbolize the hardy pioneer spirit that has made our country great. Despite the scientific sophistication of our age, we still sense the need for strong hands.

The Bible values strength for families and nations but names God as the Source of all strength. Solomon in his dedicatory prayer for the new temple in Jerusalem speaks of God's strong hands when he asks the Lord to answer the prayers of foreigners as well as those of the people of Israel. Both groups are to rely on God's strong help. God's mighty hand brought Israel out of Egypt, through the Red Sea and the wilderness, to the Promised Land. God's mighty hand brought victory after victory to Israel and made possible the completion of the temple. On her own, Israel stumbled and fell. By God's strength Israel could climb walls and storm fortresses.

You may feel weak and helpless, unable to make ends meet or hold your family together. You may have tried to succeed by your own strong hands, only to experience reverses and discouragements. Solomon points you to the mighty hand of God. He was willing to let His strong hands become tiny, helpless infant hands in the manger. Later, those strong carpenter hands would be bound by captors, then nailed to a cross. But the hands of the Savior, raised from the dead, are raised in blessing for you and the world. Strong hands to make you strong as you live for Him!

Prayer: Lord, in my weakness I seek the blessing of Your strong hands to forgive and sustain me. Amen.

Praying Hands

Before leaving one of our parishes for another call, we received a meaningful gift from a member, a brown ceramic sculpture of praying hands. The hands express an intensity of purpose. Those folded hands provided an important key to the new ministry as we frequently—pastor and laity together—went before the Lord in prayer.

That's what Paul intends for Timothy and his church as he writes, "I want men everywhere to lift up holy hands in prayer" (1 Timothy 2:8). Whether lifted up or folded, praying hands reveal a dependence on the Source of all life and strength—God the Father, Son, and Holy Spirit.

So often we first put our hands to work—baking, sewing, building, carrying. Only then do we ask why we are working or frantically playing. Restless hands. Selfish hands. Nervous hands. Hurting hands. Fearful hands. Repentance is needed.

When we fold our hands in prayer, our thoughts turn to God. We admit our confusion and hyperactivity. He assures us of His love and forgiveness in Christ. We praise Him for being God. We thank Him for His countless blessings. We ask Him for help and direction in our lives. We pray for each other. We rest in His promises and expect His power. He speaks to us through His unfailing Word and nourishes us at His Table.

Praying hands. The Upper Room. Gethsemane. Pentecost. Bedside. Dinner table. Living room. Sanctuary. Automobile. Hospital room. We rise refreshed to offer our hands in His service, but always also to pray again.

Prayer: Lord, we lift up our hands in prayer everywhere as we claim Your saving promises. Amen.

Open Hands

The little child holds the quarter so tightly, you can't get it out of his grasp. Three shoppers grab a piece of sale clothing so firmly at the same time that the cloth tears. The robber clings so tenaciously to the valise of stolen jewelry that he fails to reach the getaway car in time. What do you refuse to release? How often do you grasp for yourself? Closed hands.

The psalmist describes the opposite, the God who gives freely, the God with open hands. "You open Your hand and satisfy the desires of every living thing" (Psalm 145:16). He bountifully showers us with His blessings. Life, health, clothing, food, friends, family—the list goes on. He even opened His hand to send His only Son, Jesus Christ, into a selfish world of closed hands. Often rejected, Jesus nevertheless opened His hands to feed the multitudes and bless the children. He went to His capture, conviction, and cross with open hands of love. He reaches out to us as the risen and ascended Lord.

No wonder the early Christians after Pentecost "were together and had everything in common" and "selling their possessions and goods ... gave to anyone as he had need" (Acts 2:44–45). Forgiven and accepted as God's children, they opened their hands to each other and to a world in need.

Thanks to the God with open hands, we extend our hands to others. Received by Him because of Christ's death, we welcome others. We give. We touch. We comfort. We include. We heal. Open hands for others, an extension of His hands to "satisfy the desires of every living thing."

Prayer: O God of the open hands, use me to reach others for You. Amen.

Busy Hands

Ultimately God gave us hands to work for Him. Idleness has no place in the Christian life. The proverb says it well, "Lazy hands make a man poor, but diligent hands bring wealth" (Proverbs 10:4). Not diligent hands for selfish gain like the rich man who built bigger barns, but diligent hands for faithful stewardship of God's resources. Busy hands to work and build and help and produce.

How easy for us to sit back and watch television, to extend coffee breaks, work halfheartedly, and campaign for better working conditions. How prone we are to fill church pews, to hear, to talk, but never to do anything as a result. James questions such inactivity, "Do not merely listen to the Word, and so deceive yourselves. Do what it says" (James 1:22). Busy hands are needed to work and to help those in need.

Because Jesus Christ's busy hands were pierced for us and He made our hands clean by His shed blood, we offer Him our hands for His tasks. With praying hands we seek His will and His strength. From His open hands we receive both the opportunities and the ability to be busy. At home with dishes, garbage, and laundry; at work with wrench, word processor, and assembly line; in our community with food basket, paint brush, and snow shovel, we lend our busy hands to the ongoing opportunities for service. His saving hands. Our busy hands. A partnership of love.

Prayer: Lord, forgive us for idleness. By Your death on the cross, empower us with busy hands in Your service. Amen.

Blessing Hands

The series on "hands" from the Bible comes to a close today. We have looked at God's hands and our hands. His hands—pierced for us on the cross; clean because of His holiness and perfect life; strong as the Creator and Preserver of the universe; praying on mountains, in the wilderness, and in Gethsemane; open in abundant provision; busy in service. Our hands—bearing the imprint of His nails, clean because of His shed blood, strong from His saving strength, praying for His daily direction and empowering, open to share His bounties, busy for His purposes.

What better way to conclude than to picture Jesus' blessing hands. The disciples wanted to send the mothers away with their little children. But Jesus had time and energy to receive them. As Mark says, "And He took the children in His arms, put His hands on them and blessed them." (Mark 10:16). Blessing hands. He loves the children. He accepts them in their humility. He saves them.

And those blessing hands stretch forth to us and through us to others. The pastor speaks the benediction, "The Lord bless you and keep you." God's people come to the baptismal font with their children and to the altar to receive Christ's Body and Blood. His blessing hands at work.

And we use our hands to bless our children and others in our lives as we tenderly share the saving death and resurrection of Jesus Christ.

Prayer: Lord, thank You for Your hand of blessing. We yield our hands to You so that through us the world may be blessed. Amen.

Lesson from a Robin

Right outside our patio doors I see a robin sitting on her nest, warming two turquoise eggs. How protective the robins are against any intrusions! They guard their turf and fly away at the smallest noise to distract any threat to their young. How painstakingly the nest was built and how lovingly food is gathered!

Jesus on His way to the cross cries out pleading to Jerusalem, which has killed the prophets, "How often I have longed to gather your children together, as a hen gathers her chicks under her wings, but you were not willing" (Matthew 23:37b). He loves like a hen and offers warmth, comfort, and protection under His sheltering wings. Jerusalem rejected Him and nailed Him to a cross. But He never stopped loving them.

He cries out to us as well. The world threatens to destroy us. Enemies lurk everywhere. We live vulnerable lives, however self-sufficient we consider ourselves. Often we reject the advances of the mother hen. But God continues to love us. That death on the cross availed for our sins. Repentant, we find ourselves securely gathered under the protecting wings of the Savior. Nourished and cared for, we grow and gain strength to live for Him in a dangerous world.

Prayer: Lord Jesus, since you love me, Now spread your wings above me And shield me from alarm. Though Satan would devour me, Let angel guards sing o'er me; This child of God shall meet no harm.

Transitions

Each of us faces transition points in life. We graduate from high school or college. We begin married life. We give birth to the first child. We change jobs, move to a new community, form new friendships. Transitions often bring much pain, create anxiety, and disrupt our lives. They also present new challenges and opportunities for growth. How can we face transitions with confidence?

In Deuteronomy 31, Moses comes to the end of his life. Israel gathers at the Jordan River ready to enter the Promised Land. God chooses Joshua as Moses' successor. Truly a time of transition. Joshua may have felt overwhelmed by the new responsibilities. But Moses gives these reassuring words: "The LORD himself goes before you and will be with you; He will never leave you nor forsake you" (Deuteronomy 31:8a).

God comes to each of us in our transitions. His Son moved from heaven to earth as a human being, began His ministry with His Baptism in the Jordan, set His face toward Jerusalem, and went willingly from Gethsemane to Calvary. He faced each transition with confidence, and made the transition from death to life to demonstrate His victory over sin. That saving and helping God now says to us, in the midst of our transition anxiety: "The LORD himself goes before you and will be with you; He will never leave you nor forsake you."

Prayer: God is my comfort and my trust, My hope and life abiding; And to his counsel, wise and just, I yield, in him confiding. The very hairs, His Word declares, Upon my head he numbers. By night and day God is my stay, He never sleeps nor slumbers.

Changeless

We face many transitions in life and realize how rapidly our world changes. The book *Future Shock* details the enormous changes taking place both in number and in speed of change. We feel as though we are riding a merry-go-round that goes faster and faster until everything around us is blurry. What can we count on? What solid object can we grasp? Change can be positive or negative, but in either case we need to adjust to it.

In Malachi God says to Israel, "I the LORD do not change. So you, O descendants of Jacob, are not destroyed" (Malachi 3:6). He implies that Israel has turned from God and gone back on her covenant responsibilities. She has changed in her relationship to God. But God reaffirms His love. He does not go back on His covenant promises. He pleads, "Return to Me, and I will return to you" (Malachi 3:7b).

In this changing world we often stand guilty of changing our loyalties from God to the enticements of worldly progress. But God, who sent His Son to fulfill His covenant promise by dying on the cross for our sins, declares to us, "I the LORD do not change." He provides solid ground for us as we come to Him in repentance. Indeed, we have "a changeless Christ for a changing world." We can see God's hand in change and turn to Him for strength until He calls us home eternally.

Prayer: Swift to its close ebbs out life's little day; Earth's joys grow dim, its glories pass away; Change and decay in all around I see; O thou who changest not, abide with me.

Envy Rot

According to movie scripts, treasure hunters seeking pirate gold or jewels usually come upon hideous skeletons of greedy cutthroats who died in pursuit of ill-gotten wealth. The rotting bones bear mute testimony to the futility of greed.

Proverbs makes a similar point by saying, "Envy rots the bones" (Proverbs 14:30b). We always want what others possess—the fancier car, the more luxurious home, the high-paying job, the college scholarship, the attractive family. We daydream about enjoying these things, resenting those who prosper. No wonder Proverbs describes envy as rotting the bones. The acid of envy eats away at our insides, rotting our peace, our purpose, and our hope. Purely and simply, we sin.

But the proverb also says, "A heart at peace gives life to the body." (Proverbs 14:30a). We look to the Prince of Peace, who came with a heart only for others. He knew who He was and why He had come. He gratefully accepted the Father's provision, renouncing the kingdoms of this world. At peace with the Father, He endured the storm of suffering and death for our sins. Though dead in the grave, His bones did not rot, for He rose on the third day to bring peace to the world.

Repenting of envy, we accept His forgiveness and receive His peace. "Godliness with contentment is great gain" (1 Timothy 6:6). We gratefully accept God's provision, rejoice in the blessings of our neighbor, and live like Jesus for others. God eliminates envy rot. Peaceful hearts give our bodies new life.

Prayer: What is the world to me With all its vaunted pleasure When you, and you alone, Lord Jesus, are my treasure! You only, dearest Lord, My soul's delight shall be; You are my peace, my rest. What is the world to me!

Promises in Peril

How often we live in fear of perils! Automobile accidents, tornadoes, floods, earthquakes, house fires, robbery, and the list goes on. Israel faced many perils as well, partly from foreign nations who threatened destruction. The individual traveler took his life in his own hands by venturing on a journey to cross rivers and climb mountains.

Isaiah offers God's promises to a repentant people who look to the promised Messiah for salvation and deliverance. His words also provide real comfort to us as baptized Christians living each day for the Savior who paid for our sins. Let these vivid words of Isaiah strengthen you: "Fear not, for I have redeemed you; I have summoned you by name; you are mine. When you pass through the waters, I will be with you; and when you pass through the rivers, they will not sweep over you. When you walk through the fire, you will not be burned; the flames will not set you ablaze. For I am the LORD, your God, the Holy One of Israel, your Savior" (Isaiah 43:1b–3a).

Promises in peril. God's promises, clearly stated in His Word, promises for the New Testament church as well as Israel, promises for you as an individual child of God. Redeemed, called by name, we belong to Him, now in the midst of our trials and forever in heaven. Thank God for His powerful promises.

Prayer: God is my comfort and my trust, My hope and life abiding; And to his counsel, wise and just, I yield, in him confiding. The very hairs, His Word declares, Upon my head he numbers. By night and day God is my stay, He never sleeps nor slumbers.

Fishers of Men International

Summer is a good time to go fishing. At the beginning of His public ministry Jesus met the disciples at their own lake, then used fishing imagery to call them into His service.

Jesus unveils His fishing plan. Starting with a miracle on the lake, He calls the disciples to follow Him. For three years He trains them. Then He goes to the cross to pay for their sins, rises from the dead, and commissions them for a worldwide fishing trip. He calls us to a similar fishing trip. Made His own in Baptism, we learn from Him, and we witness in family, community, nation, and world.

But we face obstacles to our fishing. The disciples struggled with catching men, because they were provincially bound to Galilee and constantly worried as opposition to Jesus mounted. We often live provincial lives as well. How difficult we find it to picture Christ coming for people of every city, state, tribe, and nation! We become so preoccupied with unfavorable fishing conditions that we lose sight of God's international plan.

The Lord reveals His fishing method. He saturates us with His powerful, life-changing Word. Peter heard that Word from the pulpit of his boat. And we hear that Word in worship and Bible study. Jesus applied that Word to the daily experience of the disciples. How could they ever forget the miraculous catch of fish, the mountaintop transfiguration, the footwashing, the Holy Meal, the nail-pierced hands of the risen Lord? No wonder they responded to His call. We too respond to His ongoing call to be *fishers of men international.*

Prayer: *Raise up, O Lord the Holy Ghost, From this broad land a mighty host; Their war cry, "We will seek the lost Where you, O Christ, will come."*

Miracle of Birth

The birth of a child is one of the miracles of life, even in a world which daily experiences the wonders of technology. That truth becomes very personal when my wife is in the delivery room on Father's Day and I wait out the early morning hours in a father's room.

I look out the window and see a beautiful day dawning, a fiery sun rising against a clear blue sky, and my thoughts turn to God. He is making the sun rise. And He is with my wife, the doctor, and our baby. I don't know if our baby is a boy or a girl. Only God knows what abilities and potential are within the baby. But our child is in God's hands, and that means everything to me. He also cares for my wife. He is the God who loves us so much that He sent His own dear Son to be born just like our baby is being born. That Son was willing to die for me and my wife and that baby—so that all of us can be forgiven and free to serve Him.

Even before I know the results in the delivery room, I thank God for being God and for loving us. "Know that the LORD is God. It is He who made us, and we are His; we are His people, the sheep of His pasture" (Psalm 100:3).

Soon the waiting is over. At 5:49 a.m. our daughter is born. We rejoice together in the recovery room, anticipating her Baptism in the name of the Father, the Son, and the Holy Spirit. We want her to know the God who brings the miracle of birth, and who sent His Son to heal our world by His death on the cross. It is a happy Father's Day for many reasons, but most of all because of God the Father, who makes it possible.

Prayer: Dear Father, thank You for the miracles of birth and of rebirth through Your Son, Jesus Christ, our Lord. Amen.

God's Cookout

Cookouts are very popular. Almost every backyard has some sort of grill. Fathers bend over glowing charcoal as they wear a chef's hat and apron. Isaiah 25 describes heaven as a cookout on a mountain, with God spreading out a wondrous feast complete with the best of meats and the finest wines. Do you have time for God's cookout?

The description sounds inviting, but only if you are hungry. Many don't have time for God's cookout. They are busy tending to their jobs, paying bills, going on vacations, fishing, boating, golfing. Is that your problem? Could it be that you aren't hungry enough for God? Full of hamburger, one doesn't have room for even the tastiest steak. Full of ourselves, we may not be hungry for God and His love.

When we live only to satisfy our whims, we discover that everything tastes flat. Even the finest wine and filet mignon fail to satisfy. Spacious swimming pools and growing bank accounts do not satisfy. Selfishness is sin, and the wages of sin is death. When we seriously probe our lives, we admit our growing hunger for God.

And He fills us. He sent His only Son to fast 40 days in the wilderness and to drink the bitter cup of suffering by dying on the cross. By His death Jesus invites us to attend God's great cookout in heaven, freely and without charge. He not only invites us but encourages us to invite others as well.

Think about these things the next time you are gathered with your family in the backyard for a cookout.

Prayer: Lord Jesus Christ, we humbly pray: Oh, keep us steadfast till that day When each will be your welcomed guest In heaven's high and holy feast.

Flimsy Building

We Americans love outward appearances. Homes are built quickly, with little concern for quality, but the paint and the trim look impressive. Automobiles feature fancy gadgets, plush seats, and racing stripes, but rattles and vibrations come early. Poor workmanship is covered up to look good.

Unfortunately, we often build our lives in the same fashion. Not much attention to a solid foundation of Biblical truth. Not much character building. Not much quality parenting. Instead, we concentrate on bodybuilding, social graces, fashion. The flimsy building is covered up to look good.

Ezekiel uses similar imagery to describe the false prophets of Israel. They cry " 'peace' when there is no peace" (Ezekiel 13:10) and make Jerusalem falsely secure. In reality Jerusalem is like a flimsy wall built on a shaky foundation. The prophets merely cover that wall with whitewash to make it look good. But the Sovereign Lord will unleash a violent wind with hailstones and rain so that the wall collapses. Flimsy building exposed. No whitewash cover-up will help.

But God also brings hope. He sent His Son Jesus Christ as chief cornerstone of a new building. By His sin-atoning death on the cross and His resurrection, Jesus provides a solid base for the building of His church. By Baptism we are "built on the foundation of the apostles and prophets, with Christ Jesus Himself as the chief cornerstone" (Ephesians 2:20). No flimsy building. No need for cover-up. We concentrate on inner growth in the Word, which keeps us strong.

Prayer: Christ is our cornerstone, On him alone we build; With his true saints alone The courts of heav'n are filled. On his great love Our hopes we place Of present grace And joys above.

Foundational Building

Covering up a flimsy building won't work, but how can we build solidly as individuals and as a church? Paul addresses this as he writes to the church at Corinth. Troubles have developed. The Corinthians have formed factions loyal to Paul, Apollos, or Peter. Paul points them to the true Foundation.

He writes, "By the grace God has given me, I laid a foundation as an expert builder, and someone else is building on it. But each should be careful how he builds" (1 Corinthians 3:10). He refers positively to the various builders, but then adds that the only valid foundation is "the one already laid, which is Jesus Christ" (1 Corinthians 3:11).

Jesus Christ, God's Son, by His saving death and resurrection laid the only foundation for our relationship to God and our relationships with one another. The church builds only on Christ crucified.

How do we build solidly? Will we use "gold, silver, costly stones, wood, hay or straw" (1 Corinthians 3:11)? Only the Day of the Lord will reveal how solidly we have built. But all building needs to be foundational building, that is, building on Jesus Christ. As we go again and again to Jesus in Word and Sacrament, He will forgive us and lead us to choose only the finest of building materials. We will not act for self-glorification or out of party spirit, but will seek to honor Christ and share Him with others. Built solidly from the ground up, the church will stand and testify to the Savior before all the world.

Prayer: The Church's one foundation Is Jesus Christ, her Lord; She is his new creation By water and the Word. From heav'n he came and sought her To be his holy bride; With his own blood he bought her, And for her life he died.

Surface Talk

Poor communication causes relationship problems. In the next several devotions we will identify communication barriers and seek ways to break them down.

A spouse comments, "We used to talk for hours about important things. We made so many exciting discoveries about each other. Now all we ever talk about is the weather, the children's runny noses, and what we will eat for supper. Or we just sit in front of the television and never say anything."

Surface talk. A major problem in marriage and family relationships. How shallow, discouraging, and separating! We do the same thing in offices, at social engagements, and in churches. When surface talk serves to avoid more caring and honest communication, relationships deteriorate.

Our Bible reading from Proverbs suggests the wonderful potential for meaningful conversation: "The purposes of a man's heart are deep waters, but a man of understanding draws them out" (Proverbs 20:5). Proverbs also describes how to break through the surface talk: "A word aptly spoken is like apples of gold in settings of silver" (Proverbs 20:11). Speaking the caring word and listening to the heart opens up new channels of communication.

Recognizing our selfish hearts and the rut of surface talk, we turn in repentance to our Father, who speaks to us at the deepest level of our being about the forgiving love of Jesus Christ, His Son, who gave Himself for us on the cross. Listening to His Word, we can listen to one another and speak words of deep caring. Surface talk no more.

Prayer: Dear Lord, help me to move beyond surface talk to share Your love with others in my life. Amen.

Nag, Nag, Nag

A disgruntled husband complains, "All she does is nag, nag, nag. She criticizes everything. She remembers everything I have ever said and uses it against me."

If surface talk creates a communication barrier, then certainly nagging and constant criticism create an even more serious one. When one family member attacks, the others either lash back or withdraw and sulk. Over time, nagging causes deep hurts and bitter resentments.

For this reason the writer of Proverbs asserts, "He who guards his lips guards his life, but he who speaks rashly will come to ruin" (Proverbs 13:3). James in our Bible reading offers a practical way to break down this communication barrier: "Everyone should be quick to listen, slow to speak, and slow to become angry" (James 1:19). That listening ear helps us tune in to the other person's needs. Listening carefully will slow our speaking and keep our anger from rising. Good advice indeed.

But on our own, we stand helpless. Only One can forgive us our nagging and strengthen us to change long-established patterns of rash speech. He is the One who "was led like a lamb to the slaughter, and as a sheep before her shearers is silent, so He did not open His mouth" (Isaiah 53:7b). When He was being crucified, He spoke words of forgiveness. When He was suffering on the cross, He spoke words of comfort and concern for others. God's powerful remedy for nagging: quick to listen to Him and each other, slow to criticize, and slow to anger—because we have been forgiven for His sake.

Prayer: Dear Lord, forgive me for nagging and constant criticism. Fill me with love to listen carefully and speak words of healing, for Your sake. Amen.

The Silent Treatment

Strange how communication barriers generate other barriers. You may have loved yesterday's devotion which exposed the sin of nagging, especially if that problem belongs to your spouse. But don't feel too smug because today God also exposes as a serious sin "the silent treatment."

A frustrated wife says, "I come to him with my hurts and disappointments. I need his support, but he clams up. He doesn't care at all. He just buries his head in the newspaper."

How devastating! Sometimes we nag because we want some reaction from our spouse. No answer. We beg and plead. No answer. We even try to compliment. No answer. The silent treatment often becomes a weapon to frustrate and repay the other person for verbal abuse. We may feel superior for holding our tongue, but often we stand guilty of lovelessness and thoughtlessness.

Proverbs states the positive value of speaking at the right time: "A man finds joy in giving an apt reply—and how good is a timely word!" (Proverbs 15:23). Once again we come face-to-face with our need for forgiveness and our responsibility to forgive one another. Paul says it so well in our Bible reading "Be kind and compassionate to one another, forgiving each other, just as in Christ God forgave you" (Ephesians 4:32).

Yes, while Christ knew when to keep silent before His accusers, He also knew when to speak words of encouragement, caring, and forgiveness. His death on the cross and glorious resurrection makes us His own and frees us to "find joy in giving an apt reply." The silent treatment no longer.

Prayer: Dear Lord, open my mouth to sing Your praise and to speak the timely words of compassion and forgiveness, for Your sake. Amen.

Full-Scale War

Sometimes marriages exist on noncommunication, whether surface talk or the silent treatment. But with equal frequency marriages feature full-scale war.

A spouse describes their sad relationship, "We converse civilly when others are around, but when we are alone, we seem to fight constantly. Even an innocent remark leads to full-scale warfare." A well-known comedy recording introduces a couple named the Bickersons, who constantly shout at each other and outdo one another in taunts, put-downs, and insults. You laugh but wonder if you should cry as this parody unfolds. Too true for comfort!

Again Proverbs brings wisdom about the lethal potential of quarreling: "Starting a quarrel is like breaching a dam; so drop the matter before a dispute breaks out" (Proverbs 17:14). The imagery of a dam breaking and a deluge of water rolling over us accurately describes our full-scale warfare. Paul bluntly advises us in our Bible reading "Get rid of all bitterness, rage and anger, brawling, and slander, along with every form of malice" (Ephesians 4:31).

Jesus dealt with disputes among His disciples as well as the taunts, jeers, and accusations of His opponents. But He went to Calvary in full payment for our sins. Full-scale war raged between Christ and the combined forces of evil. He won the war. Peace has been established between God and humanity. Jesus says, "Peace I leave with you; My peace I give you" (John 14:27). Living in that peace, we can avoid quarrels; and when war develops, we can seek His forgiveness and establish, on that basis, a loving, quarrel-free relationship with one another.

Prayer: Lord, give us Your peace so we may live in peace together. Amen.

Empty Flattery

Angry and cutting words certainly raise communication barriers, but seemingly positive words can also cause problems if they are insincere. A discouraged wife commented, "He talks a good game. When he is trying to get on my good side, he makes all kinds of promises and whispers sweet nothings into my ear. But I know he really doesn't care about me; he is simply not being sincere."

Empty flattery, we call it. Words abound, but they mean little because the heart lies elsewhere. Proverbs castigates such insincerity: "A lying tongue hates those it hurts, and a flattering mouth works ruin" (Proverbs 26:28). How easily we slip into hollow words, flattering words, manipulative words which mask our selfish, scheming, and even vengeful hearts!

Paul describes the honest speech which God desires us to use: "Instead, speaking the truth in love, we will in all things grow up into Him who is the Head, that is, Christ" (Ephesians 4:15). As a result of our relationship to God in Christ, we speak from the heart. Sometimes we confront our loved one. Sometimes we register our concerns and problems. Sometimes we express our tender feelings. But always we speak the truth in love—honest, sincere, caring words. God speaks words of judgment against our sin, including empty flattery. He pulls no punches with us, because He loves us. But He also speaks His Word of mercy, most clearly spoken in His Son, Jesus Christ, the Word-made-flesh. On Calvary, Jesus by His death spoke the truth in love for us. Cleansed by His blood, we lay aside flattery and speak honestly and lovingly from the heart.

Prayer: Dear Lord, purge my lips of empty flattery and strengthen me to speak the truth in love. Amen.

Cold Logic

A final communication barrier deals with cold logic and a clinical approach. A wife comments sadly, "I don't feel free to talk to him anymore. When I come with my problems, he gives me a quick answer that makes me feel stupid. I feel frustrated because he tries to be so logical and rational. When he does listen, I think he is trying to play psychiatrist, and I serve as an interesting subject for analysis."

Even when we desire to help, quick answers, easy advice, or cold logic make others feel unimportant and uncared-for. We remain detached and uninvolved. Proverbs tells us: "He who answers before listening—that is his folly and his shame" (Proverbs 18:13). We fail to listen empathetically and speak caringly.

Communication barriers abound—surface talk, nagging, the silent treatment, full-scale war, empty flattery, and cold logic. At root are selfishness, jealousy, resentment, and indifference. We confess our sins toward those we love. Paul states the goal of good communication: "Do not let any unwholesome talk come out of your mouths, but only what is helpful for building others up according to their needs, that it may benefit those who listen" (Ephesians 4:29). Wholesome talk. Building others up. According to their needs. His words of life, of salvation through faith in Jesus Christ, of forgiveness, of healing. His words spoken to us, received in the Water, the Bread and the Wine. His words spoken through us to the family because we have listened with love. Communication barriers broken down.

Prayer: Dear Lord, thank You for communicating with us through Your death and resurrection. Give us wholesome words to build up those in need. Amen.

Anniversary Thoughts: Companionship

I'm preparing to take my wife out for dinner on our wedding anniversary. Memories flood my mind as I treasure our time together. "It is not good for the man to be alone" (Genesis 2:18). I remember lonely nights before I met her, times when I wondered whether God would provide a wife for me.

"I will make a helper suitable for him" (Genesis 2:18). What a delight to meet her on that spring weekend at college! Three years of daily letters followed, because we lived in different states. Communication flowed as we learned to know each other, our interests, values, common faith, family backgrounds, and dreams for the future. We rejoiced that by God's grace we completed each other.

We stood together at the altar and promised to be faithful. We began our journey together—new job, moving from school to church, the birth of children, more moves as pastor from church to church. Struggles. Challenges. Adjustments. Disagreements. But always companionship. Three children born. Ages and stages. Still companionship.

God deserves all praise and honor as we celebrate our anniversary. He made us unique individuals. He brought each of us into His kingdom through Holy Baptism. He brought us together. He forgives our sins when we strain our relationship. He constantly reminds us of His Son, Jesus Christ, who died for us. God is our Companion, though undeserved by us. Therefore we enjoy each other's companionship as we seek God's continuing purpose for our life together.

Prayer: *Oh, blessed home where man and wife Together lead a godly life, By deeds their faith confessing! There many happy days are spent, There Jesus gladly will consent To tarry with his blessing.*

Anniversary Thoughts: One Flesh

The Hebrew word for "be united" or "cleave" to his wife means "stick together like glue" When a man and woman marry, God joins them in a permanent bond. He knows what is good for us. He promises to sustain us in our marriage.

One could focus on the negative. If God joins man and woman together, why do so many marriages break up? As a society we have sown the wind and reaped the whirlwind. For generations couples have been divorcing and remarrying, and the children and grandchildren have followed suit in ever-increasing measure. Tremendous discord, emotional scars, and wounds of emptiness and bitterness have been the result. That's sin at work.

But I prefer to focus on the positive. God forgives sinful people. He provides a third partner in our marriage, His Son Jesus Christ. I can love my wife because Christ loved the church and gave Himself for her. He has washed us with water through the Word and presents us to God without blemish, because He has paid the price for our sins.

With such cleaving, uniting, bonding on Christ's part, we can cleave to each other as one flesh. I love her and she loves me. Our commitment to each other flows from His unwavering commitment to us. From the solid "one flesh" foundation comes delight in romance, intimacy, and the prospect of surprises and adventure in our future together.

Prayer: If they have given him their heart, The place of honor set apart For him each night and morrow, Then he the storms of life will calm, Will bring for ev'ry wound a balm, And change to joy their sorrow.

Anniversary Thoughts: Children

While my wife and I prepare to eat out for our anniversary, she is serving spaghetti to our three teenagers. It seems like just yesterday that they were infants. Who can forget the first shaky steps, the first children's Christmas service, the first day on the school bus? How many Halloween parties, Little League baseball games, school programs, and gymnastics meets have we attended over the years?

Oh, the joys of a family! Yes, God made Adam and Eve one flesh and so provided intimate companionship. But to many couples God also gives the gift of children. Children bring added responsibility, more than a few headaches, and an emptier pocketbook, but they also bring warmth, love, and joy.

Childbearing implies child-rearing. Parenting is an awesome task. No room for absentee parents. No room for permissiveness. No room for child abuse. Much need for time with the children, both quality and quantity. Much need for patience and a listening ear. Much need for firm discipline and Christian values. Much need for modeling worship, caring, and sharing.

I know that we have fallen short as parents in many ways over the years. We confess our sins as parents even as we commend our three to God's protective care. But we also recognize God's forgiveness in Jesus Christ and His gentle guiding of us in the parenting task. He lifts us up when we are discouraged, refreshes us with His Good News, and shows us our children's potential.

Prayer: O Lord, we come before your face; In ev'ry home bestow your grace On children, father, mother. Relieve their wants, their burdens ease, Let them together dwell in peace And love to one another.

Disneyland

When Walt Disney opened his theme park in Anaheim, a new era began in American entertainment. People flocked to the fantasy world of Mickey Mouse and the other Disney characters. Similar parks have sprung up in Florida and in various countries of the world. Disneyland offers wholesome fun for children and grownups alike. But unfortunately we sometimes expect that real life will feature a Disneyland-type experience, with no major problems and constant pleasure.

St. Peter tells a quite different story to the persecuted Christians in Asia Minor. He writes, "Dear friends, do not be surprised at the painful trial you are suffering, as though something strange were happening to you" (1 Peter 4:12). He goes on to suggest that they are participating in the sufferings of Christ. Living a clear Christian witness brings insults and persecution at times. Peter tells them that they can praise God though they're suffering.

Christ has suffered and died for us to make us His own dear children. He indeed promises us joy and an abundant life as Christians. But we may end up suffering for our faith in Christ. The Christian life is not a spiritual Disneyland, but an opportunity to praise God as we bear His name, no matter what the cost. He strengthens us in and through suffering and promises us eternal glory in heaven.

Prayer: Then let us follow Christ, our Lord, And take the cross appointed And, firmly clinging to his word, In suff'ring be undaunted. For those who bear the battle's strain The crown of heav'nly life obtain.

Heat and Humidity

In many parts of the country, summer brings sweltering heat and high humidity. One walks out of an air-conditioned building and faces a blast furnace of hot, humid air. Soon the sweat begins to pour out. We hurry to complete our business so we can again seek air-conditioned shelter. Heat and humidity create an environment that controls our life.

Christians face the "heat and humidity" of a hostile world. Our Lord repeatedly warned His disciples to expect persecution. St. Peter speaks of a "fiery trial" the early Christians could expect (1 Peter 4:12 KJV). We too face a culture that causes us as much trouble as heat and humidity. But within the fellowship of God's people we gather around Word and Sacrament, experiencing God's cool refreshment before we walk out into the hostile world. As Jesus tells His disciples in John's gospel, "In this world you will have trouble. But take heart! I have overcome the world" (John 16:33b).

When faced with the blast furnace of temptation and ridicule, we begin to sweat. But Jesus, who resolutely faced the world's hatred and went to the cross in payment for our sins, offers us strength to face the world's heat and humidity. He has overcome. We can live boldly in the midst of the world's anti-Christian culture as He continues to refresh us in the air-conditioning of worship with God's people.

Prayer: The world seeks to be praised And honored by the mighty Yet never once reflects That they are frail and flighty. But what I truly prize Above all things is he, My Jesus, he alone. What is the world to me!

Moving

Oh, the headaches of moving! A house to sell. Moving arrangements, sorting, garage sales, packing, and leaving. A house to purchase in the new community. Thousands of details concerning utilities, doctors, services, church and school choices, and adjustment to a new job. Not to mention the emotional turmoil of leaving good friends and reestablishing roots! Yet God leads us into new situations as part of His plan for our lives.

God similarly came to Abraham with a call to leave his homeland and travel long miles to a promised land. God was establishing special people who would carry out His promises for the world. Out of that special nation would come the Messiah, the Savior of the world.

No doubt Abraham must have faced major obstacles and the wrenching experience of leaving his homeland. Nevertheless, the writer to the Hebrews tells us, "By faith Abraham ... obeyed and went, even though he did not know where he was going" (Hebrews 11:8). He lived in tents, as did Isaac and Jacob, and "was looking forward to the city with foundations, whose architect and builder is God" (Hebrews 11:10).

We gain a new perspective on moving. God calls us to live for Him in a new land. By faith we obey. His promise, fulfilled in Christ's death and resurrection, stands sure for us. We live as pilgrims in this world and will someday experience the joys of living in the heavenly "city with foundations, whose architect and builder is God."

Prayer: Therefore I murmur not, Heav'n is my home; Whate'er my earthly lot, Heav'n is my home; And I shall surely stand There at my Lord's right hand. Heav'n is my fatherland, Heav'n is my home.

Unity and Power

Peru, Ind., annually hosts an amateur circus of dazzling proportions. Formerly the winter home of a major professional circus, Peru involves the youth of the community to produce "the greatest amateur show on earth." High wire and trapeze acts, jugglers, tumblers, clowns, and a band delight audiences from far and wide. Townspeople work closely with the youthful performers for at least four months of the year to make this July event possible. What unity of heart and mind is displayed by this circus community!

How much greater the unity and power of the early believing community in Jerusalem, as stated in our text! Persecuted by the religious leaders in Jerusalem, these believers nevertheless stood firm in the confession of their faith and cared deeply for one another. With great power the apostles continued to testify to the resurrection of Jesus Christ. The believers shared their possessions with one another. Only the Spirit of God, by His grace, created this unity and this witnessing power.

God established the early Christian church, and He also sustains us. As we devote ourselves "to the apostles' teaching and to the fellowship, to the breaking of bread and to prayer" (Acts 2:42), God assures us of our salvation through faith in Jesus Christ and empowers us to live in harmony and work together as witnesses of His love.

Prayer: Come, Holy Ghost, God and Lord, With all your graces now outpoured On each believer's mind and heart; Your fervent love to them impart. Lord, by the brightness of your light In holy faith your Church unite; From ev'ry land and every tongue This to your praise, O Lord and God, be sung. Alleluia, Alleluia!

America: Lost and Found

The well-known parable about the lost sheep provides a different perspective on our country as we prepare to celebrate Independence Day. Where does America stand today?

Like the Pharisees and teachers of the law in the Bible reading, we often think we have arrived. We fancy our world supremacy and our high standard of living. We may even look down upon less fortunate cultures. The Pharisees murmured that Jesus ate with tax collectors and sinners.

In reality America is lost whenever we attempt to succeed on our own power. We have chinks in our armor. We no longer control everything in world affairs or dominate industrial productivity. We struggle with moral corruption and the breakdown of our families. Personally we fall short of God's glory. We often live selfishly instead of serving Him. The Pharisees were lost but refused to admit their condition. Could we be more like the lost sheep than the ninety-nine?

But God wants to find America. The Shepherd goes out of His way to seek us. He finds us confused and lost, bruised and bleeding, tired and forlorn. He takes us in His arms and brings us home. He has given His life for the sheep. America is found. God restores us to our heritage as a nation under Him. He forgives our arrogance and helps us share our bounty. He turns the Christians of America from self to His love. Once lost and now found, we rejoice in finding the lost. God bless America!

Where does America stand? Wrong question. We kneel before God in confession and let God find us in Jesus Christ.

Prayer: Dear Father, thank You for finding us lost sheep and restoring us to the fold. Help us to seek the lost at home and abroad, for Jesus' sake. Amen.

A Beacon in the Harbor

A gift of France and the brilliant work of sculptor Frederic Auguste Bartholdi, the Statue of Liberty symbolizes basic American values of liberty and opportunity. In the 1880s ordinary citizens in the United States and France contributed their pennies, nickels, and dimes to make the Statue of Liberty a reality, and in the 1980s many across America contributed to refurbish and repair the statue. The festivities of Liberty Weekend in 1986 properly crowned this renewal project and reaffirmed the American dream of liberty for all. The Lady continues as a beacon in the harbor for all to see.

Our text speaks of national righteousness and sin. Certainly God has blessed America and we have much to be happy about. Nevertheless, America also reveals a record of sin. Selfishness, greed, prejudice, corruption, and lovelessness have reared their heads in politics, business, labor, and even in the church. We need to search our hearts and confess our sins as American citizens. Like the Lady in need of repairs, our values have been tarnished and our ideals corroded.

But righteousness is ultimately God's doing, not ours. Despite our sin, He declared the world righteous, based on the death and resurrection of Jesus Christ, who fully paid for our sins. By His Spirit God makes us righteous through faith in Jesus Christ as Savior and Lord, and we are empowered to live righteously as citizens of our land.

When we see the Lady, renewed and shining in the sun, we are reminded to let God cleanse us of our sins and renew us to live righteously for Him and for our fellow citizens. God bless America!

Prayer: *Dear Father, help us to shine as beacons of Your love. Amen.*

Fireworks or Handiwork?

Fireworks go hand in hand with the Fourth of July. Large fireworks displays bring people flocking to parks, city squares, and drive-in theaters. Watching an unfolding fireworks show from a blanket, lawn chair, or bleacher elicits oohs and aahs of appreciation as one burst of rockets follows another—towering Roman candles, multiple explosions of many-colored starbursts, pinwheels, and trailing comet tails. Everything breaks loose in a spectacular finale, with the sky full of reds, greens, blues, and golds. But the spectacle is short-lived, and life goes on as usual.

Our text and our Bible reading speak of something far more spectacular and enduring than the most dazzling fireworks— the handiwork of God. The heavens and all of creation provide a permanent display of the power and love of Almighty God— the sun traveling across the sky, the moon and the stars, the clouds as God's chariot, the winds as His messengers, springs pouring water into ravines, birds nesting by the waters and singing among the branches of well-watered trees.

We stand in awe of God's spectacular display—the mountains, the plains, the rivers, the oceans, the sky with its infinite stars, and the seashore with unlimited grains of sand. We look with new eyes of wonder. Instead of taking this world for granted, we realize that God's handiwork surpasses everything made by human hands. We praise the God who not only created the world but sent His own Son to die on the cross and to bring about a new creation of forgiven humanity.

Prayer: "*I will sing to the* LORD *all my life; I will sing praise to my God as long as I live. May my meditation be pleasing to Him, as I rejoice in the* LORD" (*Psalm 104:33–34*).

An Unlikely Champion

David describes facing an enemy with super strength. He felt overwhelmed. One could think either of David's encounter with Goliath or later with Saul, who marshaled all his official troop strength against a fleeing David with a ragtag band of followers. But David had a secret weapon which he mentions in our text—God's help. With God's strength behind him, David knew he could win. Ultimately this unlikely champion was crowned king of Israel.

How often we feel like underdogs. The opponents look tall and strong. The troops against us are hardened fighting men with superior equipment. In front of us looms a huge wall blocking our road. We lack money, education, or courage. We want to witness to our faith, demonstrate love to others, work for the Kingdom, but we feel overwhelmed by the challenges.

Then we remember that God sent His Son Jesus to face the old evil foe. He appeared to be the underdog. Born in a manger, growing up in the obscure provincial town of Nazareth, sentenced to an ignominious death on the cross, Jesus nevertheless emerged the victor. He conquered Satan, death, and the world's sin by His death and resurrection. The underdog was crowned King of kings and Lord of lords.

He lives in us by virtue of our Baptism. He forgives us our doubts, builds up our confidence, shows us the way, and goes with us into battle. We can advance against the troop and scale the wall. By His grace, we too are crowned as champions—unlikely champions in His service.

Prayer: Fight the good fight with all your might; Christ is your strength, and Christ your right. Lay hold on life, and it shall be Your joy and crown eternally.

Memories

A popular song bears the title "Memories." America seems caught in a wave of nostalgia in which "the good old days" are remembered as bright and untarnished. Antique cars, painted milk cans, barn wood, old movies, and baseball trading cards attract keen interest and stir memories. But nostalgia and history sometimes conflict. History records the problems and pain, the failures and disasters, as well as the successes and blessings.

The psalmist covers both kinds of memories when he asks God, "Remember, O Lord, Your great mercy and love, for they are from of old," then adds, "Remember not the sins of my youth and my rebellious ways" (Psalm 25:6–7). He recognizes that because of sin our past should be forgotten. Repentant, he depends on God to remember His steadfast love and forget those sins. God sent His Son to pay for them so He could say, "I will ... remember their sins no more" (Jeremiah 31:34c).

In our text we hear Jesus in the Upper Room instituting the Supper of His body and blood. He says to the disciples and to us, "Do this in remembrance of Me." We remember Him regularly as we go to the Sacrament. What a great focus for our memories—regular worship in God's house, hearing His unchanging Word, and receiving His body and blood for the forgiveness of our sins!

Prayer: All honor, thanks, and praise to you, O Father, God of heaven, For mercies ev'ry morning new, Which you have freely given. Inscribe this on my memory: My Lord has done great things for me; To this day he has helped me.

Oaks of Righteousness

Few people stand tall against the evils of our age. People talk resolutely but bend like a willow in the wind when compromise seems the better course. When forests covered the land in America, sturdy leaders pioneered the way for a fledgling nation. Now strong leaders seem harder to find.

Isaiah in a time of disobedience and compromise points ahead to the Messiah who will one day step into the synagogue at Nazareth and apply these words of Isaiah 61 to Himself as Savior. Isaiah prophesies the results of the death and resurrection of Jesus Christ for believers: "They will be called oaks of righteousness, a planting of the LORD for the display of His splendor" (Isaiah 61:3e). Oaks of righteousness—sturdy, unbending, enduring, solid, towering oaks.

God makes us "oaks of righteousness" beginning in our Baptism. Our weakness and compromise forgiven in the blood of Christ, we stand tall with His strength. As a planting of the Lord, we display His splendor, witness to His love, and speak out for Him against evil in its many forms. When the storms come and the winds blow, we can by God's grace stand tall and firm in His strength, so that others can find their strength in us, to the glory of His name.

Prayer: Fear not, I am with you, oh, be not dismayed, For I am your God and will still give you aid; I'll strengthen you, help you, and cause you to stand, Upheld by my righteous, omnipotent hand.

Pain

The pain strikes suddenly and sharply. The lower back aches. Movement increases the discomfort. Lying down helps, but sleep becomes difficult. The pain continues with no relief in sight. Why is this happening? Who can help? We often live with pain—if not in the back, then the head, chest, or stomach. When pain leaves, we often forget, but when chronic symptoms persist, we wilt and lie helpless.

The psalmist struggles under affliction and cries out, "O LORD, heal me!" He adds, "I am worn out from groaning; all night long I flood my bed with weeping and drench my couch with tears" (Psalm 6:6). No easy answers for the problem of pain. No help from philosophical answers about the inevitability of pain or the beneficial results of maturing through pain. Like the psalmist, we turn to God in our despair. We ask for healing, for relief, for strength. God understands and can help. Later the psalmist exclaims, "The LORD has heard my cry for mercy; the LORD accepts my prayer" (Psalm 6:9).

But most of all, we focus on God's Son, who took on flesh and therefore experienced pain for us. He hurt when roughly handled and scourged. The nails through His hands and feet sent pain stabbing through His nervous system. And the hours of tortured breathing on the cross took their toll. In the process, He conquered sin and death. Pain continues now, but God heals, soothes, and strengthens. Risen and ascended, Jesus will come again to take us to eternal life with Him, where there will be no more pain. He stands with us.

Prayer: But the pains which he endured, Alleluia! Our salvation have procured; Alleluia! Now above the sky he's king, Alleluia! Where the angels ever sing. Alleluia!

Failure

In our success-oriented society no word conjures up more dread than the word "failure." Students fear to take home a report card with an F. Aspiring athletes hang their heads when cut from a team. Unfortunately, high achievers condemn themselves as failures when falling short of the first prize or the highest office or the million dollar bonus. Failures abound, with divorces, bankruptcies, prison terms, unemployment, and additions. In short, every one of us lives with the reality of failure, either real or imagined.

The psalmist struggles with failure because he envies the prosperity of the wicked. He sees them with healthy and strong bodies, free from human burdens, and fabulously wealthy. He bemoans his own struggles and ill-treatment by these wicked people. Then he realizes his own foolishness and stupidity. He has failed to see God's love for him.

Are we failures? Not in God's eyes. He created us in His image. Despite the failure of our sinful rebellion, God sent His own Son into the world. Living faithfully in love, obedience, and service, Jesus was rated a failure in the eyes of the world. His crucifixion appeared to signal a final humiliating defeat. But in that sin-atoning act, Jesus won the victory. Because of Jesus' death and resurrection for us, God accepts us as His special people, headed for eternal life in heaven. Yes, God is the Strength of our hearts and our Portion forever. Failures no more.

Prayer: Jesus, all our ransom paid, All your Father's will obeyed; By your suff'rings perfect made: Hear us, holy Jesus. Save us in our soul's distress; Be our help to cheer and bless While we grow in holiness: Hear us, holy Jesus.

Obstacles

Obstacles are everywhere—bills, family challenges, demands at work, struggles with personal identity and purpose. We confidently start toward our goals, then an obstacle looms large. We fight our way over, around, or through it and continue on with less energy. When another obstacle appears, we scratch and claw to the other side, this time with less enthusiasm. Plodding on, we reach a third obstacle and sit down, exhausted and discouraged. How can we keep on going?

Judah faced obstacles because of powerful enemies and rebellion against God. She tried to face the obstacles all alone through alliances and military might. Ultimately, Judah was destroyed and her people herded into exile.

Isaiah writes to people like us, overwhelmed by obstacles and deeply conscious of sin and helplessness. But God reassures us by turning obstacles into roads. He prepared the way by sending His own dear Son. Jesus walked straight toward His goal of the cross. Obstacles loomed everywhere—crowds who sought to make Him king, disciples who didn't understand His purpose, enemies around every bend in the road. But He persisted. God turned the greatest obstacle of all, the cross, into the road to eternal life. In death Jesus brought life to the world through the forgiveness of sins.

The risen Christ goes before us as we face innumerable obstacles in life. Sometimes we circumvent them, we plow through them. But always the forgiving Christ provides the way, the strength, and the support to move on toward the goal of eternal life.

Prayer: In God, my faithful God, I trust when dark my road; Great woes may overtake me, Yet he will not forsake me. It is his love that sends them; At his best time he ends them.

Backbone

We lack backbone. We bend, give ground, and look the other way. Abortion, pornography, corruption, and ruthless business practices abound. We lack the courage to stand up and be counted. Spineless wonders!

In the first days after Pentecost Jesus' disciples faced stiff opposition from the religious establishment. Peter and John were arrested, brought before the Sanhedrin, and told to keep quiet about their faith in Jesus Christ. They could have played it safe and gone underground. They could have compromised their convictions. But by God's grace these apostles displayed backbone. Arrested again for preaching Christ crucified, they replied, "We must obey God rather than men!" (Acts 5:29). They continued boldly. Ultimately their confession of faith cost most of them their lives as martyrs. But God used their testimony to build the church on the solid foundation of the apostles and prophets, with Jesus Christ as the Chief Cornerstone. No spineless wonders, the apostles!

We confess our weak, sinful flesh. God points us to His courageous Son, who endured the cross. With backbone He drove the moneychangers from the temple and exposed the sham of the Pharisees. Risen, He offers us forgiveness and strength to stand up for Him and obey God rather than men. Reinforced by regular use of Word and Sacrament, we step forward with backbone to proclaim Jesus as Savior and Lord. No longer spineless wonders!

Prayer: Stand up, stand up for Jesus; The trumpet call obey; Stand forth in mighty conflict In this his glorious day. Let all his faithful serve him Against unnumbered foes; Let courage rise with danger And strength to strength oppose.

Complacent?

Last year's World Series champion often struggles to win again. It's so easy to rest on past accomplishments! Complacency. Top management sometimes relaxes after climbing the corporate ladder and coasts toward retirement. Complacency. Confirmed Christians frequently take it easy in worship attendance, Bible study, witness, and service. Their relationship with God and with other believers slips. Complacency.

The prophet Amos writes to both Judah and Israel with a bold message against complacency. He describes their lives of ease—lying on beds inlaid with ivory, dining on choice lambs and fattened calves, strumming away on harps, and drinking wine by the bowlful while both countries, wicked and rebellious, are headed for destruction. Amos condemns their pride and self-satisfaction. He calls them to repentance and trust in the promised Messiah.

Amos' words rock our complacency as well. We drift away from God and His Word, filling our lives with trivialities and selfish pursuits. We forget about God's plan for the world and our key missionary role in that plan. Complacency shattered by the reality of God's judgment, we turn to the One who came for us, always intent on His saving mission. Never complacent about the Father's plan or the opposition of Satan, He went to the cross and finished the work of paying for our sins. Even now He hears and forgives. And we, complacent no more, live for His purposes.

Prayer: Rise, my soul, to watch and pray; From your sleep awaken; Be not by the evil day Unawares o'ertaken. Satan's prey Oft are they Who secure are sleeping And no watch are keeping.

Complaining?

How common our complaining! The weather always seems too hot or too cold, too wet or too dry. We always need more money and more time. We complain about sickness, job stress, family conflict, church coldness, and garbage collection. Then when serious problems of an extended duration arise, we complain on a deeper level.

You know the serious plight of Job, who suddenly lost his possessions, his children, and his health. Sitting in rags on a dung heap, he faced stark reality and cried out in the words of our text. He did not understand, and asked God why he was suffering. He tried to maintain his own innocence and wondered when God would vindicate him.

Ultimately Job learned not to complain but to accept God's authority as Creator. He also learned to trust in God's love for him. No human arguments can suffice. We sin and deserve nothing but punishment. Like Job, we voice our complaints against God and others. We despair of ourselves and wish to place the blame on someone else. God also silences our complaints. We realize that we are sinful and that God is holy. But with our complaints silenced, we listen to His voice and hear a word of love. His Son endured all the pain, injustice, and punishment of a sinful world. No complaints from His lips. Silent before His tormentors, He went willingly to death on the cross for us. He lives, and so shall we. Complaints transformed to thanksgiving and praise!

Prayer: "My heart is rich in lowliness; My soul with love is glowing; My lips the words of grace express, Their tones all gently flowing. My heart, my mind, my strength, my all To God I yield; on him I call."

Confused?

Confusion reigns. So many conflicting facts are reported. So many contradictory ideas are expressed. So many lifestyles surround us.

Are you also confused about your faith? Do you wonder why we have so many different religions and denominations? Do you struggle as to whom to believe? Do you have difficulty understanding God's will for your life?

The disciples also got confused. Jesus had just told them that He was going to Jerusalem, where He would be arrested, beaten, and killed, and then would rise again. Luke tells us, "The disciples did not understand any of this" (Luke 18:31). Why the confusion? They had walked with Jesus for an extended period. He had communicated quite clearly about Himself and His purpose for coming. Still they were confused. Why? As sinners, their minds were clouded. They could not grasp that Jesus must suffer and die to save them. Thank God that Jesus journeyed to the cross and saved them anyway! Then they began to understand the Scriptures correctly.

We often don't understand either, despite the fact that as baptized Christians we hear His Word on a regular basis. We, too, are sinners with clouded minds. Thank God that Jesus still died for us! He opens our minds to understand the Scriptures as we gather around Word and sacraments. The more we look to Jesus and absorb His Word, the more the confusing, contradictory ideas of the world fade away and we clearly see our Savior. Confused no more!

Prayer: Restrain, O Lord, the human pride That seeks to thrust your truth aside Or with some man-made thoughts or things Would dim the words your Spirit sings.

A Well-Watered Garden

Summer gardens take much work before yielding good produce. Gardeners plow, plant, hoe, and weed to prepare for harvest. But the garden needs adequate water to grow. A well-watered garden produces an abundance of beautiful vegetables.

Isaiah describes Israel as a well-watered garden. What great promise! She would first become a dry desert because of her rebellion. But then God would bring deliverance and supply the water of life to His people by bringing them back from captivity. By making them a well-watered garden, He would enable them to produce much fruit as they rebuilt the walls of Jerusalem.

In our sun-scorched world of sin, we are helpless to produce an abundant crop. But God sent His own Son as the water of life to die for our sins. Through our Baptism God has made us a well-watered garden so we might produce a bountiful harvest of souls won for the Savior. We receive His watering regularly as we worship with Word and Sacrament. We depend on Christ for life and respond with a joyful, caring, witnessing lifestyle. A well-watered garden indeed!

Prayer: I heard the voice of Jesus say, "Behold I freely give The living water, thirsty one; Stoop down and drink and live." I came to Jesus, and I drank Of that life-giving stream; My thirst was quenched, my soul revived, And now I live in him.

Trophies

I just glanced at some trophies on my bookshelves. So many have been discarded over the years, but a few remain to remind me of tennis victories or basketball participation. I remember working hard to win them, then displaying them proudly. Now they seem forgotten except for an occasional glance and the fleeting memory of a triumph.

How avidly we collect trophies, not just the kind that stand on bookshelves but houses, cars, jewelry, club memberships, and perhaps even church memberships. We work hard, look for opportunities, meet the right people, take risks, then savor the victories. Very impressive.

But then we hear Paul writing about dedicated athletes training for the Isthmian games to win a coveted garland crown. "They do it," he says, "to get a crown that will not last" (1 Corinthians 9:25a). And only one gets the prize. How futile the pursuit of fading crowns or trophies that will gather dust.

Paul goes on to describe a much more worthwhile pursuit. "But we do it to get a crown that will last forever" (1 Corinthians 9:25b). He describes the Christian life as a race or a boxing competition. Rugged training and great self-discipline are needed for a life of service to God. But the crown of eternal life comes only from God by His grace. God's Son came to earth for us, obeyed the Father's will, endured suffering, pain, and death to pay for our sins. Risen from the grave, He freely offers us the crown of life. We respond by living for Him, never taking our eyes off Jesus Christ and our crown of life. Our trophies gather dust. His trophy shines forever.

Prayer: *Sinners, whose love can ne'er forget The wormwood and the gall, Go, spread your trophies at his feet And crown him Lord of all.*

Humble or Harried?

We often make a virtue of rushing around and leading hectic lives. Full calendars, frequent business trips, and endless meetings are considered marks of success. Is it any wonder that we often feel harried?

St. Peter sounds a warning that living harried lives may signal a lack of humility. Are you humble or harried? Peter refers to anxiety as one source of harassment. We worry about money, health, family, job. Peter adds that we are harried by the devil, who "prowls around ... looking for someone to devour" (1 Peter 5:8). Finally, Peter suggests that harassment takes the form of suffering for Christ. Persecutions came to the early Christians because of their faith. We also may suffer when we stand up for the faith in family and community.

Peter in our text suggests that we humble ourselves. Admitting our need for help, we turn to Christ, who "humbled Himself and became obedient to death—even death on a cross" (Philippians 2:8b). We humble ourselves by casting all our anxieties on Him, for He cares for us (1 Peter 5:7). He bears the burden. We rest in Him. We humble ourselves by resisting the devil (1 Peter 5:9). We know that God has caged Satan, the roaring lion, in the death of Jesus. We humble ourselves by seeing God's hand in suffering. He makes us "strong, firm, and steadfast" after we "have suffered a little while" (1 Peter 5:10).

Are you humble or harried? By God's grace you can humbly rest in Him.

Prayer: Rely on God your Savior And find your life secure. Make his work your foundation That your work may endure. No anxious thought, no worry, No self-tormenting care Can win your Father's favor; His heart is moved by prayer.

In the Wilderness

I'm free from Egypt. What a great miracle at the Red Sea! I walk into the wilderness with a spring in my step. We're headed for the Promised Land! God is wonderful!

Wait a minute. I'm hungry and thirsty. How long will we have to walk? My feet hurt. Where is Moses anyway? The clouds and fire from Mount Sinai were impressive. But now with Moses gone, I'm ready for that golden calf and some joyful celebration in this dreadful place.

You say we are near the Promised Land? Spies are returning. "A land flowing with milk and honey" (Exodus 3:8). Sounds great! Giants? Fierce warriors? Why did God bring us here? We can't risk entering the land. Forty more years of wandering! What a blow!

I'm grumbling again. What a horrible life here in the wilderness! Food the same. Water scarce. Rebellion. Oh, no, fiery serpents! We'll all perish! I'm looking at the serpent of brass. Thanks, God, for saving me!

I can't believe it. The Promised Land at last! God is faithful to His promises. We have arrived at our destination.

So it is with us. We journey with high hopes. The hopes are shattered. Weary trudging sets in. We grumble and complain. We seek religious thrills outside the church. We're afraid to risk discipleship. But a faithful God leads us from slavery to eternity along a wilderness road marked with the sure promises of salvation and lighted by the cross of Christ.

Prayer: Guide me ever, great Redeemer, Pilgrim through this barren land. I am weak, but you are mighty; Hold me with your pow'rful hand. Bread of heaven, bread of heaven, Feed me now and evermore; Feed me now and evermore.

Passing By on the Other Side

You know the story. A man in need. Fallen among thieves. Left half dead. Two people in a position to help—a priest and a Levite, both tied to the temple and the worship conducted there. Both passed by, leaving him to die.

Can you relate their inaction to your life? Wife in need of caring time with you. Newspaper and television sports take precedence. You pass by on the other side. People hurting and struggling at work or school. Business comes first. Tasks pile up. No time. You pass by on the other side. National and local issues scream for your attention. Abortions increase. Hate crimes rise. Refugees need help. But yardwork beckons. Vacations are scheduled. Making money takes precedence. You pass by on the other side.

The story, though, doesn't end with the priest and Levite passing by. It goes on to describe the grace of stopping to help. A despised Samaritan cares enough to risk his safety and attend to the man's wounds. We all recognize him as the Good Samaritan. We could think of him as a type of Jesus, the One who endured suffering, pain, and death for us to save us. His stopping to help us, "God's enemies" (Romans 5:10), demonstrates pure grace and forgiveness.

And helped, we stop for others. Forgiven, we receive the grace to help. Not "Who is my neighbor?" (Luke 10:29) but "To whom can I be a neighbor?" becomes our question. The answer comes back: "Go and do likewise" (Luke 10:37). With God's help, no more passing by on the other side!

Prayer: In sickness, sorrow, want, or care, Each other's burdens help us share; May we, where help is needed, there Give help as though to you.

Sitting at the Lord's Feet

In the Good Samaritan story, the priest and Levite are criticized for passing by instead of helping the injured man. In today's reading, Martha is criticized for helping prepare food for Jesus instead of sitting at His feet like Mary. What is the difference?

Perhaps Martha serves selfishly, wanting to be recognized as a good hostess. Certainly she serves anxiously. Jesus chides her gently, "Martha, Martha ... you are worried and upset about many things" (Luke 10:41). Caring for Jesus, wanting genuinely to serve Him, she grows fretful and troubled, showing open irritation toward her sister.

Are we sometimes guilty of trying to serve without sitting at Jesus' feet? We may be serving for selfish reasons—looking good in people's eyes, trying to soothe our conscience. Certainly we often serve anxiously. We push ourselves, rush around, worry and fret as we do the Lord's work. Like Martha we don't sit enough at the Lord's feet listening to His Word.

Mary sits at Jesus' feet and learns to serve. The rabbis had only men "sitting at their feet." Mary finds it a great joy to be included by Jesus. She knows the value of living not "on bread alone, but on every word that comes from the mouth of God" (Matthew 4:4). She no doubt hears about her sin, God's forgiving love in the Messiah, and the joy of serving God every day.

We also need to sit at Jesus' feet, listening to His Word. All distractions put aside, we worship, commune, and study the Word. We see Jesus as the One who became a servant for us, fully paying for our sins on the cross. Thus we let Him prepare us for joyful, genuine service.

Prayer: Dear Lord, make us Marys sitting at Your feet so we can serve generously, as Martha wanted to serve. Amen.

Spiritual Aerobics

Physical fitness is a much higher priority today than in the past. Along with greater attention to nutrition, aerobic exercise has received widespread endorsement. Such exercise demands careful discipline to bring results.

St. Paul in Romans 8, his great chapter on the Holy Spirit, stresses the importance of what we might call spiritual aerobics. By nature we live the wrong kind of lifestyle—selfish, rebellious, disobedient. But God sent His Son in the likeness of sinful humanity to be a sin offering. He fed on the Word of God, obeyed the Father, exercised spiritually in prayer and worship, and went to the cross for us. The Spirit of God brought Jesus into our hearts in our Baptism and nurtured our spiritual life through whatever Christian education we received. The Spirit of life has set us free from sin and death.

We are now free in Christ to choose a lifestyle of spiritual aerobics. We put to death the old nature and let the Spirit control our minds. We come to God in prayer. We read and study His Word. We worship with fellow believers. We confess our sins, breathing out the stale air of sin and breathing in the fresh air of God's forgiveness in Christ. As Paul puts it, "the mind controlled by the Spirit is life and peace" (Romans 8:6).

We need careful planning, discipline, regularity, and positive motivation in order to grow in God's peace and joy. But the Spirit testifies with our spirit that we are God's children. Jesus Christ has won the victory for us. Spiritual aerobics, letting Christ live in us and through us, works to the glory of God.

Prayer: Dear Father, discipline my spiritual life so I may serve You freely and joyfully. Let Your Spirit fill my mind with life and peace through Jesus Christ. Amen.

Walking

Spiritual aerobics suggests the importance of exercise in the Christian's life. The next five devotions will apply physical activities associated with exercise to the spiritual disciplines of the life in Christ. We start with walking. Most fitness manuals recognize the value of regular, brisk walking for good health. I personally derive great pleasure from lengthy walks throughout the year, combining wholesome exercise with an enjoyment of God's creation.

Scripture uses walking imagery to describe the believer's relationship to God. Micah, for example, condemns superficial sacrifices of burnt offerings, hiding wickedness and the exploitation of people. Instead, he tells us "to walk humbly with ... God" (Micah 6:8). John communicates the same truth when he contrasts walking in darkness with walking in the light: "If we ... walk in the darkness, we lie and do not live by the truth. But if we walk in the light, as He is in the light, we have fellowship with one another, and the blood of Jesus, His Son, purifies us from all sin" (1 John 1:6–7).

Jesus walked the road that led to Calvary because we had stumbled in sin and could go no farther. He completed His walk by dying for our sins and rising again from the dead. Made His children through faith, we now receive His power to walk humbly with our God in service to others. Proverbs tells us, "I ... lead you along straight paths. When you walk, your steps will not be hampered" (Proverbs 4:11–12a).

Prayer: I am the light; I light the way, A godly life displaying; I help you walk as in the day; I keep your feet from straying. I am the way, and well I show How you should journey here below.

Running

Running always gets high marks as a vigorous form of physical exercise. Jogging has both zealous advocates and detractors, but millions purchase jogging equipment and pursue a rigorous program of regular exercise.

The writer to the Hebrews uses running imagery as a key to spiritual aerobics. Having reviewed for us the great heroes of faith in chapter 11, he calls for a lifelong race with the necessary quality of perseverance. Paul echoes the same thought when he writes, "Run in such a way as to get the prize" (1 Corinthians 9:24b). Hebrews further points to the only One who can save us, "Jesus, the author and perfecter of our faith, who for the joy set before Him endured the cross, scorning its shame, and sat down at the right hand of the throne of God" (Hebrews 12:2). He ran the race for us and won the victory. On our own we grow weary and lose heart. We cannot continue. We sin daily. But God supplies the strength, through Christ's death and resurrection, so we can "run with perseverance the race marked out for us" (Hebrews 12:2). Proverbs assures us, "When you run, you will not stumble" (Proverbs 4:12b). And Isaiah beautifully promises, "Those who hope in the LORD will renew their strength ... they will run and not grow weary" (Isaiah 40:31a, c).

And so we run for physical exercise, disciplining our bodies for good health. And we run spiritually with eyes fixed on the cross of Christ which alone saves us and the world. Spiritual aerobics at work in the body of Christ.

Prayer: Run the straight race through God's good grace; Lift up your eyes, and seek his face. Life with its way before us lies; Christ is the path, and Christ the prize.

Leaping

Leaping provides a more strenuous form of physical exercise. Aerobic dancing features leaps into the air along with stretching and jogging in place. Long jumping, high jumping, and pole vaulting take great conditioning and muscles in the legs like coiled springs. Leaping ability helps greatly in basketball, football, and baseball.

The spiritual aerobics parallel to leaping with joy connotes a somewhat different imagery, though difficult to achieve. We think of happy reunions or jubilant football or basketball players after a victory leaping for joy. What makes Jesus' words so difficult is His point of reference. He has been describing the inevitable persecutions which will come to faithful believers. "Blessed are you when men hate you, when they exclude you and insult you and reject your name as evil, because of the Son of Man" (Luke 6:22).

What a challenge—to leap for joy when we are being hated and rejected because of our faith in Jesus. On our own, we cannot leap in such circumstances. We have no spring in our step or joy in our heart. But Jesus "for the joy set before Him endured the cross, scorning its shame" (Hebrews 12:2). He brings forgiveness and new life to us with the promised great reward in heaven by His grace alone. We can join the lame man healed by Peter and John outside the temple, "walking and jumping, and praising God" (Acts 3:8). We can exclaim with the psalmist, "My heart leaps for joy and I will give thanks to Him in song" (Psalm 28:7c).

Prayer: Zion hears the watchmen singing, And in her heart new joy is springing. She wakes, she rises from her gloom.

Climbing

Climbing fits well as a physical exercise. Children's monkey bars and swing sets provide opportunities for using many different muscles and developing coordination. Public parks provide ingenious equipment designed to encourage safe climbing. High school gymnasiums often feature a climbing rope. Military basic training usually features obstacle courses requiring superb conditioning and climbing skills.

Spiritual aerobics also include climbing imagery to describe the disciplines of the Christian life. Think of all the mountains in the Bible, and Moses, Abraham, Elijah, and Jesus Himself climbing mountains in obedience to God.

Luke, though, describes a memorable climbing incident. Zacchaeus the tax collector, an outcast and a sinner, wants to see Jesus. No doubt he feels a need for rescue from his predicament. Since he is a short man, he runs ahead and then climbs a sycamore tree for a better glimpse of the Man from Galilee. Jesus then seeks him out and brings salvation to his house. Repentant, Zacchaeus believes in Jesus as his Savior.

What a marvelous example! Are we willing to climb for a glimpse of Jesus? Do we sense our own helplessness and need for His grace? He freely offers us the salvation won for us as He climbed Mount Calvary and was lifted on the cross. Through regular Word-and-Sacrament communion with Him, He supplies the strength for us to climb every mountain in our lives and scale every wall as we serve Him and witness to others regarding our Savior.

Prayer: *Calv'ry's mournful mountain climb; There, adoring at his feet, Mark that miracle of time, God's own sacrifice complete. "It is finished!" hear him cry; Learn from Jesus Christ to die.*

Sitting

Walking, running, leaping, and climbing obviously qualify as physical exercises leading to better health and an aerobic lifestyle. At first, sitting doesn't seem to fit. In the exercise cycle, however, sitting suggests needed rest between exercises. We all need a breather before resuming exercise.

The psalmist talks about refusing to sit with the wicked (Psalm 26:5) and says the man is blessed who does not "sit in the seat of mockers" (Psalm 1:1c). Amos criticizes those who lounge on couches to dine on fattened calves (Amos 6:4).

But Moses gives important advice to Israel ready to enter the Promised Land. He asks them to worship the Lord our God as one Lord and to love Him with heart, soul, and strength. He instructs them to share God's teaching with their children in every aspect of life. Moses tells Israel, "Talk about them when you sit at home" (Deuteronomy 6:7). Sitting at home provides opportunity to study the Word of God and teach the whole family about God's love in Jesus Christ.

We remember Jesus commending Mary for sitting at His feet and hearing the one thing needful. We sit to rest and let God refresh us through worship and study of the Word so we can rise to serve Him through walking, running, leaping, and climbing. Through Christ we can anticipate the promise of Revelation, "To him who overcomes, I will give the right to sit with Me on My throne, just as I overcame and sat down with My Father on His throne" (Revelation 3:21).

Prayer: New graces ever gaining From this our day of rest, We reach the rest remaining To spirits of the blest. To Holy Ghost be praises, To Father, and to Son; The Church its voice upraises To you, blest Three in One.

Before They Call ...

Sometimes when we make a telephone call the other person says, "I was about to call you!" Always surprising. But God says something far more surprising through the prophet Isaiah: "Before they call I will answer; while they are still speaking I will hear" (Isaiah 65:24).

Israel would go through great trouble because of rebellion against God. In captivity far away from home, they would cry out in anguish. Now God is making the tremendous promise that He will answer Israel's prayer even before they call. He was already planning to send His Son as the promised Messiah to save the world from sin.

How often we wonder whether our prayers will be answered. We struggle because of our sins. We feel overwhelmed by circumstances. We cry out in despair. But even before we call, God has already answered by sending His Son, who is with us always, "to the very end of the age" (Matthew 28:20).

Jesus says, "Ask and it will be given to you; seek and you will find; knock and the door will be opened to you" (Matthew 7:7). We can go to God regularly with all our needs, small or large, and we can be certain that He will hear our prayer and answer in His own way and at His own time. How comforting to know about God's personal, immediate attention!

Prayer: Christians, while on earth abiding, Let us never cease to pray, Firmly in the Lord confiding As our parents in their day. Be the children's voices raised To the God their parents praised. May his blessing, failing never, Rest upon his people ever.

When I Called ...

Yesterday we heard about God's great care for us: "Before they call I will answer" (Isaiah 65:24). In the very next chapter of Isaiah, from which today's text comes, we learn of how people despise the love of God: "When I called, no one answered, when I spoke, no one listened" (Isaiah 66:4b).

God details the disobedience of His people. Their sacrifices do not come from the heart but display only an external obedience. They choose to go their own way and delight in abominations. They do evil and choose what displeases God. In these ways they refused to answer when God called to them and failed to listen when He spoke His Word.

How tragic that we often fail to listen and refuse to answer the God who calls us with His love! Like Israel we sometimes go through the motions of worship while inwardly pursuing our own selfish agenda. But God's Word has a way of hitting us like a hammer, and He calls us again to repentance and faith in His Son, the Crucified One. Then by His grace we rewrite the verse of our text: "When I called, they answered in faith, when I spoke, they listened with thanksgiving."

Prayer: Today your mercy calls us To wash away our sin. However great our trespass, Whatever we have been, However long from mercy Our hearts have turned away, Your precious blood can wash us And make us clean today.

Earthquake

The other day my wife and I were upstairs and noticed everything shaking on the dresser top. Unusual in the Midwest, the shaking turned out to be tremors from a moderate earthquake centered in southern Illinois. While for the world as a whole such tremors are not that unusual, they gave us pause for reflection. How easily and unexpectedly nature can unleash destruction upon thousands of people!

Jesus describes signs of His second coming in Matthew 24 and includes this reference: "There will be famines and earthquakes in various places" (Matthew 24:7). He refers to such signs as "the beginning of birth pains" (Matthew 24:8). We can easily live for the moment, forgetting about the second coming of Christ. Then a slight earth tremor calls us to account as we look to the One who lived, died, and rose again for us and will come again in glory at any moment.

While earthquakes can strike fear into the hearts of people, we also recall the solid foundation of God, our Refuge and Strength, who dwells in the midst of all the turmoil. Thank God for His control of nature and for His redemptive plan, which will soon bring the whole creation "into the glorious freedom of the children of God" (Romans 8:21).

Prayer: The seas shall waste, the skies in smoke decay, Rocks fall to dust, and mountains melt away; But fixed this Word, this saving pow'r, remains; Thy realms shall last, shine own Messiah reigns.

Painful or Painless?

I sit in the dentist's office getting two teeth filled. Is it painful or painless? Thanks to modern dentistry, the affected areas are numbed once the needle penetrates the gums with the anesthetic. But few people enjoy the process. This minor procedure causes me to reflect on the purpose of pain in our lives.

Jeremiah, rejected and discouraged in his ministry, cries out to God, "Why is my pain unending and my wound grievous and incurable?" (Jeremiah 15:18a) He compares his discouragements with a terminal illness, bringing unending pain. God answers, "If you repent, I will restore you that you may serve Me" (Jeremiah 15:19b). God doesn't promise an easy, pain-free life. He doesn't let him engage in self-pity. He simply promises to be with him as he speaks the Word of God.

To understand the purpose of pain, look to Jesus, who endured untold pain and suffering. He suffered physically, emotionally, and spiritually. But through it all, God the Father made His Son the instrument of salvation for the world. Saved by Christ's painful death, we begin to see the value of pain in our lives. Pain turns us to God for help. Forgiven and restored, we then serve Him as we reach out to others. He promises to be with us in the midst of pain. And He understands our pain, because He Himself suffered for us.

With Him at our side, trusting in His promises, we find it easier to endure the pain that comes to us in this fallen world.

Prayer: When I suffer pains and losses, Lord, be near, Let me hear Comfort under crosses. Point me, Father, to the heaven Which your Son For me won When his life was given.

The Sower and His Powerful Seed

If you have planted a garden, you are harvesting or anticipating the harvest. But it all begins with sowing the seed. Jesus knew that, as He told the parable of the sower. Over the next several days we focus on the parable and its meaning for. Ask yourself the question, "Is my soil receptive to God's seed?"

Jesus moves from the synagogue to the seashore, where large crowds gather to hear Him. He teaches about the Kingdom by using parables, all down-to-earth examples with application to the people who hear and understand.

He begins with the parable of the sower. Two common methods of sowing were used. In the broadcasting method, the farmer threw the seed to either side of him and let the wind carry it. Sometimes a sack of seed was placed on a donkey. A hole cut in the bag permitted the seed to fall to the ground as the donkey meandered through the field. Either method would account for the sowing described.

Clearly the seed represents the Word of God, described by Jesus as "the message about the kingdom" (Matthew 13:19). That Word is powerful and effective, always producing a harvest. God, the Sower, provides the Good News that the Kingdom comes in Jesus Christ, who suffers and dies for the world's sin.

We now enter the parable. The Sower wants to sow the good seed of the Word on our soil so He can produce an abundant harvest in us. Will we be receptive soil? What a joy to receive that seed of the Kingdom in action! Thank God for His powerful Word and His victorious Son! Tomorrow we begin to consider the kinds of soil upon which the seed falls.

Prayer: Almighty God, your Word is cast Like seed into the ground; Now let the dew of heav'n descend And righteous fruits abound.

The Wayside Soil of a Closed Mind

The parable of the sower continues. God, the Sower, sows the powerful seed of His Word, with some falling by the wayside. This wayside or path probably refers to a narrow strip of land used as a common walking ground between the fields. This path was trampled down by many feet and therefore totally hardened against the sprouting of any seed. Birds could easily see and take the seed for themselves.

Jesus identifies the wayside soil as follows: "When anyone hears the message about the kingdom and does not understand it, the evil one comes and snatches away what was sown in his heart" (Matthew 13:19). The wayside soil tells a grim story. Some hearers of the Word do not understand, because they have a hardened, unteachable spirit.

Pride rears its ugly head: "I don't need to study the Word. I feel quite satisfied spiritually. I come from a long line of church people, so I heard all of it years ago!" Fear may also intervene: "I don't want to hear anything new that will challenge my way of life. I'm quite content with my lifestyle. Certainly I'm no worse than others. Frankly, I'm afraid the Word might upset me, so I'd rather not have anything to do with it." Both pride and fear spring from hardened hearts, and the evil one easily sees and takes the seed away.

Do I ever hear like seed sown on wayside soil, rejecting the Word of God? Or is my soil receptive to that seed? Thank God for Jesus Christ, who died also for those with hardened hearts. Thank God for sending His Holy Spirit to break down my stubborn refusal and my hardened spirit.

Prayer: O Lord, help me listen with an open mind so Your Word can take root in my heart as I trust You alone for salvation. Amen.

The Rocky Soil of Shallow Faith

God sows the powerful seed of His Word. Some of that seed, according to the parable, falls on rocky soil. In parts of Palestinian fields a thin layer of earth lies on top a shelf of limestone. The seed falling on this rocky soil would quickly germinate in the warm soil, but no roots penetrate the limestone shelf. The promising young plant quickly withers and dies when the sun scorches it.

Jesus describes the rocky soil as follows: "The one who received the seed that fell on rocky places is the man who hears the Word and at once receives it with joy. But since he has no root, he lasts only a short time. When trouble or persecution comes because of the Word, he quickly falls away" (Matthew 13:20–21).

This description strikes at the heart of modern religious life. We often grow tremendously excited over fads and trends. We make a faith commitment with good intentions. But when the good beginning fades, we lose our initial enthusiasm. We have experienced a shallow and emotional faith, with no lasting roots in the promises of God.

Am I ever like seed on rocky soil, or is my soil receptive to the seed? Thank God that the powerful seed of His Word produces roots that go deep into the soil of His love. Thank God that Jesus Christ, lived in a world of rocky soil, yet committed Himself to death on a cross and offers forgiveness to those hearers who, at least at times, resemble rocky soil. Thank God for His gift of deep and solid faith in Jesus Christ as Savior.

Prayer: O Lord, strengthen my shallow and emotional faith by pointing me to the sure promise of salvation through Your death and resurrection. Ground me solidly in Your saving Word. Amen.

The Thorny Soil of Conflicting Interests

God, the Sower, sows the powerful seed of His Word. Some of the seed falls on soil with thorns. This soil looks clean at the outset but is deceptive. When one tills a garden with fibrous roots still in the ground, similar trouble lies ahead. When the seed germinates and the young plant begins to grow, thorns and weeds grow up right alongside the plant and choke the life out of it.

Jesus describes thorny soil: "The one who received the seed that fell among the thorns is the man who hears the Word, but the worries of this life and the deceitfulness of wealth choke it, making it unfruitful" (Matthew 13:22).

How devastating to us the thorny soil! We grow as young plants in good soil but all the while permit conflicting interests to grow beside us. We lead busy lives filled with activities. We earn a living. We buy appliances, gadgets, and recreational equipment. We plunge our children into activities. We build a social life—all alongside our hearing the Word of God. Most of these interests may not be wrong in themselves, but second best is always the enemy of the best. Gradually the thorns begin to choke off the life of God in us.

Do I hear like thorny soil or is my soil receptive to the powerful seed of God's Word? Thank God that Jesus was not distracted by conflicting interests but shunned Satan's temptations and went to the cross. In His death He won life for a sinful world attracted by thorns and weeds. Thank God for the priceless gift of His life and His Word for us.

Prayer: Lord, forgive me for letting the thorns of conflicting interests sap my strength. Restore to me the saving life that flows from Your Word. Amen.

The Good Soil of a Receptive Heart

Jesus is teaching by the seashore. In the background a sower is sowing seed in the fields. The people gather to hear, but with different attitudes and motivations. They listen spellbound to His parable from a familiar scene in their lives. As He describes each kind of soil—the wayside soil of a closed mind, the rocky soil of a shallow faith, and the thorny soil of conflicting interests—the Spirit of God convicts them of sin, poor hearing, and false understanding. Now comes the fourth kind of soil.

"Still other seed fell on good soil, where it produced a crop—a hundred, sixty or thirty times what was sown" (Matthew 13:8). Good soil. Deep, clean, soft soil. Nourishment for the germinating seed. An abundant harvest.

God's grace at work. He sent His Son to live and die for a world which represented all the wrong kinds of soils. The seed of God's Word alone contains the power to create receptive soil and bring about a growing plant and an abundant harvest. Even our fruit-bearing comes only from God's grace. The mighty seed explodes in our lives. He gives us receptive and obedient hearts. We learn to listen and understand, to trust and obey.

May we always be good soil and produce abundant fruit. And may God also make us participants in sowing the seed, so many may be won for Christ's kingdom.

Prayer: On what has now been sown Your blessing, Lord, bestow; The pow'r is yours alone To make it sprout and grow. O Lord, in grace the harvest raise, And yours alone shall be the praise!

A Chariot Witness

The award-winning film *Chariots of Fire* describes the 1924 Olympic success of the United Kingdom track team. They ran with the intensity of fiery chariots. Eric Liddell, a Church of Scotland believer, anchored that track team and shocked the press by refusing to run on Sunday at the Olympics because of his religious convictions. One year after winning an Olympic gold medal, Liddell journeyed to China as a missionary. In addition to teaching science at an Anglo-Chinese college, he served as an evangelist, traveling many miles on foot and bicycle. During World War II he spent two years in a Japanese prison camp, dying there of a brain tumor in 1945. Throughout his career he served as a tremendous inspiration—a chariot of fire in his witness to Jesus Christ.

In Acts we read about the evangelist Philip, who was asked to seek out a dignitary from Ethiopia traveling by chariot. "Then Philip ran up to the chariot and heard the man reading Isaiah the prophet" (Acts 8:30a). Philip ran in order to witness to Christ. The Ethiopian believed and was baptized through Philip's witness. No doubt the Gospel came to Ethiopia as the man's chariot reached his home.

We can also be "chariots of fire" for the Lord. God sent His Son to run the race for us and win the victory on the cross. He endured persecution, suffering, and death to pay for our sins. He chooses us as His own forgiven children. By His power we can run like Philip and Eric Liddell to tell others about Jesus the Savior. What chariot witness does God plan for you?

Prayer: *Give me a faithful heart, Likeness to thee, That each departing day Henceforth may see Some work of love begun, Some deed of kindness done, Some wand'rer sought and won, Something for thee.*

The Shadow of God's Hand

What could be worse than walking under a mercilessly hot sun with no shade in sight? Skin grows dry and parched. Headache begins. We feel faint. Many times our daily life brings temptations and problems which beat down on our heads like the blazing sun. We try to cover up and protect ourselves but fail to dispel the heat.

Isaiah describes God's salvation with the words, "I have ... covered you with the shadow of My hand" (Isaiah 51:16). God with His powerful hand reaches down to us and provides refreshing, cool, life-giving shade to protect us from sin and temptation. Our Bible reading emphasizes both God's might and His mercy. He, the great, merciful God, will take care of His own and will save us, His children, from our enemies.

Alone, we die in sin. But God's Son went to Calvary for us, where He endured the blazing wrath of God on our sins. He won the victory. Now forgiveness is ours through Jesus Christ. God's hand shades us from all guilt and shame.

By speaking the words God puts in our mouth, we can also bring the good news of God's shading hand to others. Repenting of their sins, they too can rest in the shade of God's protecting hand. The next time you seek the shade of a large tree, remember the gracious hand of God available at all times for you in a hot, desert land.

Prayer: I heard the voice of Jesus say, "Come unto me and rest," Lay down, O weary one, lay down Your head upon my breast." I came to Jesus as I was, So weary, worn, and sad; I found in him a resting place, And he has made me glad.

The Vault without Fault

A dramatic moment occurred during the 1984 Olympics. Competition in women's gymnastics reached a climax in the vault event. America's first opportunity for a gymnastics gold medal rested on the shoulders of 16-year-old Mary Lou Retton, With confidence and dynamic energy, Mary Lou exploded on the vault into not one but two perfect scores. Her clutch performance has been called "the vault without fault."

Young gymnasts throughout the country aspire to achieve like Mary Lou Retton, but few succeed. We would like to accomplish in our lives at home, in school, and on the job a "vault without fault," but we also fall far short. How many dreams are shattered, goals unreached, and opportunities lost!

The writer to the Hebrews, though, points us to a high priest who brings hope to us all. Other priests, themselves weak and sinful, offered daily sacrifices in the temple for their own sins and the sins of the people. But Jesus Christ, the great High Priest, came down from heaven to earth and lived among us without fault. He was tempted as we are, yet was without sin. In a climactic moment on Calvary, with the future of the whole human race at stake, He needed to make a perfect sacrifice for us. And He did just that!

Now, through His sacrifice, we are perfect in God's eyes—forgiven and cleansed. Now, like Mary Lou Retton, we seek to reach our God-given potential. Therefore, as the Hebrews writer suggests, "Let us consider how we may spur one another on toward love and good deeds" (Hebrews 10:24).

Prayer: Fight the good fight with all your might; Christ is your strength, and Christ your right. Lay hold on life, and it shall be Your joy and crown eternally.

Spiritual Dryness

In the old West, desert travel was perilous—hot, dry conditions; miles of wilderness; prickly cactus; volcanic rock; precious canteens of water for horses and travelers; scarce water holes, sometimes empty, sometimes filled with brackish water; the body dehydrated, weary, tested beyond human endurance. Imagine the utter gratitude at journey's end with an unlimited supply of cool, clear water!

In Psalm 63:1 the writer uses this desert imagery to describe spiritual dryness. David knew the meaning of desert travel from his experiences in fleeing from Saul. He had endured physical thirst and desperation. Here he applies these physical realities to his spiritual thirst for God. Alone, rejected, hopeless, discouraged, he wants a close relationship with the God of Abraham, Isaac, and Jacob, "the spring of living water" (Jeremiah 2:13).

Do you know the reality of spiritual dryness? Have you felt isolated from God? Troubled on the job, in your family, perhaps even in your church, you wander around desperately seeking a drink of cool, clear water. You cry out to God, but He does not seem to hear. You are spiritually exhausted. You can barely face the next day with its people, problems, and demands. You try to live on what you have within, but you are dry and parched. From time to time you think you see a lake of water ahead, only to discover a mirage. Spiritual dryness has overwhelmed you. Where is God's cool, clear, thirst-quenching refreshment?

Come to Jesus, the Living Water!

Prayer: Lord Jesus, I am spiritually dry. Let me drink Your life-giving water. Amen.

A Drink of Living Water

Yesterday we left David "in a dry and weary land where there is no water" (Psalm 63:1c). But he finds his spiritual thirst quenched by God alone, his Rock and Salvation. The Son of David, Jesus Christ, says to the disciples and to us many years later: "If anyone is thirsty, let him come to Me and drink. Whoever believes in Me, as the Scripture has said, streams of living water will flow from within him" (John 7:37b–38).

Having spent 40 days and nights in the wilderness, where He was tempted, Jesus relied on the Father and refreshed multitudes with living water. Having cried out in agony from the cross, "I thirst," Jesus won the victory over the evil wilderness forces of sin, death, and the devil.

He offers us the cool water of His Word and Sacrament to quench our spiritual thirst day by day. Spiritual dryness will occur because of our sin and the circumstances around us. But the great Thirst-Quencher stands ready to help us and through us to pour forth a stream of living water to a dry, thirsty world. With the desert traveler we still cry out for "water, cool, clear water." But God supplies us with an endless drink of living water through Jesus Christ. How wonderful that we have water from our spiritual canteen to share with others!

Prayer: I heard the voice of Jesus say, "Behold I freely give The living water, thirsty one; Stoop down and drink and live." I came to Jesus, and I drank Of that life-giving stream; My thirst was quenched, my soul revived, And now I live in him.

Common Clay Pots

Movie premiere. Limousines arrive. Stars in glittering evening wear sweep through the crowds as cameras flash. Who knows what lies behind the smiling faces—loneliness, fear, arrogance, immorality, emptiness? How often we try to maintain a glittering exterior while hiding what lies inside!

Paul takes an opposite approach in describing his apostolic ministry. He refers to himself as a jar of clay, a common clay pot—ordinary, weak, sinful, no glitter. Why? He wants his treasure, "the light of the knowledge of the glory of God in the face of Christ" (2 Corinthians 4:6b), to shine brightly for all to see. That light can shine through the cracks in a common clay pot. No one will mistake the clay jar for the treasure. Everyone will see that "this all-surpassing power is from God and not from us" (2 Corinthians 4:7b).

We have the same treasure, Jesus Christ, crucified and risen, God's Light in our lives. Admitting that we are common clay pots, sinful but forgiven, calls attention away from ourselves to the treasure of Christ. Others will know that "this all-surpassing power is from God and not from us." Which do you prefer—a glittering exterior like a movie star with nothing inside or the marvelous treasure of Christ in a common clay pot?

Prayer: Wisdom's highest, noblest treasure, Jesus, is revealed in you. Let me find in you my pleasure, Make my will and actions true, Humility there and simplicity reigning, In paths of true wisdom my steps ever training. If I learn from Jesus this knowledge divine, The blessing of heavenly wisdom is mine.

A Driving Force

What causes people to climb formidable mountains, explore unknown frontiers, and push toward scientific discoveries? What motivates us to condition our bodies, fight for a higher rung on the career ladder, and struggle to accumulate wealth? Driving forces within us. All too often these driving forces are desire for recognition, greed, and lust for success. At root is selfishness and pride.

But Paul describes a far more powerful motivation. This driving force led the apostles to travel the world, testify boldly, and face obstacles, persecution, and death. They loved their enemies, helped ungrateful churches, and proclaimed Jesus Christ as the only way to salvation. What motivated the apostles? Paul simply says, "Christ's love compels us, because we are convinced that One died for all" (2 Corinthians 5:14). Paul knew that Jesus went to the cross to pay for the world's sin. Not interested in personal gain and wanting only to obey the Father, Jesus loved us to the death. Paul lived boldly and joyfully because Christ's love compelled him.

Thank God for the driving force of Christ's love! We confess our selfish drives and rest in the forgiving love of the Savior. We look to the cross and see the Christ, compelled by love to hang there for us. We soak in His love through Word and Sacrament, daily offering His forgiveness. Then we rise to face the challenges of the day—people to love, goals to reach for Him, opportunities for Christian witness. And without striving or struggling, we realize that Christ's love moves us to willing and joyful action. What a driving force!

Prayer: Lord, thanks for Your saving love, which compels us to serve You! Amen.

Internalizing His Death

Smoking causes lung cancer according to research reports. No doubt true. An external fact. Yet people continue smoking. America provides unprecedented freedom for all citizens. No doubt true. An external fact. Yet people take freedom for granted. When Dad dies of lung cancer or I cough dangerously, I may internalize the research and quit smoking. When I live in a foreign country and experience its lack of liberty, I may internalize America's precious freedom.

"He died for all" (2 Corinthians 5:15). Paul writes. True. An external fact. Jesus Christ died on the cross for the sin of the entire world. God declared the whole world righteous for Jesus' sake. I live because God has brought me to faith through the waters of Baptism. Dead to sin, I live in the death and resurrection of Christ. True. An objective fact. But I often live each day as though dead in sin. I fear. I build my own kingdoms. I hate. I reject. I withdraw.

Paul describes internalizing Christ's death, "And He died for all, that those who live should no longer live for themselves but for Him who died for them and was raised again" (2 Corinthians 5:15). "For all"—external, objective. "For them"—internal, subjective. For us. For me. Because He died for me, a poor sinner, I know God's love and forgiveness. Undeserving, I have eternal life now. I no longer want to live for myself but for Him who died for me and rose again. What a life—rich, challenging, surprising, open, other-directed, praise-filled—when by God's grace I internalize Jesus' death!

Prayer: All that I am and have, Thy gifts so free, In joy, in grief, through life, Dear Lord, for thee! And when thy face I see, My ransomed soul shall be Through all eternity Something for thee.

Godly Sorrow—Worldly Sorrow

Sin brings sorrow every time. The immediate result may appear to be exciting, enjoyable, even exhilarating. But in the long run there is guilt and anxiety. Worldly sorrow over sin seeks superficial ways to deal with guilt. We try to blame others. We insist that everyone else does the same thing. We try to make up for sin by doing something good. Worldly sorrow leads to death.

Paul talks about godly sorrow. He writes to the Corinthians, "Godly sorrow brings repentance that leads to salvation and leaves no regret" (2 Corinthians 7:10). The Corinthians had sinned in many ways. Paul confronts them with their sin in his first letter. Initially, they seemed reluctant to listen to his admonition. They displayed only a worldly sorrow.

But in these verses Paul rejoices. A visit by Titus has revealed that God has worked true repentance in their hearts. No longer covering up, they admit their sin and turn to Jesus for forgiveness. Relying on His mercy, their sorrow has produced earnestness, eagerness to be cleared, indignation over wrongdoing, longing to see the wrongs righted, and genuine concern. "Godly sorrow ... leads to salvation."

God addresses each of us through Paul. Are we dealing with our sin by worldly sorrow, striving desperately to cover up and avoid the truth? Or do we open our lives to the Word of God, admitting our guilt and applying to ourselves the full forgiveness of Christ, won on the cross? "Godly sorrow brings repentance that leads to salvation."

Prayer: Lord, open my heart to sorrow over my sin so that I may receive Your free forgiveness. Amen.

Olympic Torch: Goals

Since 1936 the Olympic torch has been transported from Greece to the Olympic site. In 1984 a torch relay moved across the United States. Providing many dramatic and inspiring moments, the relay involved Americans from every walk of life in a common goal. Proceeds from the torch relay helped local sports programs across the country.

Covering 9,000 miles, the relay started May 8 and ended at the opening ceremonies in Los Angeles on July 28. This major effort required careful planning and the cooperation of groups nationwide. Some runners had the goal of running a kilometer with trained runners covering much more territory in less populated areas of the country.

In running the race of the Christian life, goals provide awesome power. Paul writes to the Philippian Christians, "I press on toward the goal to win the prize for which God has called me heavenward in Christ Jesus" (Philippians 3:14). He knew that Jesus had run the race before Him to die on the cross for the world's sin. Forgiven by Christ's sacrifice, Paul now strains ahead to live for Christ by serving others every day. He lives with purpose—sharing Christ's salvation with others.

We join other Christians to press on toward the goal for which God has called us in Christ Jesus. By grace He will lead us to heaven. In the meanwhile, we live with purpose each day, joining hands to carry the torch of Christ's love to every person on the path of life.

Prayer: Run the straight race through God's good grace; Lift up your eyes, and seek his face. Life with its way before us lies; Christ is the path, and Christ the prize.

Olympic Torch: Determination

The Olympic torch relay in 1984 not only provided challenging goals but also developed determination in organizers and runners alike. On Atlanta's Peachtree Street, with crowds four and five deep, a disabled child takes the torch, almost falls off balance, and then moves slowly toward his goal, concentrating on holding the torch aloft. Stumbling several times, he reaches his goal to the crowd's thunderous cheers. Such determination hardly left a dry eye in the crowd.

We who carry the torch of Christ's love also find our faith tested. James writes, "Consider it pure joy, my brothers, whenever you face trials of many kinds, because you know that the testing of your faith develops perseverance" (James 1:2). At the race's start serving Christ seems glorious and exciting, but as the road lengthens and our energy wanes, we struggle and feel like quitting. Then God helps us develop determination. He reminds us of the agony and bloody sweat of His only Son on the final march to Calvary. He supplies us with the encouragement of brothers and sisters in the faith. And we learn to focus on Him and move on toward the finish line.

That determination, developed within us by His grace, serves to strengthen the crowds who watch and equips us to meet even greater challenges that lie ahead. We live triumphantly on God's staying power, for His Word endures forever in us, and through us to others. Thank God for the determination of His Son.

Prayer: Jesus, Lord, my heart renew, Let me bear my crosses, Learning humbleness from you, Peace despite my losses. May I give you love for love! Hear me, O my Savior, That I may in heav'n above Sing your praise forever.

Olympic Torch: Support

The Olympic torch relay promoted teamwork among the American people. Runners supported each other and likewise received support from the crowds. In Kansas City a beautiful mentally disabled girl struggled her way up an incline while her entire class waved balloons and shouted, "Run, Amy, run!" Delayed by a severe thunderstorm in Kentucky, the relay team arrived in a small community at 2 o'clock in the morning, expecting everyone to be in bed. Instead, they were greeted by several hundred townspeople holding candles to light the way. Giving and receiving support.

Paul writes to the Philippians, "Each of you should look not only to your own interests, but also to the interests of others" (Philippians 2:4). How easily we become self-absorbed, settle into our selfish routine, and look out for number one. We want to star on the team and make the headlines.

Paul points to Jesus, who took on the role of a servant and became obedient to death on the cross. Before we can give support, we need support—His total self-giving sacrifice on the cross for us. And we need the strength of fellow Christians to grow in faith. Then by God's power we can live for Him and for others. He helps us see the needs around us and respond with specific, practical aid. We learn to encourage, commend, sustain, and uplift others as they also support us. The Christian fellowship in action far surpasses any Olympic torch relay and bears eloquent testimony to the saving work of Jesus Christ, the Servant whom God exalted as Lord.

Prayer: We share our mutual woes, Our mutual burdens bear, And often for each other flows The sympathizing tear.

Hold High the Torch

The Olympic torch symbolizes the spirit of the Olympics—international friendship, national pride, and the pursuit of athletic excellence. Setting goals, developing determination, and sharing support through the torch relay contributed to the Olympic spirit. The runners held high the torch across America, and when Rafer Johnson ignited the permanent Olympic torch in the Los Angeles Coliseum, the games began with high spirits.

As Christians we are called to hold high the torch of our Lord Jesus Christ. Hebrews describes us as running the race surrounded by all the great heroes of the faith who have gone before us. We are to throw off the weight of our sin and run with determination. But the focus of our running always rests on Jesus: "Let us fix our eyes on Jesus, the author and perfecter of our faith" (Hebrews 12:2a). Jesus went joyfully to the cross for us and was raised to the right hand of the Father.

Far from seeking glory or fame, we lift high the cross of our Lord Jesus Christ for all to see. Saved by His death, we set our life's goals to serve Him. Relying on His promises, we develop determination to run the race. Surrounded by the fellowship of believers, we give support to all who alongside of us bear witness to Christ's love. In the darkness of a sinful world, hold high the torch!

Prayer: In the cross of Christ I glory, Tow'ring o'er the wrecks of time. All the light of sacred story Gathers round its head sublime. When the sun of bliss is beaming Light and love upon my way, From the cross the radiance streaming Adds more luster to the day.

Favorite Things: Brown Paper Packages

In the Broadway musical *The Sound of Music* Maria comforts the von Trapp children during an evening thunderstorm by singing them a song about her favorite things. She includes in her list "brown paper packages." We delight to receive a package in the mail, even when it's wrapped in plain brown paper. We eagerly open it to see what treasure lies inside. Whatever the contents, we appreciate receiving the gift with its mystery inside.

In a very real sense God's greatest gift, Jesus Christ, came to us in the equivalent of a brown paper package. The eternal Son of God slipped into this world as a baby wrapped in swaddling clothes in Bethlehem's manger. Although He was and is the most priceless Treasure possible—the Son of God who has won forgiveness for the world—He did not display His glory (except for occasional glimpses) in the cities and towns of the Holy Land or on the ugly road to Calvary. Rather that Treasure remained hidden in the "brown paper package" of His humility and servanthood. Only in His resurrection and ascension did Jesus Christ shine forth as King of kings and Lord of lords.

The next time you receive one of your favorite things in a brown paper package, think of Christ, your greatest Treasure, for now and for eternity!

Prayer: Dear Lord, thank You for coming into this world for me as a "brown paper package." Let me never be offended by the lowly outward form You took when You were here on earth. Amen.

Favorite Things: Ice-Cream Cones

One of my favorite things is an ice-cream cone. Our family used to live on Main Street. On warm summer evenings we would walk several blocks together to our favorite ice-cream stand. There we would order double dips of the best ice-cream in the world. Those delicious cones would last all the way home.

An ice-cream cone for me symbolizes God's special favor. Yes, He provides bread, meat, and potatoes for the supper table. Daily bread indeed. And I suppose many people enjoy gourmet meals in fashionable restaurants by His grace. But an ice-cream cone represents a simple extra blessing of God, a taste treat available to most people, a testimony to God's over-flowing care.

God speaks of Zion in Psalm 132:15b: "I will bless her with abundant provisions." Abundant—over and above what is needed for survival. Abundant—delicious and delightful. Abundant—like the overflowing gift of eternal life through Jesus Christ, crucified and risen, who said, "I have come that they may have life, and have it to the full" (John 10:10b).

Favorite things—ice-cream cones for a growing family on a hot summer evening and abundant life through faith in Jesus Christ, the Savior!

Prayer: Dear Lord, thank You for Your life freely given for us and for the extra delight of ice-cream cones on a summer evening. Amen.

Favorite Things: Thoughtful Notes

How often I have been encouraged by a thoughtful note written by someone who cares—an unexpected thank you, an encouraging word in time of trouble, an invitation to a family gathering, a newsy letter and word of wisdom. I would place thoughtful notes high on my list of favorite things.

Paul wrote many letters to Christian congregations in Europe and Asia Minor. No doubt they brought much encouragement and counsel to embattled believers. But in his letter to the Corinthians, Paul makes a startling statement, "You yourselves are our letter, written on our hearts, known and read by everybody" (2 Corinthians 3:2). He considers them letters of recommendation, attesting to the validity of his apostolic ministry. In their daily lives of purity and service they witness to Christ and encourage both Paul and others.

In short, thoughtful notes become an extension of the sender. We show thoughtfulness by the way we live for Christ each day. Jesus Christ by His death and resurrection is God's love letter to us. We receive that love letter in faith and pass it on to others by the life we live and, yes, by the thoughtful notes we send to others. What a privilege for Paul to say of us, "You yourselves are our letter, written on our hearts, known and read by everybody." Thoughtful notes—one of my favorite things!

Prayer: Dear Lord, thank You for Your love letter to us. Help us to be letters of Your love and to send thoughtful notes to others. Amen.

The Seasons

Vivaldi's *The Four Seasons* provides ongoing delight to lovers of baroque era music. His musical imagery using violin and orchestra portrays spring, summer, autumn, and winter in succession. Four descriptive sonnets accompany the music.

How much a part of life itself, the seasons. We can count on their regularity, their uniqueness, and their individual character. God describes the seasons to Noah as a promise of His loving presence after the Flood: "As long as the earth endures, seedtime and harvest, cold and heat, summer and winter, day and night will never cease" (Genesis 8:22).

Year after year we experience the rebirth of spring, the heat of summer, the colors of autumn, and the cold of winter. While varying in intensity from climate to climate, the seasons nevertheless remind us of God's creative power and His orderly rule in nature.

With the passing of years they remind us also of the reality of death and the ultimate end of this world. We recognize our sinfulness and rebellion against God, even as the Flood marked God's punishment of sin.

For this reason we rejoice that God has sent us a "Man for All Seasons," His Son Jesus Christ. Born at winter's midnight hour, He grew up to walk the roads of Palestine at seedtime and harvest, including a winter visit to Jerusalem (John 10:22). He went to death for our sins and rose from the dead during a glorious springtime and offers us eternal life with Him long after the seasons end.

Prayer: Your bountiful care what tongue can recite? It breathes in the air, it shines in the light, It streams from the hills, it descends to the plain And sweetly distills in the dew and the rain.

Summer and Fall

God provides the seasons as a demonstration of His creative power and His love. The warmth of summer brings delight. Crops grow and ripen into maturity. People enjoy being outside. Golf, swimming, picnics, baseball, and fishing trips abound. Withering heat may also take its toll, and drought may cause serious problems. But the God who causes the sun to shine also sends rains to water the earth. God reigns during summer. The writer of Proverbs encourages us to the example of the industrious ant which "stores its provisions in summer" (Proverbs 6:8). We are to make the most of our summer opportunities to serve God.

Fall brings unique beauty. The days grow shorter and cooler. The first frost comes. The leaves change colors, creating a breathtaking panorama. Farmers gather the harvest in preparation for winter. The leaves fall. The cold increases. Again the writer of Proverbs holds up the ant, which "gathers its food at harvest" (Proverbs 6:8). God wants us to enjoy autumn but also to make the most of the time so we are ready for winter.

As we reflect on summer and fall, we recognize on the one hand God's magnificent creation and His boundless provision. On the other hand we come face-to-face with our own laziness and need for God's help. How thankful we are that God sent His Son to pay for our sins and make us His own. Together with all of God's people we praise Him for summer and fall!

Prayer: You forest leaves so green and tender That dance for joy in summer air, You meadow grasses, bright and slender, You flow'rs so fragrant and so fair, You live to show God's praise alone. Join me to make his glory known.

Winter and Spring

Of all the seasons, winter seems the most threatening. While snow can create a winter wonderland and winter sports enthusiasts love it, winter nevertheless suggests cold, darkness, and death. Paul writes to Timothy and asks him to "do your best to get here before winter" (2 Timothy 4:21).

Winter reminds us that we will all die, even as leaves wither and fall and green grass grows brown. We rejoice that Jesus Christ died for us. We rejoice that in winter we have always with us the warmth of God's love and that of His people gathered around Word and sacraments.

Spring follows winter. The beloved exclaims the words of our Bible reading. Winter is bleak. Spring is glorious. Nature comes alive. Warmth and gentle winds return. God showers us with His love.

Because spring gives way to summer, summer to fall, and fall to winter, we cannot base our eternal hope on the beauty of spring. But we can anchor our hope on the resurrection of Jesus Christ from the dead, an event which occurred in springtime. Jesus Christ conquered death for us. His death was all-sufficient for our salvation, His life guaranteeing eternal life for those who believe in Him as Savior.

Thank God for the seasons! As we move through life from the springtime of youth, the summer of maturity, and the autumn of aging to the winter of death, we rejoice in the constant presence of the crucified and risen Christ.

Prayer: *This the spring of souls today: Christ has burst his prison And from three days' sleep in death As a sun has risen; All the winter of our sins, Long and dark, is flying From his light, to whom is giv'n Laud and praise undying.*

Sin and Salvation in Story Land: Peter Rabbit

You will remember that Mrs. Rabbit dressed her children one morning in good clothes and sent them out to play. Only one thing was forbidden—to sneak into Farmer McGregor's garden patch and eat his vegetables. Flopsie, Mopsie, and Cottontail obeyed. Not so Peter Rabbit. He immediately slipped under the fence into Farmer McGregor's garden patch. How good those vegetables tasted!

But soon, to his horror, he found himself right under the accusing eye of Farmer McGregor. "Stop, thief!" the farmer cried out as he chased Peter with a hoe. Peter ran as fast as he could, but he got caught in a gooseberry net. He barely managed to pull free, but he was forced to leave behind his brand-new coat with shiny brass buttons. He raced into Farmer McGregor's shed and jumped into a half-full water can. At last, Peter—exhausted, wet, tired, frightened—managed to wriggle under the fence and escape home. He was sent right to bed without supper, while Flopsie, Mopsie, and Cottontail had a delicious meal of fresh blackberries and milk.

Aren't we like Peter Rabbit? God has placed us in this beautiful world to enjoy as we serve Him. Yet we go beyond the fence and indulge ourselves. We enjoy these forbidden pleasures until we start feeling sick. God, the righteous Judge, pursues us. We know He will find us and that we are guilty. We cannot escape.

Recognizing our sin against God, we repent and turn to Him. He sent His Son, Jesus Christ, to rescue us from our sins. We can stop running and let Him heal and forgive us.

Prayer: Dear Father, help us sinners to stop running away and to receive Your Son as our Savior and Lord. Amen.

Sin and Salvation in Story Land: Belling the Cat

Once there was a cat who constantly attacked a group of mice. Eventually the mice decided to summon a council to discuss the problem. A young, self-assured mouse said, "Let's put a bell around the cat's neck. Then whenever he comes near us, we will hear the bell and be able to escape."

The mice nodded their approval. "A wonderful plan, brilliantly conceived. It's bound to work," they cried. "Shall we select a silver bell, a gold bell, or a brass bell? What color ribbon should we use to fasten the bell around the cat's neck?"

At length, a very old, wise mouse spoke. "Wait a moment! I have one question: Who will put the bell on the cat's neck?" Complete silence. Several mice nervously cleared their throats. A few shuffled their feet. No one stepped forward to volunteer, least of all the young, self-assured mouse. The elder mouse said, "That shows it's not enough just to talk about something unless you can also do something about it."

Despite what we learned from Peter Rabbit about our rebellion against God, we somehow think we can come up with a brilliant plan to atone for our failures. But can we? We talk a great deal about how our lives will change. But how often do we back up our talk with actions? How often we sit at church for hours in meetings and make plans for evangelism, education, and service. Often we believe our task accomplished because we have talked about our responsibilities. As Proverbs says, "Mere talk leads only to poverty" (Proverbs 14:23).

Our attempts to justify ourselves before God are futile. We need to turn to God's Son, Jesus Christ. He alone can save us.

Prayer: Dear Father, forgive us for empty talk. Turn us to Your saving action in Jesus Christ. Amen.

Sin and Salvation in Story Land: The Emperor's New Clothes

There was once an emperor who loved beautiful clothes. One day two men came to him claiming to be weavers and promising the world's most beautiful suit of clothes. So he hired them. Day after day they labored, although they had no cloth. After a time the emperor sent his advisers to check their progress. They saw nothing, but not willing to risk the emperor's wrath, they returned with glowing praise. Finally the weavers summoned the emperor to see the finished product and to march in a special parade. Eager to wear the new suit, the emperor came. The weavers talked about the suit and fitted it to his body with a flourish. "Could I be ignorant?" he thought. "I can't admit such a thing." And so the emperor permitted the men to dress him in nothing.

When he walked in the parade, no one dared say a word. Finally a young boy cried out, "Look at the emperor, he doesn't have any clothes on!" But the proud emperor continued to walk with his head high, wearing nothing but his birthday suit.

We laugh at the emperor, at his pride and stupidity. But doesn't he mirror our relationship to God? Pointing a finger at others, we pat ourselves on the back. Proudly we walk before God sporting our "fine" clothes. But God sees us as we really are—poor, miserable, sinful human beings.

But we need not stand naked before God. He offers us brand-new clothes. He sent His Son to die for our sins and rise again. We can put on the robe of Christ's righteousness and stand before God as His well-dressed children.

Prayer: Gracious Father, forgive us for our pride and foolishness. Clothe us in Christ's righteousness. Amen.

Sin and Salvation in Story Land: The Ugly Duckling

Once a mother duck hatched her eggs. Little fuzzy ducklings joined her, one at a time. One egg looked different from the others. When it hatched, an ugly duckling emerged. This duckling didn't look or act like the others. The others ridiculed her for being different. Finally, the duckling set out on her own. She tried to be a chicken, a dog, and other animals. But she failed to belong. Alone and unhappy, the ugly duckling weathered the winter.

In spring the duckling came to a pond where beautiful white swans were swimming. As she swam toward them, she expected them to avoid her, but they invited her to stay. Then she looked down and saw her own reflection—not the reflection of an ugly duckling, but of a beautiful swan.

We are all ugly ducklings at first, because of our sinful nature. But God cares about us. He sent His own Son, Jesus Christ, to be an ugly duckling for us. "He was despised and rejected by men" (Isaiah 53:3). They nailed Him to a cross to die. He did not stay in the grave, however, but rose from the dead on the third day as a beautiful white swan.

He makes us beautiful swans too in our Baptism. "If anyone is in Christ, he is a new creation" (2 Corinthians 5:17). Unfortunately, some of our ugly duckling nature is still with us, but gradually He is transforming us into something new. And someday He will permit us to take our places at His throne forever as beautiful white swans.

Prayer: Gracious Father, thank You for transforming us ugly ducklings into beautiful white swans by the death and resurrection of Jesus Christ. Amen.

You Feed Them

The scene: a lonely wilderness place. The situation: a hungry crowd of 5,000 men plus women and children. The startling command: You feed them. The disciples ask Jesus to send the crowds to the villages where they can buy food. Jesus says, "They do not need to go away. You give them something to eat" (Matthew 14:16). Taken aback, the disciples reply, "We have here only five loaves of bread and two fish" (Matthew 14:17). Impossible!

Is the scene familiar? We live in a world of hungry people—physically and spiritually hungry. We recognize their hunger and want to send them somewhere else for help. Then Jesus startles us with the words of our text. Taken aback, we look at our checkbook, our cupboard, and our calendar. Reporting, we say, "We have only $2, a can of beans, and 15 minutes a week." Impossible! What is that for a hungry world?

But Jesus replies, "Bring them … to Me" (Matthew 14:18). He works a miracle. He takes the loaves and fish, gives thanks to the Father, and then the disciples distribute it. The entire crowd eats, with 12 basketfuls remaining. Impossible? Not for Jesus.

Jesus says to us, "Bring them here to Me." We invite the hungry to come and sit. He takes our gifts and multiplies them. Then He asks us to feed them. He has fed us. He gave His body as bread for the world. He feeds us with His body and blood in the Sacrament. And He asks us to distribute our physical and spiritual blessings to the hungry. Impossible? On our own, yes, but with His bountiful grace, no. The Crucified and Risen One supplies us and then commands, "FEED THEM!"

Prayer: *O Bread of Life, help us to feed the hungry! Amen.*

A Lesson in Faith: Jesus on the Water

Feeding the 5,000 was a heady miracle for the disciples who saw the loaves multiply—surely a faith-strengthener. But immediately afterward they experience paralyzing fear. Asked by Jesus to travel at night by boat to the other side of the lake, they run into strong winds and high waves. Though seasoned fishermen, they are gripped by fear. Add a ghostlike figure walking on the water, and they cry out in terror. Faith tested.

Do we need a lesson in faith? We participate daily in God's Word-and-Sacrament miracles among His people. We see others come to saving faith and experience His daily providence in our own lives. But then stormy circumstances arise—difficult family situations, illness and death of loved ones, mountains of bills. We feel surrounded by the eerie darkness of loneliness. When a shadowy figure appears which we understand as a judging and condemning God, fear paralyzes us too. Faith tested.

Help is in sight through the darkness. Jesus says to them, "Take courage! It is I. Don't be afraid" (Matthew 14:27). Their Friend. Their Savior. The darkness remains. The wind blows and waves buffet the boat, but they need fear no longer. A lesson in faith.

Jesus walks on the water in the midst of our paralyzing fears and says, "Take courage! It is I. Don't be afraid." He came into this dark world in the little town of Bethlehem. He triumphed over sin and fear in the darkness of Good Friday. Faith tested, the darkness remains. The wind continues. The waves buffet the boat. But our Savior says, "It is I." We need fear no longer. For us too, a lesson in faith.

Prayer: Dear Jesus, thank You for teaching us a lesson in faith on the night waves of Galilee. Reassure us with Your presence. Amen.

A Lesson in Faith: Getting Out of the Boat

The lesson in faith continues. Reassured by the voice of Jesus, Peter boldly asserts, "Lord, if it's You, tell me to come to You on the water" (Matthew 14:28). Then he gets out of the boat and walks toward Jesus. Impetuous? Yes. Nevertheless it is a genuine faith response to do the impossible.

"Get out of the boat to serve others," Jesus tells us. "Don't just play it safe." Reassured by His voice, we get out of the boat and walk on the water to Him as we serve Him.

But fear returns. A second test of faith. Peter looks at the waves and feels the wind. Afraid and beginning to sink, he cries out, "Lord, save me!" (Matthew 14:30b). Problems enough in the boat, but on the water there is only a watery grave!

We, too, learn the meaning of fear when we step out of the boat. We reach out to others, take risks for the Lord, testify to our faith in Christ. In the process we often take our eyes off Jesus and look at the waves. We begin to sink. Desperately afraid, we cry out, "Lord, save me!"

Immediately Jesus reached out His hand and caught Peter. When they climbed into the boat, the wind died down. A third lesson in faith. Jesus said to Peter, "You of little faith, why did you doubt?" (Matthew 14:31). Those in the boat worshiped Him, saying, "Truly You are the Son of God" (Matthew 14:33). And they traveled on to land, where they continued ministering to people.

Recognizing our fear and weakness, Jesus reaches out His hand and guides us safely to the boat. Our sin of doubt rebuked, we see Jesus as our Savior. We follow Him to land and get out of the boat to minister to people in need.

Prayer: Dear Jesus, sustain me in the stormy waves and strengthen my faith in Your salvation so I may serve You daily. Amen.

Faith That Works

With Jesus traveling nearby, the Canaanite woman demonstrates her God-given faith by crying out, "Lord, Son of David, have mercy on me!" (Matthew 15:22b). And she is an outsider. We often feel that God is for pastors and "strong" Christians but not for us. But this woman looks not to her faith but to her God. Faith in Jesus Christ as Savior works because we have a great God.

The woman comes with faith in God to meet a specific need: "My daughter is suffering terribly from demon possession" (Matthew 15:22b). Her faith is severely tested. "Jesus did not answer a word" (Matthew 15:23a). The disciples urge Him to send her away. She hears discouragement from Jesus. "I was sent only to the lost sheep of Israel. … It is not right to take the children's bread and toss it to their dogs" (Matthew 15:24–26). But the woman, believing that Jesus can heal her daughter, persists. "Yes, Lord, but even the dogs eat the crumbs that fall from their masters' table" (Matthew 15:27). The woman's God-given faith works. Jesus answers, "Woman, you have great faith! Your request is granted" (Matthew 15:28).

Blessed with God's gift of saving faith, we come to Him with our specific needs—strength in financial crisis, restored health, wisdom in difficult decisions. Our faith is tested when there is no apparent answer from God. There is ridicule when others mock our faith as they seemingly prosper. There is discouragement: "Maybe your faith isn't strong enough." By God's grace we persevere. Christ's death and resurrection brings us forgiveness, life, and salvation. We continue to pray with the woman, "Lord, help me!" And He does—in His own way and at His own time, because He has given us freely a faith that works!

Prayer: *Lord, thank You for a faith that works. Amen.*

Learning Still?

School days finished, you may feel saturated with learning and content just to live a little. However, we never stop learning as long as we live. In our rapidly changing society, everyone struggles to keep abreast. If learning stops, we can scarcely adapt to modern life.

Unfortunately, we also may think of our knowledge of God and His Word in terms of graduation. We attended Sunday school and we received confirmation instruction. We think we have arrived!

The writer of Proverbs disagrees. Mockers refuse to learn or accept correction. But Proverbs 9:9 tells us, "Instruct a wise man and he will be wiser still; teach a righteous man and he will add to his learning." The righteous person, declared righteous by Christ's death on the cross, rejoices in salvation and never ceases to want more knowledge about God's love in Christ. Humbly and simply, the wise come to the waters of life again and again for a drink. Not like a cup, which fills with water and can hold no more, but rather like a sponge, which absorbs more and more water, the wise keep learning and sharing with others.

God's Spirit creates in us the desire to absorb more and more of God's good news. The more we live for Christ like a sponge emptying, the more we need to learn like a sponge absorbing. Jesus Christ fills our lives with His forgiving love. Yes, as God's wise and righteous people, we are learning still!

Prayer: Preserve your Word and preaching, The truth that makes us whole, The mirror of your glory, The pow'r that saves the soul. Oh, may this living water, This dew of heav'nly grace, Sustain us while here living Until we see your face.

Prisoners of the Law

Prisons restrict and confine. The days stretch into endless weeks. Oh, to live freely again and make choices!

Paul speaks of a different kind of prison. He knew personally the bondage of living by the Law. As a Pharisee he attempted to live in total obedience to God's commands to earn God's favor. After his experience on the Damascus road, he realized that he had been a prisoner of the Law, trying to bear the burden of his sin all alone.

Are you a prisoner of the Law? Are you filled with rules and expectations which run your life? Do you act out of obligation, guilt, or fear of reprisal? Are you determined to try harder but afraid you will fall short? How painful and discouraging to live by the Law! Oh, to live freely again!

Paul discovered the freedom of faith in Jesus Christ. He writes: "You are all sons of God through faith in Christ Jesus, for all of you who were baptized into Christ have clothed yourselves with Christ" (Galatians 3:26–27). Christ lived perfectly under the Law and then died on the cross to break its bondage. He now frees from prison all who trust in Him for salvation. Paul didn't have to be burdened with the demands of the Law, because Christ carried those burdens.

You, too, can live freely through faith in Jesus Christ. Admitting your inability to keep the Law, you turn to Jesus, who kept it for you. You can now live freely and joyfully.

Prayer: *I lay my sins on Jesus, The spotless Lamb of God; He bears them all and frees us From the accursed load. I bring my guilt to Jesus To wash my crimson stains Clean in his blood most precious Till not a spot remains.*

Bodies Offered as Living Sacrifices

We are encouraged to be organ donors. A heart, a kidney, or a liver can bring new life to a seriously ill person.

St. Paul in Romans 12 urges the early Christians to offer their bodies as living sacrifices. He asks them to commit themselves totally—body, mind, and spirit—to the service of Christ, which he calls a "spiritual act of worship" (Romans 12:1b). In many respects a living sacrifice requires much more than a sacrifice of body organs at the time of death. A living sacrifice means daily commitment. It is not always or even usually dramatic. It is sometimes dull and routine, time-consuming, unpopular at times, often unnoticed, and contrary to human nature. Living sacrifices demand more than we can possibly give on our own power.

That's why Paul makes this a Gospel appeal: "... in view of God's mercy" (Romans 12:1a). Paul has described God's mercy in the 11 glorious chapters of Romans preceding this text. He is "not ashamed of the Gospel" (Romans 1:16). He faces the ugly reality of sin and the Law which condemns the whole human race, but rejoices in God's free "gift of ... eternal life in Christ Jesus our Lord" (Romans 6:23b). Jesus presented His body as a living sacrifice in perfect obedience to the Law. He then sacrificed Himself in payment for the world's sin.

In view of this mercy of God, Paul urges us to offer our bodies—ourselves—as living sacrifices. Forgiven and empowered by the Gospel, we freely and joyfully give ourselves to the Lord. We love, care, give, share, witness, and obey in view of God's mercy. Falling short, we repent and receive Christ's forgiveness; then we offer our bodies again as living sacrifices.

Prayer: Dear Lord, based on Your sacrifice of mercy, help us to offer ourselves as living sacrifices each day. Amen.

Metamorphosis

Paul urges us to offer our bodies as living sacrifices. Negatively, he asks us not to conform to the pattern of this world. The Greek word for "conform" suggests a rigid, assembly-line in which we look and act like everyone else. How boring, drab, and restricted! Paul admonishes, "Be transformed by the renewing of your mind" (Romans 12:2a). The Greek word for "be transformed" suggests an interesting illustration from the world of nature—metamorphosis.

How does the lowly caterpillar become a beautiful butterfly when it looks nothing like the adult butterfly? We are helpless to bring about this change. Someone quipped, "You can't change a caterpillar into a butterfly by taping on wings and sending it to aviation school." But God provides a marvelous transformation to accomplish the metamorphosis. The caterpillar or larva passes through a stage in which changes occur inside a cocoon. When the cocoon opens, out flies the butterfly, totally transformed.

We are by nature lowly caterpillars. But God sent His Son to live and die for us. From the cocoon of His grave He emerged on the third day as a beautiful butterfly, triumphant over sin and death. God transforms us by a spiritual metamorphosis. He works faith in our hearts through His Word and sacraments. Christ lives in us. We are transformed into butterflies, free to serve Him with our lives. Through our regular exposure to His Word, God renews our minds. We can shun conformity and be transformed to offer our bodies as living sacrifices. Thank God for His metamorphosis!

Prayer: *Dear Lord, transform us to serve You. Amen.*

By the Sweat of Your Brow

In September Americans pause to observe Labor Day. How does Scripture view work?

God created human beings to work in the Garden of Eden and care for it. Work must have been a joyful blessing. With the fall into sin, work became more of a burden. God tells Adam, "By the sweat of your brow you will eat your food" (Genesis 3:19a). Now thorns and thistles would complicate farming. Much sorrow would enter the picture.

Work still represents God's purpose for people. Much blessing and fulfillment accompanies faithful labor. But, like Adam, we toil by the sweat of our brow because of sin in the world. Work problems multiply. Labor-management strife develops. Unemployment affects many. Some work takes a tremendous physical toll. Other work exacts a serious mental and emotional price. Sometimes we let work rule our lives with no room for God or people's needs. Sometimes we devalue work and become lazy, expecting others to provide for us. Both distortions reveal our sinful rebellion against a loving God.

But in our labor we remember Jesus Christ. He is the One who worked with His hands as a carpenter and called to Himself rugged fishermen and tax collectors. He did the work of God who sent Him (John 9:4). In prayer His sweat was like drops of blood (Luke 22:44). He completed His saving work on the cross and rose from the dead.

Jesus knows our needs and our labor problems. He promises to be with us. He restores our work to its joyful significance in God's creation. We continue to toil by the sweat of our brow, but through the sweat we see His face.

Prayer: Father, move us to work joyfully for Jesus' sake. Amen.

The Discipline of Work

There is a lazy streak in all of us. We glorify Tom Sawyer for cleverly getting his friends to do his fence painting. Our nation, founded on the Puritan work ethic, has experienced a breakdown in moral fiber.

Paul writes the Thessalonian believers regarding a similar problem, "We hear that some among you are idle" (2 Thessalonians 3:11a). They expected the immediate second coming of Christ. Therefore many quit their jobs, sat around idly, became busybodies and gossips. Paul strongly condemns idleness: "If a man will not work, he shall not eat" (2 Thessalonians 3:10).

The problem of idleness stands in sharp contrast to God's purpose of work. Paul urges them "to settle down and earn the bread they eat" (2 Thessalonians 3:12). Work involves a daily discipline—quiet, steady, positive effort to serve God and others. However, in the routine and drudgery of everyday life we often lose sight of God's purpose for work.

Only God can supply the power for work in our lives. Paul writes, "We command and urge in the Lord Jesus Christ to ... earn the bread they eat" (2 Thessalonians 3:12). God sent His Son to work for the world. A carpenter, Jesus worked tirelessly to proclaim the kingdom of God, heal the sick, and teach the disciples. He endured the suffering of the cross for us. His saving work complete, He offers us free salvation based on faith and not the works of the Law. Free from earning salvation, we can work while it is day to serve Him before the night comes when no man can work (John 9:4). Yes, the discipline of daily work is the foundation for a life of Gospel service.

Prayer: *Dear Father, bless our daily work to Your glory because of the finished work on the cross of Your Son, Jesus Christ. Amen.*

Witnessing Excuses: Moses and You No. 1

What a challenge God gives us to be His witnesses to the ends of the earth! We have opportunities among family and friends, neighbors, co-workers, and even church members.

What a challenge God gave Moses to free Israel from bondage. A shepherd in the Sinai desert for 40 years, Moses is now asked to return to Pharaoh and free his people.

Moses makes excuses because he fears the awesome challenge. When God tells Moses to go to Pharaoh, Moses replies with the words of our text. In effect Moses tells God that he is a nobody. What sounds like humility on the surface turns out to be cowardice. Moses, once a prince of Egypt, reared in Pharaoh's household, now feels inadequate for the task.

We often ask with Moses, "Who am I that I should witness about my faith in Jesus Christ to others?" We may have a college education and hold a responsible job, but we feel like a nobody when it comes to witnessing.

God answers Moses, "I will be with you" (Exodus 3:12a). He was preparing him in the wilderness. He would send the Messiah to save Moses from his sin. He promises to be with Moses constantly. Hence Moses' first excuse is countered. Because of God, Moses is a somebody, able to go to Pharaoh.

God answers us, "I will be with you." He made us as special people with gifts and abilities. He sent His Son to be our Savior. He made us His children in our Baptism. And He promises to be with us each day. We are somebodies, able to witness to others about our faith in Jesus Christ.

Prayer: Dear Father, thank You for making us special in Your sight through Jesus Christ. Empower us to witness to Your love every day. Amen.

Witnessing Excuses: Moses and You No. 2

Moses presents a second excuse which stands in the way of the liberation challenge: he questions God's identity. He wants to know God's name. Moses really wants that certainty for himself, so he can go to Israel and Egypt's leader.

When God presents us with the witnessing challenge, we also raise the question about His identity. We may frame the question in terms of other people, "What if they ask me who my God is? What if they ask me theological questions I can't answer?" But we want that certainty about God's identity for ourselves.

God answers Moses' second excuse by telling him: "I AM WHO I AM. This is what you are to say to the Israelites: 'I AM has sent me to you' " (Exodus 3:14). He is Yahweh, the eternal, all powerful God who gives life to the world. He will continue to act in the history of His people, bringing them salvation through His Son, the Messiah.

God answers our second excuse with the same clarification: "I am who I am." We see Him as the covenant God of the Old Testament. We see Him in Jesus Christ, the Word-Made-Flesh, who said: "I am the Bread of Life" (John 6:48), "the Resurrection and the Life" (John 11:25), "the Way, the Truth, and the Life" (John 14:6). Crucified and risen, Jesus also said, "I am with you always" (Matthew 28:20). Assured of God's identity, we have fresh power to witness to His love within our church and out in the world where we live daily.

Prayer: Dear Father, thank You for revealing Yourself to us in Your Son, Jesus Christ. Continue to deepen our understanding of Your identity so that we may witness more boldly about Your love. Amen.

Witnessing Excuses: Moses and You No. 3

Moses has questioned his own identity and God's identity. Both excuses failed to relieve Moses of his awesome challenge to free Israel from slavery.

Now Moses has a third excuse: "What if they don't believe me?" What if people are skeptical about my message?

Don't we raise a similar excuse? We want to witness to our faith, but we fear that others will doubt our message. They may question the Bible or doubt God's power in today's world. How can we possibly accept the witnessing challenge?

God answers this excuse not with words but with actions. He asks Moses to throw his staff on the ground. Moses complies, and the staff becomes a snake. Recoiling, Moses is asked to pick up the snake by the tail, and it becomes a staff again. Moses is then asked to put his hand inside his cloak. Withdrawing it, he sees that it is leprous, like snow. Repeating the procedure, Moses' hand is restored. God also tells him about a third sign—taking water from the Nile and turning it to blood. These signs confirm God's powerful words as authentic.

God likewise shores up His powerful words for us with actions. God delivered His people from Egypt, led them to the Promised Land, and at the right time sent His Son as the Word-Made-Flesh to live, die, and rise again for the world. He acts today in the fellowship of His people through Word and sacraments. He changes lives, restores people to health, and works in wonderful ways among His people. God's actions confirm His powerful words.

Prayer: Dear Father, thank You for Your marvelous actions in Jesus Christ, which reinforce Your powerful words. Help me to speak Your words boldly. Amen.

Witnessing Excuses: Moses and You No. 4

Excuses abound when a challenge seems overwhelming. Moses tried to avoid the challenge of liberating Israel. We try to avoid witnessing. But God persists. We are part of His plan.

Moses tries one more excuse, and God becomes angry with him. He claims that he is a poor speaker, lacking eloquence, slow of speech and tongue.

Before we condemn Moses for a feeble excuse, do we not plead the same deficiency? We often claim that we don't have the right words or feel awkward. We may be able to discuss current events, sports, and the weather at great length, but we freeze when trying to witness about Christ.

God reminds Moses that He is the One who gives us a mouth to speak. He also promises that He will help Moses speak and even teach him what to say. After Moses tries to bow out, God arranges for Aaron to be his spokesman. All excuses exhausted, Moses heads for Egypt to face his greatest challenge. God brings the victory.

The same God comes to us with His promise of help. He will help us speak and teach us what to say. He provides others to go with us and support us. He sent His Son to the cross for us. He has opened our eyes to see the cross and the empty tomb, the baptismal font and the bread and wine. We have seen, heard, tasted, and touched the living Christ. We have something to share with others. All excuses exhausted, we head for our witnessing challenge. God will bring the victory.

Prayer: *Dear Father, thank You for giving me the words to speak and the courage to speak them. Help me to accept the witnessing challenge without excuses, so many may come to know Jesus Christ as their Savior and Lord. Amen.*

Abraham: Test of Obedience

Whom do you hold dearest in life—a spouse, a child, a friend? Imagine being asked by God to give this person up at a moment's notice as evidence of your loyalty to Him.

That's precisely what God asked in our text. Yes, Isaac was Abraham's only son from his marriage to Sarah. What a special joy when Isaac was born in their old age! But beyond that, Isaac represented the fulfillment of God's promise to Abraham that he would have many descendants and be a blessing to the world through the promised Messiah.

Now God tests Abraham to the limit, asking him to offer Issac as a sacrifice. How does God test you? He knows vulnerabilities—health, family, financial stability. Problems in these areas are tests of obedience for us.

How does Abraham respond to God's test? He obeys without question. He saddles his donkey, cuts enough wood for the offering, takes his son to the offering location, binds his son, places him on the altar, and raises the knife. What obedience! An obedience based on Abraham's God-given faith. He had told Isaac, "God Himself will provide the lamb" (Genesis 22:8). God did spare Isaac and supplied a ram for the burnt offering. He then reaffirmed His promise to Abraham.

God likewise provides for our needs. He sent His Son Jesus to be the Sacrificial Lamb in our place. He died for our sins so that we might live forever. God gives us faith in His promises so that we can obey Him in the midst of trials.

Prayer: The God of Abr'am praise, Whose all-sufficient grace Shall guide me all my pilgrim days In all my ways. He deigns to call me friend; He calls himself my God. And he shall save me to the end Through Jesus' blood.

Joseph: God Uses Evil for Good

Evil stops us. Others treat us unfairly. We try hard but receive little recognition. Power-hungry people use us and then discard us. How easy to grow cynical and depressed!

Joseph could have felt that way. He was left in a pit by his brothers and sold as a slave. A slave in Egypt, he was thrown into prison when he refused the advances of Potiphar's wife. But he doesn't complain or grow bitter. He served faithfully in Potiphar's household. In prison he gained trust and respect. When the time came, he was ready to help the country through a famine and bring his family to Egypt.

How often we permit problems and troubles to consume, discourage, and destroy us! Unlike Joseph, we complain and grow bitter. We forget to trust God and fail to obey Him.

Near the end of his life, Joseph's brothers beg forgiveness for the evil they have inflicted on him. In tears, Joseph tells them, "You intended to harm me, but God intended it for good to accomplish what is now being done, the saving of many lives" (Genesis 50:20). Joseph recognized God's loving hand in his life. God used evil for good.

Turn from Joseph to Jesus. He was surrounded by evil—tempted by Satan, opposed by the scribes and Pharisees, convicted and crucified unjustly by Pontius Pilate. Yet He trusted faithfully, lived obediently, and died to defeat the combined forces of evil. God used evil for good.

He has a plan for your life too. He promises His constant presence. And He wants to use you to carry out His plan for the salvation of the world. God uses evil for good.

Prayer: Dear God, help us to see how You use evil for good in our lives, for Jesus' sake. Amen.

Aging: Prospects for Long Life

America is growing older. As the postwar baby boomers age, the population is steadily turning gray. Because of public health and medical advances, we live longer. Our society is changing as a result. Work, leisure, housing, finance, advertising, health, education, and religion—all are experiencing the impact of the aging of America.

According to God's Word, what are the prospects for long life? The Scriptures seems to link long life with a vital relationship to God. The psalmist says of the God-fearing person: "With long life will I satisfy him and show him My salvation" (Psalm 91:16). Of the righteous the psalmist says: "They will still bear fruit in old age, they will stay fresh and green" (Psalm 92:14). According to Proverbs 10:27, "The fear of the Lord adds length to life." God seems to promise long life to those who trust in Him. That long life includes both quantity and quality. "Gray hair is a crown of splendor; it is attained by a righteous life" (Proverbs 16:31). Only God makes joyful long life possible.

How do you face the aging process? Do you anticipate problems in your old age? Or do you picture long years of high-quality life? Only God knows your future. He alone can grant long life and joyful years. He sent His Son to die for you so that you might live for Him now and with Him eternally in heaven. He invites you to call upon His name and rest in His shadow. He promises you long life and salvation.

Prayer: Take my life, O Lord, renew, Consecrate my heart to you; Take my moments and my days; Let them sing your ceaseless praise.

Aging: Problems of Growing Old

Many glowing words can be spoken about retirement, travel, leisure time, and enjoying the fruits of our labor. However old age brings many problems as the body deteriorates. Who has not felt the pain of a loved one suffering physical or mental torment as the result of the aging process?

The writer of Ecclesiastes describes aging in a grim, poetic fashion. He labels old age as "the days of trouble." He writes, "When the keepers of the house tremble, and the strong men stoop [once-strong arms now weak and trembling, strong legs now bowed and gnarled], when the grinders cease because they are few [loss of teeth], and those looking through the windows grow dim [eyesight failing]; when the doors to the street are closed and the sound of grinding fades [hearing loss]; when men rise up at the sound of birds, but all their songs grow faint [insomnia and poor hearing]; when men are afraid of heights and of dangers in the streets ... Then man goes to his eternal home and mourners go about the streets" (Ecclesiastes 12:3–5). Pessimistic, yet realistic. We can make use of medicine, diet, and exercise, and wear eyeglasses and hearing aids, but we cannot prevent aging.

Our problems remind us of our need for God. He wants us to trust Him for each problem. He has saved us by the suffering and death of Jesus on the cross. We can remember our Creator, not only in our youth but also as we grow older. And we know that the deterioration of our bodies is followed by the resurrection to eternal life, where "there will be no more death or mourning or crying or pain, for the old order of things has passed away" (Revelation 21:4).

Prayer: *In mercy, Jesus, bring us To that dear land of rest!*

Aging: Promises of God's Presence

Problems abound for the aging population. But God promises His presence. Through the prophet Isaiah, God speaks the words of our text to the faithful remnant of the house of Judah. God's people were forced into exile. Seventy years elapsed before they could return to Jerusalem. Many grew old and died in a foreign land, separated from the temple of God. How discouraged they must have felt! Yet God promised His presence. He said, "I am He" (Isaiah 46:4a). Words similar to those He spoke to Moses at the burning bush "I am He who will sustain you." He gave them the staying power to make it through difficult times. He promised to carry them when they faltered. He rescued them with His salvation.

Whatever your problems, God is present with you also. You may be concerned about money, with a meager fixed income and future expenses. You may be experiencing failing health and wonder about the possible need for a nursing home. You may have lost your spouse and struggle with loneliness. You may sense that you are becoming forgetful. Whatever your concerns, listen to God's promises. "Even to your old age and gray hairs I am He, I am He who will sustain you. I have made you and I will carry you; I will sustain you and I will rescue you" (Isaiah 46:4a). The "I am" God came to earth in the person of Jesus Christ. He carried our burdens, problems, and sins on His own shoulders as He went to the cross. He promised, "Surely I am with you always" (Matthew 28:20b). He sustains you in the hour of trial and will carry you home to heaven.

Prayer: Dear Lord, thank You for Your promise to be with me always. Amen.

Aging: Purpose of Long Life

All too often society looks at the aging as a special-needs group. What programs should be provided so the aging will survive this difficult period?

Aging can be difficult, but we can all grow old with real purpose. The psalmist suggests a profound purpose for living: to declare God's power to the next generation. That's what aged Jacob did when he gathered his 12 sons for a final blessing before he died. He reminded them of God's promise to Abraham by asking to be buried with his fathers in Canaan.

How exciting to picture the elderly reaching out in service to one another and telling the following generations about the power of God! Simeon and Anna, waiting for the Messiah, rejoice at Jesus' birth. John, the beloved disciple, in his later years provides the comforting vision of God's kingdom in the Revelation. Veteran pastors help younger colleagues face the demands of pastoral ministry. Elder statesmen continue to provide leadership for our country. White-haired men and women take their grandchildren by the hand and show them love and guidance. Retired businessmen offer advice to young people starting in business.

These examples share a common thread: the aging living with a purpose—declaring the love of God to younger people by word and deed. When we become self-absorbed and self-pitying, He shows us our sin and points us to His Son. Forgiven, we look beyond ourselves to others who need forgiveness and love. We declare God's power until He takes us to continue praising Him before the heavenly throne.

Prayer: Dear Father, fill us with Your purpose all the days of our life. Amen.

Life in a Mini-World

To many people bigger is better—skyscrapers, domed stadiums, corporations. But in reality we live in a mini-world. Much of our progress traces to the microscope, the transistor, the atom, and the computer chip. Small automobiles, phones, and calculators have real value in today's world.

As Paul suggests in Corinthians, God has not worked through the wisdom and power of the world but through lowly and despised things. Jesus Christ was born in a lowly manger in a small town in a subjugated nation. He lived only 33 years. While He walked the dusty roads of Palestine, the Roman legions were marching proudly and successfully through the world. But that one man, Jesus Christ, the Son of God turned the world upside down. He came to give His life on a despised cross. His death brought forgiveness of sins as a gift to the world. By historical accounts at the time, His death was a mini-happening. The big news events occurred in Rome. But Christ's death cost God the precious blood of His Son. And it brought about a new breed of people called Christians, dedicated to glorifying God and serving others. Though initially not wealthy or influential, they changed history.

You may view your Christian life as a mini-event, but the example of your life and the testimony of your lips will influence the world. Drawing on the Savior's sacrifice for you and feeding regularly on His Word, you can live boldly for Him in a huge world. God's Son can take your mini-life and use it to help write the story of His salvation large across the world.

Prayer: Dear Father, help me to value my life, though seemingly small, as Your instrument for reaching others. In Jesus' name. Amen.

Living on the Growing Edge

Although we know little about Jesus' childhood, we do have the story of His visit to the temple at the age of 12. Luke tells us at the end of that story: "And Jesus grew in wisdom and stature, and in favor with God and men" (Luke 2:52).

On the trip to Jerusalem He no doubt grew in many ways. He heard more of the Word of God, which He had been studying. He learned to relate to adults on the pilgrimage and then teachers in the temple. He was challenged to question the teachers and to speak the Word. He was being prepared for His public ministry of salvation for the world. If Jesus grew in His relationships to His Father, Himself, others, and His world, should we not also be growing every day?

Bruce Larson in *Living on the Growing Edge* describes a teacher who year after year produces classes of children who are motivated to achieve their potential. Her secret: She meets them on their "growing edge," where they are ready and able to learn.

Are you living on your growing edge? What is God teaching you right now? Are you growing "in wisdom ... and in favor with God and men"?

God knows your needs and has a plan for your growth. His Son lived on the growing edge in daily ministry and on His way to the cross, where He won the victory over Satan. God has made you His own dear child through faith in Christ. You have eternal security. Therefore He frees you to live on the growing edge of service and witness.

Prayer: *Dear Father, help me to live on the growing edge in my relationships to You, myself, others, and the world so I might serve You more joyfully and faithfully. Amen.*

A Key to Miracles: Accepting His Timing

Jesus changes water to wine at a wedding in Cana of Galilee. Notice how Mary accepts His timing. First, she recognizes and admits a need. The wine supply is short. Jewish wedding celebrations lasted for a week, and hospitality dictated an abundance of wine. Mary admits the need for more wine and feels inadequate to handle the problem. Though we claim self-sufficiency in our public and private lives, we come to the point where we must recognize and admit our need for help.

Then Mary brings her need to Jesus. She trusts Him. She simply says, "They have no more wine" (John 2:3). We need to bring all needs and problems to the One who died for our sins and asks us to come to Him. Personal, church, and vocational needs all can be handled by Jesus.

But Jesus seemingly rebukes Mary by saying, "My time has not yet come" (John 2:4). He is saying, "Let Me handle your problems My way and at My time." His action in this instance relates to His whole mission on earth, ultimately to His greatest hour, being glorified on the cross. Led by the Spirit, Mary instructs the servants to do whatever He tells them. She accepts His timing in faith.

We hear the same words from Jesus, "My time has not yet come." He wants us to participate in His plan of salvation and uphold His cross as we humbly trust Him to meet our needs. By faith we accept His timing.

And Jesus changed water into wine in a magnificent way, giving glory to God. We, too, witness God at work in a miraculous way in our lives as He brings many to faith and uses us to point others to His redeeming love.

Prayer: *Lord, help us to accept Your timing in our lives. Amen.*

A Key to Miracles: Accepting His Authority

A Roman centurion comes to Jesus on behalf of his servant who suffers at home. Jesus offers to go with him and heal his servant. The centurion demonstrates genuine compassion. He cares but knows he needs help from Jesus.

Now comes the remarkable part. The centurion tells Jesus that he is not worthy to have Him under his roof and adds, "But just say the word, and my servant will be healed" (Matthew 8:8b). He explains that he has authority over soldiers to whom he can issue orders. In effect the centurion is saying, "I believe that You, Jesus, have authority to heal my servant. I accept Your authority." He then obeys by accepting Jesus' word and returning home to a healed servant.

How often we, like the scribes and Pharisees, challenge Jesus' authority. We value our own authority over others but question our obedience to Him. We doubt His Word, then we wonder why we seem to be ineffective Christians.

The key to miracles—accepting His authority. Jesus Christ accepted the Father's authority and lived as a servant. He exercised that authority by reaching out to others. He preached with authority, cast out demons, stilled the storm, and defeated Satan on the cross by His humble obedience.

Jesus likewise healed us, His servants, by paying for our sins, and now He empowers us to trust and obey Him. We accept His authority in Word and Sacrament. We help those under our care. We live effective Christian lives as instruments of God's miraculous power. We accept both His timing and His authority as we tell the world about Jesus Christ, our Savior and Lord!

Prayer: *Lord, help us to accept Your authority in our lives. Amen.*

Jeremiah's Call: The Word of the Lord

What is God calling you to do with your life? How can you best serve Him? How do you know whether you are responding to your own desires or to His purposes for your life? These questions challenge every Christian. In the next several devotions we will examine Jeremiah's call into prophetic ministry. While he as an Old Testament prophet received God's call directly from Him, and New Testament ministers of the Word receive their call through the church, we will seek guidelines in Jeremiah for every Christian's calling.

Living in a definite historical setting, "the thirteenth year of the reign of Josiah, son of Amon king of Judah" (Jeremiah 1:2), "Jeremiah son of Hilkiah, one of the priests at Anathoth" (Jeremiah 1:1), received a call from God. Not Jeremiah's personal whims, not a carefully worked out vocational plan, not a radical vision of his own, but the clear, direct Word of the Lord. That Word provided both direction and power to answer God's call. Ultimately, the Word of the Lord was made flesh and dwelt among us, full of grace and truth, Jesus the crucified and risen Savior.

In our specific historical situation, with our own personal background, we turn not to our own whims, or to a carefully contrived plan. We simply seek the Word of the Lord speaking to our heart. In that Word, received corporately among God's people and individually in our solitude, we find both direction for daily service and power flowing from the cross of our Lord Jesus Christ, the Word-Made-Flesh. Yes, Jeremiah's call and ours begin with the Word of the Lord.

Prayer: Dear Father, direct and empower me for service through the Word of Your Son, Jesus Christ. Amen.

Jeremiah's Call: Set Apart as Prophet

We listen to the Word of the Lord, addressed to us for our lives. What do we hear? God's Word to Jeremiah issues a jarring call. "Before I formed you in the womb I knew you, before you were born I set you apart; I appointed you as a prophet to the nations" (Jeremiah 1:5).

Jeremiah lived in a troubled time. There was much turmoil for Judah, with mighty nations seeking to control and destroy her; much wickedness within Judah, including idolatry, injustice, and reliance on political manipulation rather than on God. Jeremiah a prophet of God in such a time? A prophet to Judah? Overwhelming. A prophet to the nations? Impossible. Yet the Word of the Lord clearly tells him of his call. And God reveals that he has been set apart for this role even before he was born. He has been appointed and prepared all his life for this prophetic ministry. What a call indeed!

And your call? Not exactly like Jeremiah's. Different historical situation. Different person. Different calling. Yet before God formed you in the womb, He knew you. He knew you with His tender love as Creator and with His forgiving love as Redeemer. Christ's death and resurrection avails for you. And before you were born, He set you apart. That's what "holy" means, set apart for God's purposes. Baptized in the triune God, you have been set apart. He has called you in a sense as prophet, as one who "speaks forth" His Word in daily life, and yes, as proclaimer to the nations with a "make disciples of all nations" (Matthew 28:19) scope. What a call, indeed!

Prayer: Father, thank You for setting us apart as Your forgiven children. Help us to answer Your call as proclaimer of Jesus' saving love to the nations. Amen.

Jeremiah's Call: Doubts Expressed

The Word of the Lord speaks. We hear. "Set ... apart ... as a prophet to the nations" (Jeremiah 1:5). A tremendous challenge for Jeremiah. A difficult application for us as modern-day proclaimers of Christ's love. We hear. But now what?

Jeremiah expresses serious doubts about his own ability to answer God's call. He responds, "Ah, Sovereign Lord, I do not know how to speak; I am only a child" (Jeremiah 1:6). He trembles. What good is a prophet who can't speak? How can an immature teenager (which Jeremiah may have been) stand before kings and princes? Good questions. Serious doubts. And Jeremiah would indeed be tested beyond human endurance—physically, emotionally, and spiritually. He would suffer rejection after rejection. Assurance and maturity would come from God's words and His steady presence, but for the moment Jeremiah's doubts remain.

Do you have serious doubts about your ability to speak God's Word and stand boldly as a Christian in difficult situations? Do you feel like a child in your spiritual maturity even though you may have gray hair and a solid standing in society? Like Jeremiah, we can also expect stiff tests of our faith as we answer God's call to service—possible rejections, day-by-day temptations, and flagging zeal. "Ah, Sovereign Lord, I do not know how to speak; I am only a child."

We may have serious doubts, but God will supply the words to speak, and His forgiving presence in Jesus Christ, the Crucified, to mature us. The call stands.

Prayer: *Dear Father, quell our doubts with Your love in Jesus Christ. Amen.*

Jeremiah's Call: God's Assurance

Jeremiah has real doubts about his ability to serve as a prophet to the nations. He hears God's call, yet afraid and uncertain, he needs reassurance. The Lord declares, "Do not be afraid of them, for I am with you and will rescue you" (Jeremiah 1:8). Words of promise and comfort. Jeremiah takes the assignment and begins to speak God's Word of judgment and mercy. How he will need those words of assurance as he faces kings and priests! They plot against his life. They arrest and imprison him. They beat him and leave him to die. He wants to die. He complains against God. But he keeps speaking the Word of the Lord. And always there are those words of assurance for him: "Do not be afraid of them, for I am with you and will rescue you."

We need those words too. We hear God's call and know that He speaks to us. We also see the world in which we live—immorality, cheating, scoffing at religion, power plays, social climbing. Real doubts grip our hearts when we try to proclaim the Word of the Lord to our age. But the Lord declares, "Do not be afraid of them, for I am with you and will rescue you." We see the Lord come into a world that rejects Him. We hear the taunts and feel the whip gouge His back. We observe His faithfulness on the cross and hear His loving Word of forgiveness. We experience His forgiveness in our lives and dwell on His continuing Word of comfort. We falter. We speak hesitatingly. We wince at rejection. But we keep speaking His message, for those words of assurance continue, "Do not be afraid of them, for I am with you and will rescue you."

Prayer: Thank You for Your words of assurance to Jeremiah and us. Amen.

Jeremiah's Call: God's Words in My Mouth

The Word of the Lord came to Jeremiah. He learned he was set apart as a prophet to the nations. Doubts rose within him that he could not speak. God's assurance came. Now the Lord provides Jeremiah with the words he will speak as a prophet. "Then the Lord reached out His hand and touched my mouth and said to me, 'Now I have put My words in your mouth'" (Jeremiah 1:9).

That Word consumes Jeremiah. He later writes, "His word is in my heart like a fire, a fire shut up in my bones. I am weary of holding it in; indeed, I cannot" (Jeremiah 20:9). He obeys God and speaks powerfully against Judah's sins. Sometimes he illustrates the Word with symbols of God's message. But always he communicates God's message. The result—God's Word of judgment is vindicated in the destruction of Jerusalem, and His Word of promise materializes in the new covenant ushered in by Jesus Christ, the Crucified One.

What a powerful description of God's call! He specially entrusted Jeremiah with His very own words of judgment and mercy. He also gives His Word to called and ordained servants as they publicly preach the Word and administer the sacraments. They are to speak God's Word, not their own message. He also touches the mouth of each Christian and puts in His words. We are touched by the Word in Baptism and made new creatures in Christ. We feed on that Word as proclaimed by pastors. And we share that Word with others in our daily calling. Yes, Jeremiah's call has much to teach us about God's call in our lives. And His Word holds the answers.

Prayer: Father, thank You for touching my mouth with Your words of life. Open my mouth to speak to others. Amen.

Living Water and Broken Cisterns

Jeremiah speaks to a sinful Judah with powerful imagery. Precious water meant life to ancient peoples in the dry Near East. Attacking military forces laid siege to walled cities and tried to cut them off from their water supply. Now Jeremiah suggests Judah's twofold foolishness. First, they have forsaken Him, their "spring of living water" (Jeremiah 2:13b). Second, they have dug their own cisterns, which turn out to be unable to hold water. Their own efforts have failed miserably.

Don't we often try to construct our own cisterns to hold the water of this world? We want wealth, pleasure, success, happiness, recognition. But these cisterns don't hold water. All the while we have forsaken the never-ending spring of living water provided by a loving God.

Jesus refers to Himself as Living Water which will forever quench our thirst. Our selfish attempts to trap water for ourselves result in broken cisterns. But He offers us Himself. He lived, died, and rose again for us. In the waters of Baptism we receive Him as our spring of living water. The Spirit flows from us as we regularly use His Word and sacraments. Broken cisterns abandoned, we come in faith to God's spring of living water, where we invite others to drink as well.

Prayer: I heard the voice of Jesus say, "Behold I freely give The living water, thirsty one; Stoop down and drink and live." I came to Jesus, and I drank Of that life-giving stream; My thirst was quenched, my soul revived, And now I live in him.

Bush in the Wastelands?

Our town has a botanical conservatory. One walks from a seasonal display room through a tropical forest into a desert with barren terrain and cactus. The contrast is startling. Jeremiah stoutly addresses a wicked Judah with the real possibility of eternal life in a wasteland.

He writes against their idolatry: "Cursed is the one who trusts in man, who depends on flesh for his strength and whose heart turns away from the LORD. He will be like a bush in the wastelands; he will not see prosperity when it comes. He will dwell in the parched places of the desert, in a salt land where no one lives" (Jeremiah 17:5–6). How stark and hopeless these words are for those who trust in themselves.

Would Jeremiah describe you as a bush in the wastelands? You may be seeking prosperity, fashioning success on your own, but if you turn away from the Lord and depend on flesh for your strength, you will be like an isolated bush in the wastelands, with no hope for the future.

Shocked to attention, we realize our pride and our foolishness. We look to the One tempted in a wilderness to depend on flesh for strength by changing stones into bread and to turn away from the Father by bowing down and worshiping Satan. But we know how Jesus overcame these temptations. On our behalf He was willing to hang on a lonely tree in the wastelands, where He fully paid for our sins. Because He thirsted and died, we need not dwell alone in the wastelands but can sing His praises forever in heaven.

Prayer: *When I survey the wondrous cross On which the prince of glory died, My richest gain I count but loss And pour contempt on all my pride.*

Tree Planted by the Water?

In the botanical conservatory, one leaves the desert and enters the tropical forest complete with waterfall and lush greenery. What a refreshing contrast to the arid wasteland! Jeremiah offers a similar contrast to Judah.

While disobedience and rebellion against God lead a person to be cursed like a bush in the wastelands, Jeremiah describes the opposite hope: "But blessed is the man who trusts in the Lord, whose confidence is in Him. He will be like a tree planted by the water that sends out its roots by the stream. It does not fear when heat comes; its leaves are always green. It has no worries in a year of drought and never fails to bear fruit" (Jeremiah 17:7–8). How glorious and inviting this description of one who trusts in the Lord!

Would Jeremiah identify you as by God's grace a tree planted by the water? The Savior died for you on that barren tree in the wastelands. A stream of living water flows forth from Him—a stream of healing, forgiveness, and refreshment. God has planted you as a flourishing tree by the waters of Baptism. Repentant of sin, your roots reach out to that living stream. Despite the heat and drought of temptation around you, your leaves remain green, and through God's never-failing supply of living water in Word and sacraments, you bear fruit daily among family and friends, co-workers, and fellow Christians. What a joy to trust in the Lord "like a tree planted by the water"—His water of life!

Prayer: He like a tree shall thrive, With waters near the root; Fresh as the leaf his name shall live; His works are heav'nly fruit.

The Potter and the Clay

We seek control of our own destiny. We want to shape our future and often the lives of those around us. We forget the Creator and claim that role for ourselves.

In Jeremiah's time Judah is headed away from God and toward gods of human making. So God sends Jeremiah to the potter's house to observe the potter shaping the clay on his wheel. He takes a marred piece of clay and totally reshapes it into a new pot. Unless Judah repents, Jeremiah cries, she will be destroyed like this clay pot and another nation fashioned in her place. Strong words of divine judgment on sin!

Isaiah offers a beautiful prayer on the other side of God's judgment. A repentant Judah in exile will pray, "Yet, O LORD, You are our Father. We are the clay, You are the potter; we are all the work of Your hand" (Isaiah 64:8). Willing to let God shape her, God's people will return home to rebuild.

God, who formed man from the dust of the ground, also sent His own Son in human form. Begotten of the Father from eternity, Jesus lived a perfect life of obedience and even yielded to death on the cross. Because of Jesus' death, we are now perfect in God's eyes. He also desires to make us a new creation in Christ and to mold us according to His will. He wants to use us in His service. He continues shaping and reshaping us, removing the blemishes and rough spots. By His grace, He continues to make us what in His eyes we already are.

Prayer: "Yet, O Lord, You are our Father. We are the clay, You are the potter; we are all the work of Your hand. Amen."

Ordinary Days

Special days stand out in our memory—birthdays, graduations, weddings. Terrible days likewise sear our minds—the death of a close friend, a serious auto accident, or loss of a job. But what of ordinary days? Same old routine, normal ups and downs, the hours dragging a bit, not much excitement. Most days qualify as ordinary days. How we handle them probably determines how well we live.

Psalm 90 offers us a perspective for ordinary days. We are reminded of God's eternal presence. The One who always has existed dwells in our midst. As New Testament Christians we recall how "the Word became flesh and made His dwelling among us" (John 1:14). Jesus Christ, crucified and risen, dwells with us. The psalm goes on to expose the reality of our sinfulness and the shortness of our days on earth. We have reason to number our days.

From this perspective on God and the human life span comes our text's approach for dealing with ordinary days. God's unfailing love awaits us every morning. His love in Jesus Christ cleanses us from our sins and refreshes us for another day of service. We daily remember His unfailing love in the waters of Baptism. As a result, we "sing for joy ... all our days" (Psalm 90:14). The good ones and the bad ones, the special ones and the terrible ones, and, oh yes, the ordinary ones. In fact, because of God's unfailing love a good case can be made for labeling them extraordinary.

Prayer: Let each day begin with prayer, Praise, and adoration. On the Lord cast every care; He is your salvation. Morning, evening, and at night Jesus will be near you. Save you from the tempter's might, With His presence cheer you.

Man's Best Friend

You've heard the saying, "A man's best friend is his dog." There's a degree of truth in that. Our lovable "B.J." of mixed breed brings much love into our household. B. J. delights each member of the family in a special way. He greets us at the door, romps for his ball, cuddles up close, begs for scraps, and offers to help whether help is desired or not. He accepts us when no one else will.

We need accepting friends and spontaneous relationships because we don't always deserve acceptance. We often wear masks and put up barriers, lest we get hurt. With our dog, we can "let our hair down" and not worry about the response.

But dogs don't replace people in our need for lasting friendship. Our best friend is Jesus Christ. In the Upper Room He said to His disciples, "I no longer call you servants .... Instead, I have called you friends, for everything that I learned from My Father I have made known to you" (John 15:15).

Despite our enmity with God because of our sinfulness, Jesus laid down His life for us. He covers us with His righteousness and, as a result, God accepts us as His own. Friends of God through Jesus Christ, we can also be best friends to others by accepting them as they are and loving them with God's love. We learn from dogs like B. J. how to receive Christ's undeserved friendship for us and how to become "best friends" to others.

Prayer: What a friend we have in Jesus, All our sins and griefs to bear! What a privilege to carry Ev'rything to God in prayer! Oh, what peace we often forfeit; Oh, what needless pain we bear—All because we do not carry Ev'rything to God in prayer!

Coming to the Well

A woman comes to Jacob's famous well near Sychar around noon to draw water. A Samaritan woman, despised by the Jews, she has deeper needs than getting drinking water. She is living in sin. After five husbands, her current lover is not her husband. Does she feel guilty, lonely, and rejected down deep? But she prepares to meet her immediate need for water.

We come to the well often, always trying to quench our thirst for physical things—food, shelter, money. Like the woman, we have deeper needs. We too have sinned because we have rebelled against God. We feel guilty, lonely, and rejected. Yet we continue quenching our immediate thirst.

The woman meets a Stranger at the well who unexpectedly asks her for a drink and then offers her living water that will forever quench her thirst. Not understanding at first, she grows skeptical. Then He exposes her sin and she learns that He is the Messiah. He probes her deeper needs, and now at the well she discovers Him as the living water that refreshes her soul. No longer guilty but forgiven, no longer rejected but accepted, she rejoices at her new life.

When we come to the well, we meet Jesus who offers living water. Uncomprehending and skeptical, we probe further. He exposes our sin and our deepest needs. Repentant, we see Him as the Messiah, the One who died and rose again for our sins. Guilt forgiven, loneliness and rejection replaced by belonging and acceptance, we rejoice in our new life. We continue coming to the well to meet Jesus.

Prayer: Lord Jesus, thank You for bringing me to the well of Your salvation and giving me the living water which forever quenches my thirst. Amen.

Returning from the Well

She came to the well for physical water, with deep spiritual needs. She returns from the well with those deep needs met by her encounter with Jesus Christ, the Water of Life. Transformed, she has good news to tell the very people who previously looked down upon her for her sinful life. She tells them, "Come, see a man who told me everything I ever did. Could this be the Christ?" (John 4:29). The living water is flowing through her, for many made their way toward Jesus. We are told, "Many of the Samaritans from that town believed in Him because of the woman's testimony" (John 4:39a). Later, after talking with Jesus, they are confirmed in their belief that "this man really is the Savior of the world" (John 4:42c).

How do we return from the well? There our deepest spiritual needs have been met. We have seen Jesus and drunk deeply of the living water. The water flowed in our Baptism and continues quenching our thirst through the Word, Wafer, and Wine. Like the woman, we return from the well with good news to share. We need to tell people, "Come, see a man who is the Christ." Living water flows through our testimony. Others will come and see. Others will hear the Word preached and will read, study, and learn for themselves that Jesus Christ is their crucified and risen Savior. The more we come to the well, the more powerfully and lovingly we can return with a never-ending stream of living water for the world.

Prayer: Lord Jesus, as I return from the well, let Your living water flow through my words to a thirsty world. Amen.

The World Series: Thoughts for the Faith Life

Hebrews 11 and 12 illustrate the faith life by presenting examples of great heroes of faith. Baseball's World Series with heroes galore sparks some thoughts on our faith in Jesus Christ.

There's something almost religious about a World Series. The true fan radiates undying loyalty toward a favorite team, year in and year out, no matter what the record. Along with loyalty comes a sense of trust. In the fire of intense World Series competition, the fan believes in the popular slugger, fastball pitcher, or manager, even after they fall short a time or two. For every dyed-in-the-wool baseball fan there is a future hope. If the team doesn't make the Series, even if they finish in the cellar, the fan always looks ahead to next year.

Loyalty, trust, and hope for the future are joined by a type of exciting ritual service—a half hour of pregame activities, the formal introduction of players, the singing of the National Anthem, the first pitch, the home team taking the field, the first batter digging in at the plate, the seventh-inning stretch, the sweet taste of victory, and then retelling the story of victory to everyone within earshot.

The same ingredients characterize the life of faith. Loyalty to God, unswerving even when the going gets tough and we are outnumbered by the skeptics. Trust in God's promises. We believe firmly that God loves us and has freed us by sending His own Son to suffer and die for our sins. A future hope, that God will complete our joy and give us eternal life in heaven.

Prayer: *Dear heavenly Father, graciously fill us with loyalty, trust, hope, and joyful worship so we may live as Your forgiven children. Amen.*

Friends in the Name of the Lord

What makes a true friend? Common interests, convenience, mutual gain will bind people together for a time. But when trouble arrives, friends can quickly become enemies.

Jonathan and David stand out as a great model of true friendship. King Saul burned with an insane jealousy of David, the slayer of Goliath, the one anointed by Samuel to succeed Saul. David trusted God and obeyed His commands. Jonathan was caught in the middle. As Saul's son, he stood in line to become king and owed his father obedience. As David's friend, he wanted to help him.

The moment of testing arrives. Saul seeks to kill David. David waits in hiding to get word of Saul's intent. Jonathan stands up for David and becomes a target for Saul's spear. He realizes David must flee. At a prearranged signal, he warns David, then runs to him for a final embrace. In the words of our text he reaffirms their friendship. They were loyal friends because they trusted in the same Lord and called on Him as witness. Jonathan remained loyal until his untimely death on the battlefield. David grieved for his friend and later welcomed Jonathan's son at his own table.

Only God can bind two people together in a lasting friendship. Because of our rebellion, we shun God's friendship. Similarly, we betray friends when selfishness takes over. But God sent His Son as Friend of sinners to die on the cross. Through Christ, God has changed us from enemies into His friends. We then can make friends with others.

Prayer Thought: Discuss the qualities of a good friend. Describe someone you consider a friend. Thank God for friends and ask Him to make you a friend for Jesus' sake.

Sow the Seed Worldwide!

My wife and I planted tulip bulbs yesterday before the rain. The bulbs were of high quality. We followed the instructions carefully. Next spring we hope to enjoy some colorful tulips and share their beauty with others.

In Luke 10 Jesus describes a plentiful harvest before sending out the 70 into Galilee. Sowing and harvesting both involve sharing God's love with others. When we sow the seed of God's Word, sometimes we are privileged to harvest a soul for Christ, and sometimes someone else reaps the harvest. In either case, He asks us to sow the seed worldwide!

The harvest is plentiful. Seventy suggests the whole number of nations—a worldwide mission. We start sharing the Good News of salvation through faith in Jesus Christ at home but expand our vision to include people from all over the world. God is preparing a bountiful harvest.

The laborers are few. Starting with 12 disciples, and now 70, Jesus sends them on a seemingly impossible task. How precious He regards each worker! We ask the Lord of the harvest to send laborers, then make ourselves available for that task. He died to pay for our sins. He gives us new life and then sends us out on His mission.

How very much like planting tulips! We sow the seed. The powerful Word of God is of high quality. We follow the instructions carefully by praying and going. We place our planting in God's hands. Next spring we will rejoice to see everything in full bloom.

Prayer: So when the precious seed is sown, Your quick'ning grace bestow That all whose souls the truth receive Its saving pow'r may know.

Going Nowhere?

Have you ever felt that you were going nowhere? You started out with enthusiasm but soon encountered discouragement, danger, or dull routine. For every step forward, you seemed to take four steps backward. The Lewis and Clark expedition experienced "going nowhere" when they tried to row their huge flatboat *Discovery* up the Missouri River against the current. A few yards of hard-won progress up the river quickly disappeared as the boat hit a sandbar or plunged into rapids. The tired men had to start all over again.

In our text Israel felt they were going nowhere. Excited to leave Egypt, they now found themselves boxed in by the Red Sea and the desert, with Pharaoh's army converging. They railed against Moses, "What have you done to us by bringing us out of Egypt?" (Exodus 14:11b). Seemingly trapped, the people quickly forgot about God. On their own, they were going nowhere. A familiar problem!

But God was clearly leading His people somewhere—to the Promised Land. He took the initiative. He instructed Moses to stretch out his hand over the sea, and the Israelites walked through on dry land while Pharaoh's army perished. God's grace makes the difference. When bogged down and discouraged, we look to God for strength and direction. He sent His Son Jesus as "the way" (John 14:6a). He leads us. Ultimately He brings us to eternal life in heaven. Going somewhere indeed!

Prayer: I walk with Jesus all the way, His guidance never fails me; Within his wounds I find a stay When Satan's pow'r assails me; And by his footsteps led, My path I safely tread. No evil leads my soul astray: I walk with Jesus all the way.

Going Astray?

"I'm going somewhere in life. I make my own choices. I have confidence in myself." Sometimes we come to a crossroads. One path looks broad and straight, with much promise. The other looks narrow and winding, with an unknown destination. Relying on our own judgment, we may quickly choose the broad path which leads to destruction. As the proverb says, "There is a way that seems right to a man, but in the end it leads to death" (Proverbs 14:12).

We examine our current path. Are we living mostly for ourselves? Do we value material possessions more than we should? Do we seek recognition, success, and power? Did we start on the right path only to stray away on a yellow brick road which leads to danger? Are we depending on our own wisdom?

God directs us to the only way that leads to life. His own Son walked the narrow path of the cross. Tempted to go astray, He never wavered. Because of His atoning death, God opens to us the narrow way of salvation. He offers protection along the way through His Word and sacraments. He brings us back when we go astray and will bring us at last to heaven.

Prayer: I walk in danger all the way. The thought shall never leave me That Satan, who has marked his prey, Is plotting to deceive me. This foe with hidden snares May seize me unawares If I should fail to watch and pray. I walk in danger all the way.

Going Straight

The prison doors clank shut for the last time, and the paroled convict marches out into the blinding sunlight carrying his few belongings. The words of the warden still ring in his ears, "We know you have served as a model prisoner in here. Now you have a chance. Are you going straight? It's up to you."

Going straight. Words ridiculed by those who are intent on fighting the system. Words treasured by others, determined to make good, to conquer the alcohol or drug problem, to turn over a new leaf. What of us? We have admitted at times going nowhere, bogged down by routine, trapped in our own lifestyle. We have also confessed at times going astray on the alluring road to destruction.

The proverb simply states, "In all your ways acknowledge Him, and He will make your paths straight" (Proverbs 3:6). We can't go straight on our own. The devil, the world, and our sinful flesh conspire to defeat us. But God can make our paths straight. He acknowledges us as His children because His Son traveled that straight path to the cross where He defeated the unholy trinity mentioned above. In our Baptism and Christian education God places our feet on the straight path and gives us the desire and the strength to acknowledge Him in all our ways. Prison doors of sin and death clank behind us, and we walk out into the sunlight of a new life—going straight, by God's grace—with heaven as the destination.

Prayer: My walk is heav'nward all the way; Await, my soul, the morrow, When God's good healing shall allay All suff'ring, sin, and sorrow. Then, worldly pomp, begone! To heav'n I now press on. For all the world I would not stay; My walk is heav'nward all the way.

A Lesson in Grace:

A landowner goes out early in the morning to hire men to work in his vineyard. He agrees to pay each worker one denarius for the day. He then goes out again at 9:00 a.m., noon, 3:00 p.m., and finally at 5:00 p.m., each time hiring additional laborers. When day is done, the workers collect equal wages. The full-day workers complain but are told they are receiving exactly what has been agreed upon.

We learn a lesson in grace with three parts. First, working in God's vineyard (kingdom) is a privilege. Workers gathered in the marketplace, needing work because one denarius was required to feed a family. God gives us the privilege of entering His kingdom and serving Him there. The alternative is spiritual hunger.

Second, workers are chosen by grace alone. In the parable the owner chose workers not on their merit but because he desired to give them work. We are not chosen for God's kingdom because we are such good workers. Our work record cannot stand before God for a moment. No, we are chosen by God's grace for Christ's sake through faith.

Third, workers are compensated by grace alone. In the parable all the workers were given the same pay no matter how long they worked. Each, therefore, had enough to put bread on the table that day. Yet the all-day workers complained. We often complain too as we compare ourselves with others. But God gives eternal life in heaven to all who believe in Jesus Christ as Savior, whether they are lifetime believers or deathbed converts. All by grace.

Prayer: Dear Father, help me to work for the Kingdom joyfully and willingly, by Your grace. Amen.

Enlarge Your Tent

Israel struggled to survive. Her territory was shrinking. First, a divided kingdom, then enemy attacks. Gone are the glory days of David and Solomon. In this pessimistic setting Isaiah cries out the Word of the Lord, "Enlarge the place of your tent, stretch your curtains wide, do not hold back" (Isaiah 54:2). The Messianic kingdom is coming! Many will be added to the people of God. Even though current conditions look bleak, do not be afraid. Reach out. God cares.

Today's church often seems outnumbered by her enemies. Christians fight each other. Christian morality appears to lose ground in every generation. We may spend time remembering sadly the glory days of our congregation. But God says also to us through Isaiah, "Enlarge the place of your tent, stretch your tent curtains wide, do not hold back." Jesus Christ has come. He has paid the price for the world's sin. The Holy Spirit works powerfully in the church through Word and sacraments. Don't be afraid. Reach out. Believe God's promise of a mighty church with believers added daily.

Open the doors. Give generously. Tell others of Jesus' love. Prepare your tent for more people. Think worldwide in your vision. God cares. God brings in the harvest of souls. He strengthens us for the great task. Enlarge your tent!

Prayer: Jesus shall reign where'er the sun Does its successive journeys run; His kingdom stretch from shore to shore Till moons shall wax and wane no more. People and realms of ev'ry tongue Dwell on his love with sweetest song; And infant voices shall proclaim Their early blessings on his name.

The Rain and Snow of God's Word

Words, words, words. So many words bombard us that we take them lightly. We may also trifle with God's Word—spoken by the pastor on Sunday morning, read aloud, sung in worship, taught in Bible classes, or read silently at home. "The same old words," we say. "I already know that."

But the Word of God creates and saves, as Isaiah says so poetically, "As the rain and the snow come down from heaven, and do not return to it without watering the earth and making it bud and flourish, so that it yields seed for the sower and bread for the eater, so is My Word that goes out from My mouth: It will not return to Me empty, but will accomplish what I desire and achieve the purpose for which I sent it" (Isaiah 55:10–11).

God spoke, and the world was created. "In these last days [God] has spoken to us by His Son" (Hebrews 1:2a). "The Word became flesh and made His dwelling among us ... full of grace and truth" (John 1:14). The apostles spoke God's Word regarding Jesus as the Savior, and many believed and were baptized. As surely as rain and snow water the earth and bring about abundant crops, so surely God's unfailing Word brings new life to His people.

No wonder Paul admonishes us to "let the Word of Christ dwell in [us] richly" (Colossians 3:16). God accomplishes His purposes for us individually and for His Church through His unfailing Word.

Prayer: Preserve your Word and preaching, The truth that makes us whole, The mirror of your glory, The pow'r that saves the soul. Oh, may this living water, This dew of heavenly grace, Sustain us while here living Until we see your face.

One Thing Desired

Many fairy tales revolve around a central character receiving an opportunity to choose one thing. One wish is granted by a genie. Or the king offers one request, up to half of his kingdom. Scripture contains some interesting verses where "one thing" receives attention.

David writes, "One thing I ask of the LORD, this is what I seek: that I may dwell in the house of the LORD all the days of my life, to gaze upon the beauty of the LORD and to seek Him in His temple" (Psalm 27:4). Aware of many enemies and major problems confronting him, David nevertheless rejoices at the opportunity to worship the Lord. There in God's presence he finds shelter and safety; he experiences victory over his enemies; he sings and makes music to the Lord. The one thing he asks of the Lord is to worship Him perpetually in His house. A rather interesting choice for a warrior and political leader.

Would you choose, as your one thing desired, to dwell in the house of the Lord all the days of your life? Problems loom large. Challenges occupy our attention. But nothing brings greater joy than focusing on the God of our salvation, the One who gave His life as a sacrifice for the world. Dwelling in His house means living for Him each day aware of His saving presence and rejoicing with praise to Him. How thrilling to gather with God's people around Word and Sacrament each Sunday in the house of the Lord! It is the one thing desired!

Prayer: Open now thy gates of beauty, Zion, let me enter there, Where my soul in joyful duty Waits for God, who answers prayer. Oh, how blessed is this place, Filled with solace, light, and grace!

One Thing Needed

What one thing do you most need? A difficult question. You might answer—a steady job, a marriage partner, a close friend, money for your children's college education. Your answer probably would differ depending on the circumstances. A man lost in the desert might most need a drink of water. The hospital patient awaiting major surgery probably needs the assurance of life. What one thing do you most need?

Martha worried about many things as she tried to host her friend Jesus. Mary sat and listened to what Jesus said. Jesus, referring to Mary's choice, commented: "But only one thing is needed" (Luke 10:42). Hearing God's Word is the one thing needed. Mary no doubt learned about Jesus as the Messiah bringing in the kingdom of God. The Word offers salvation and strength for living.

No matter what our worries and problems, Jesus offers the one thing needed—His Word, which offers us forgiveness and life through His death on the cross for our sins. Taking the time to listen, we learn to live joyfully for Him. His Word helps us to place our other needs in perspective and to receive comfort and direction for daily living. One thing is needed!

Prayer: One thing's needful; Lord, this treasure Teach me highly to regard; All else, though it first give pleasure, Is a yoke that presses hard. Beneath it the heart is still fretting and striving, No true, lasting happiness ever deriving. The gain of this one thing all loss can requite, Can teach me in all things to find true delight.

One Thing Lacking

What do you give to the person who has everything? Quite a problem these days in our affluent society. The rich young man in our text seemed to have everything. He was wealthy. He had a solid religious background, even claiming that he had kept all the Commandments since he was a boy. He therefore assumed that he would inherit eternal life.

Imagine his shock when Jesus said to him, "One thing you lack" (Mark 10:21a). He must have wondered what in the world could be lacking. Jesus proceeds, "Go, sell everything you have and give to the poor, and you will have treasure in heaven" (Mark 10:21b). He lacked treasure in heaven because he was placing his trust in earthly possessions. Sadly he went away because he had great wealth. He preferred lacking heavenly treasure to lacking earthly treasure.

Do you have one thing lacking? Do you trust earthly wealth instead of Jesus Christ as your only Savior from sin? One thing lacking means eternal punishment in hell. Possessing that one thing means lacking nothing else. As Paul writes, "He who did not spare His own Son, but gave Him up for us all—how will He not also, along with Him, graciously give us all things?" (Romans 8:32). Yes, believers in Christ lack nothing!

Prayer: Therefore you alone, my Savior, Shall be all in all to me; Search my heart and my behavior, Root out all hypocrisy. Through all my life's pilgrimage, guard and uphold me, In loving forgiveness, O Jesus, enfold me. This one thing is needful, all others are vain; I count all but loss that I Christ may obtain!

One Thing Known

Often we feel ignorant about theological matters. We hesitate to speak up in Bible class because others might regard our question or comment as foolish. We falter in our witness to a neighbor or friend because we fear they will raise religious questions beyond our ability to answer. We wish we knew more about God and His Word.

The man blind from birth, healed miraculously by Jesus, could have worried about his theological knowledge. Neighbors asked him about the healing in skeptical tones. The Pharisees with their superior knowledge grilled him and tried to discredit Jesus as a sinner who defiled the Sabbath. But the humble man doesn't hesitate to testify of Christ. "Whether He is a sinner or not, I don't know. One thing I do know, I was blind but now I see!" (John 9:25b)

Whether or not we have memorized the entire Scripture and have mastered Christian doctrine, we can say, "One thing I know, I was blind but now I see!" Jesus Christ through His atoning death and resurrection has brought us out of darkness into His marvelous light. God's Spirit has restored our spiritual sight so we know Him as our Savior and Lord. Unafraid we can witness. One thing known!

Prayer: He lives, all glory to his name! He lives, my Savior, still the same; What joy this blest assurance gives: I know that my Redeemer lives!

One Thing Remembered

Time runs our lives. Either our hectic schedules drive us to race frantically from one day to the next or because of troubles and boredom time drags on endlessly. In either case we easily lose perspective. We live for the moment and forget God's eternal plan.

St. Peter writes to Christians who wondered why Christ had not yet returned for judgment: "But do not forget this one thing, dear friends: With the Lord a day is like a thousand years, and a thousand years are like a day" (2 Peter 3:8). On the one hand, the Lord loves us so much that He shows great patience. He wants everyone to come to repentance. Each day also spells fresh opportunities to witness to our faith in Jesus as Savior and to serve God with our lives. What a blessing to fill our days with praise, service, and witness!

On the other hand, the day of the Lord will come like a thief. Every day may be the last day. Urgency prevails. We want to maximize each hour to live thankfully for Him in service to others. Jesus redeemed the time. His short public ministry was filled with obedience to the Father and service to people in need. On the cross the hours must have seemed like years. Yet He endured patiently to save us for eternity. One thing remembered—all time is God's time.

Prayer: A thousand ages in your sight Are like an evening gone, Short as the watch that ends the night Before the rising sun. Time, like an ever-rolling stream, Soon bears us all away; We fly forgotten, as a dream Dies at the op'ning day. Our God, our help in ages past, Our hope for years to come, Still be our guard while troubles last, And our eternal home.

Fainthearted?

What an opportunity for Israel! God sends 12 men to explore Canaan, a land flowing with milk and honey. They come back with a report of a good land, but a land inhabited by powerful peoples and fortified cities. Joshua and Caleb favor trusting God to capture the land. But the other 10 explorers disagree. Israel responds in a grumbling, fainthearted manner: "Why is the Lord bringing us to this land only to let us fall by the sword? Wouldn't it be better for us to go back to Egypt?" (Numbers 14:3). You know the result of their faintheartedness—40 more years of wandering in the wilderness!

What opportunities we have to live for God today—people ripe for our Christian witness, churches to be planted, missionaries to be sent, Christian schools to expand. We hear about the great possibilities but also about the problems, dangers, obstacles, and high costs. Are we fainthearted as we complain and say no? Do we prefer standing still or going backward to the good old days? This rebellion against God brings serious consequences.

God's Son saw the plan of His Father for saving the world. He also knew the dangers, the opposition, and the high cost of faithfulness. But with a strong heart He depended on the Father and went boldly to the cross, where He won the victory against incredible odds. Through Him and strengthened by His Word and sacraments, we need be fainthearted no more. We can move forward in service and participate in Christ's saving action for the world.

Prayer: Faint not nor fear, his arms are near; He changes not who holds you dear; Only believe, and you will see That Christ is all eternally.

Halfhearted?

One of the greatest ills of American society is apathy. Many citizens do not bother to vote on election day. Civic organizations struggle to find volunteers. People express strong opinions about needed changes, but then do little about making those changes happen. We give only halfhearted support.

Jeremiah writes against Judah for being halfhearted. Her sister nation Israel has openly rebelled against God with adultery and immorality. But Judah stands equally guilty, pretending to love God but not returning to Him with all her heart. In fact, Jeremiah says, "Faithless Israel is more righteous than unfaithful Judah" (Jeremiah 3:11). Halfhearted service to God deserves eternal punishment.

Even as we confess our halfhearted response to God, He promises to be our faithful Husband. He gives us shepherds after His own heart to care for us. They point us to the Chief Shepherd, Jesus Christ, who wholeheartedly obeyed the Father and died for our sins. Jesus draws us to Himself. Forgiven and restored, our love for God increases. The Spirit fills us with enthusiasm to live for God and others. By grace God fills our hearts with praise to Him. With God's heart in us, we are halfhearted no more.

Prayer: On my heart imprint your image, Blessed Jesus, king of grace, That life's riches, cares, and pleasures Never may your work erase; Let the clear inscription be: Jesus, crucified for me, Is my life, my hope's foundation, And my glory and salvation!

Whom Do You Serve—God or Money?

Headlines feature news about unemployment, inflation, or the stock market. We rejoice or weep, based on the news as it affects our pocketbook. Who says the Bible doesn't speak to the issues of today? Jesus makes the point in clear terms: "You cannot serve both God and money" (Matthew 6:24).

Mammon is the Aramaic word for material possessions. Unfortunately, many people trust in *mammon* or money like a god. Trusting money leads to either wanting more or worry about food, drink, and clothes.

While money has a legitimate use as a gift entrusted to us by God, we must not put our trust in it. Money can easily gain a stranglehold on us. We end up serving money instead of God. The root sin is unbelief.

Serving God means regarding Him as the Pearl of Great Price, worth everything we have. Instead of self-seeking, Kingdom-seeking. Instead of worry, trust. Serving God means using our money for Him—joyfully, sacrificially.

With the choice clear, we confess our self-seeking greed and faithless worry. Who can help us? The God who asks us to serve came to us in the form of a servant. Jesus Christ refused Satan's offer of worldly kingdoms and chose to serve the Father. He went to the cross. "Though He was rich ... He became poor, so that [we] through His poverty might become rich" (2 Corinthians 8:9). Made God's children in Baptism, we now serve Him as He freely supplies faith to replace our worry, and Kingdom-seeking to replace our self-seeking.

Prayer: Dear Father, transform our greedy, anxious hearts (pursuing money) into serving, trusting hearts (seeking only You), through Your Son, Jesus Christ our Lord. Amen.

Greed: A Dead End

Greed is ugly. A deadly vice recognized in the ancient world, condemned by the New Testament. The Greek word means simply "wanting more." How deceptively simple, yet how deadly! Just one more piece of candy. Just one more amusement park ride before heading home.

Jesus tells of the rich man with a good crop who tears down his barns and builds bigger ones to store his grain and goods. Relishing his plenty, the man plans to take life easy. Then comes the proof that greed leads only to a dead end. God says to him, "You fool! This very night your life will be demanded from you" (Luke 12:20).

There are two lessons here: (1) Don't seek material wealth instead of God's riches. (2) Selfish acquisition leads to death, generous giving to life. Think about our culture. Greed prevails under the guise of the good life. Professional athletes receive high salaries. Television game shows encourage greedy contestants who hunger for winnings. And we quest for more—savings, investments, cars, and appliances. Selfish acquiring replaces generous giving to God and others. A serious sin to confess.

Comes Christ with life. "For you know the grace of our Lord Jesus Christ, that though He was rich, yet for your sakes He became poor, so that you through His poverty might become rich" (2 Corinthians 8:9). We receive the riches of full and free forgiveness. Greed-forgiven saints rising to new life. There is no need for new barns, because we already have glorious riches in Christ. "Giving more" is possible now from His inexhaustible supply.

Prayer: Lord, replace my greed with contentment in Your forgiveness. Amen.

An Investment for Eternity

What kinds of investments do you have—insurance, savings, property, stocks, bonds? How secure are they? How well do they prepare you for the future? In preparing the disciples for their future, Jesus describes God's eternal investment in us.

God made a major investment in His kingdom on earth. He placed human beings on earth as managers of His kingdom. Initially God received a very poor return on His investment. Adam and Eve fell into sin. The world rebelled against Him. But God continued investing His love and mercy. Eventually He invested the ultimate—His own dear Son, who paid the price with His life. That costly investment produced rich dividends.

God makes all believers in Christ's death and resurrection co-managers in His kingdom. And to us beleaguered managers, wrestling with worries, burdens, and temptations, Jesus says, "Do not be afraid, little flock, for your Father has been pleased to give you the kingdom" (Luke 12:32).

Jesus moves us to examine our investment portfolio. He urges us to get rid of the investments that fail—purses that wear out, treasures that can be stolen, and clothes eaten by moths. And, He directs us to safeguard those eternal investments from God—purses that will not wear out, heavenly treasures that will not be stolen, and clothes no moth can destroy. He means the gift of eternal life based on the forgiveness of sins through His death on the cross. God's eternal investments move us to share our possessions with the poor. We joyfully serve others, witness to our faith, rear a Christian family, and give our financial resources to the Lord's work.

Prayer: Father, help me to live unafraid because of Your eternal investment. Amen.

What's Your Measuring Stick?

When my son was growing up, he was constantly measuring to see how tall he was. The marks on the wall told the story. How do you measure your place in life? John the Baptizer uses an unusual measure when he says of Jesus, "He must become greater; I must become less" (John 3:30).

Jesus had arrived on the scene and was calling disciples, some of them John's followers. As He gained popularity, some of John's disciples became concerned. "Everyone is going to Him," they said (John 3:26). By their measuring sticks, John was failing in his competition with Jesus.

Is your measuring stick "I must become greater"? Are you seeking recognition, success, advancement, higher income, greater social standing? Do you view your relationship to Christ and the church as an opportunity for personal gain? Are you jealous when others outshine you or Christ receives the credit? An I-must-become-greater measuring stick simply measures our sin and selfishness.

But John was using a totally different measuring stick. He rejoiced that Jesus was active in ministry to save the world—the Lamb of God taking away our sins (John 1:29). He saw his own mission as pointing to Jesus and our need for Him. John now wanted to become less so Jesus could become greater. That was his great joy (John 3:29).

The best measuring stick for us is "He must increase." Jesus loves us, died to save us, and lives to strengthen us in His service. He is our life and hope. The greater He becomes, the greater is our joy.

Prayer: Lord, help me to become less, so that in the eyes of many You will become greater as Savior and Lord. Amen.

The Need for Spiritual Healing

As Jesus teaches in Galilee, crowds gather in a house to hear Him. Four men bearing a paralytic on a stretcher lower the man to Jesus from the rooftop. What is this man's greatest need? Obviously he is paralyzed. Yet Jesus sees that he needs forgiveness. Dead in sin, he needs a miracle of spiritual healing. He cannot lift a finger to help himself. The need for spiritual healing always comes first.

Are you willing to let Jesus diagnose your needs? He comes with sure knowledge of your condition. He explores every nook and cranny of your life. You may identify physical needs—illness, injuries, financial problems, family difficulties—all very real and painful. But Jesus probes beneath the obvious to your need for forgiveness and spiritual healing.

Jesus says to the man, "Take heart, son; your sins are forgiven" (Matthew 9:2). What sweet music—sins forgiven! Still physically paralyzed, the man feels unburdened, clean, and whole. Jesus has authority to forgive sins because He is God. He earned forgiveness for the world by dying on the cross in full payment of sin. Spiritual healing accomplished!

Jesus says to us, "Take heart; your sins are forgiven." He announces it every Sunday in the liturgy, bestows it through the preached Word and the Holy Supper. Physical problems may remain, but we have peace with God through Jesus Christ. We feel unburdened, clean, and whole. Thank God for daily forgiveness. Spiritual healing accomplished!

Prayer: Today your mercy calls us To wash away our sin. However great our trespass, Whatever we have been, However long from mercy Our hearts have turned away, Your precious blood can wash us And make us clean today.

The Need for Physical Healing

Teachers of the Law accuse Jesus of blasphemy for daring to forgive sins. They don't think about the man's need for spiritual healing, or rejoice in his forgiveness. They just complain about Jesus exceeding His authority.

Jesus, knowing their thoughts, prepares to address the man's other need, the need for physical healing. "Which is easier: to say, 'Your sins are forgiven,' or to say, 'Get up and walk'? ... Then He said to the paralytic, 'Get up, take your mat and go home' " (Matthew 9:6). He demonstrates His authority to perform the greater miracle (forgiveness) by performing the lesser miracle (healing the man's paralysis).

The physical miracle is recorded simply and powerfully, "The man got up and went home" (Matthew 9:7). No fanfare. No vivid, detailed account of the miracle. "The man got up and went home." Yet in those few words we see a man given a new lease on life. No longer helpless, depending on others to carry him, he is now able to walk and care for himself. His physical need is supplied. A precious gift, but not as great or as profound as the spiritual healing of forgiveness.

Jesus still heals both physically and spiritually. When He heals physically through doctors or in unexplained ways, He reminds us of His authority to forgive sins and change lives. We can come to Him with our hurts, our diseases, our problems, our concerns—physical and spiritual. He will meet our needs. He always offers full and free forgiveness—spiritual healing. Sometimes He provides the physical healing, meeting our needs on both levels. Jesus still has the power He demonstrated when He healed the paralytic.

Prayer: Lord, grant Your total healing, that I may praise You. Amen.

Giving vs. Hoarding

All we have comes from God, and He expects us to share with others what has been entrusted to us. We are to give generously and sacrificially to the Lord and to those in need. And God blesses, not because we have earned it but simply because He loves us.

Or we can choose a lifestyle of hoarding: "Another withholds unduly, but comes to poverty" (Proverbs 11:24b). We started hoarding when as children we kept our blocks from our playmates. That same hoarding spirit leads us to withhold gifts from the Lord. Hoarding should be labeled for what it is—sin. Though we withhold to gain riches, the proverb is correct in saying that hoarding leads to eternal poverty.

How can we learn to give generously? St. Paul gives the answer, "For you know the grace of our Lord Jesus Christ, that though He was rich, yet for your sakes He became poor, so that you through His poverty might become rich" (2 Corinthians 8:9). God freely gave us His Son, Jesus, to become poor so we might be rich—rich in forgiveness, grace, and mercy. Because of His death, we are motivated to give.

Giving is living. Hoarding is death. God gives us His Son so that we might adopt a lifestyle of giving. Keep that in mind as you respond to the many opportunities for giving that are all around us.

Prayer: Grant us hearts, dear Lord, to give you Gladly freely of your own. With the sunshine of your goodness Melt our thankless hearts of stone Till our cold and selfish natures, Warmed by you, at length believe That more happy and more blessed 'Tis to give than to receive.

Wanted: Stewards of God's Gifts

The scene: first-century Asia Minor. Christians were persecuted for their faith. A world to be won for Christ, there was desperate need for light in the darkness. "Wanted: stewards of God's gifts. Long hours. Hard work. Purpose: serving others and praising God through Jesus Christ. Reward: probably more suffering." An unlikely want ad? God's people responded with love and service, using their unique gifts within the fellowship to reach an alien world with the saving news of Jesus Christ.

The scene: 20th-century America. Christians are ignored for their faith. There is growing secularism and pluralism. A world to be won for Christ, there is desperate need for light in the darkness. "Wanted: stewards of God's gifts. Not just an hour on Sunday. Long hours. Hard work. Purpose: serving others and praising God through Jesus Christ. Reward: probably less credibility with the world." How will you respond? Will you use your unique gifts of God's grace to reach an alien world with the saving news of Christ? Or will you be a spectator, safe and removed from the battle?

Peter describes the key to faithful stewardship of God's gifts: "Do it with the strength God provides" (1 Peter 4:11). Any gift points to the giver. God freely gave His Son for us all. He lived in a hostile world, used His gifts in love and service, died to pay for our sins, and rose triumphantly from the grave. "The gift of God is eternal life in Jesus Christ our Lord" (Romans 6:23b). He provides us with His strength to live for others to His praise and glory. "Wanted: stewards of God's gifts!"

Prayer: Lord, make me a good steward of Your varied grace in my daily life, so that others may trust in You as their Savior. Amen.

Unemployed?

How difficult to be unemployed! You want to work, to earn a living, to pay your bills, to support your family. But you have lost your job through unforeseen circumstances. You are trying so hard to find something, anything, but no one seems willing to hire you. The days stretch out endlessly. The bills mount. Every "no" in an employment line reduces your hope a little more. You feel helpless and worthless. You doubt your ability to perform adequately. You turn inward and spend hours moping. Others try to comfort you, but their words seem hollow. They pity you and don't understand. You begin to envy those who have a job and to question why God is letting this happen to you.

The psalmist must have felt similarly when he compared his own poverty to the wicked people's success. He cries out, "When my heart was grieved and my spirit embittered, I was senseless and ignorant" (Psalm 73:21). He recognizes his own self-pity and bitter attitude. His answer comes from his faith in a caring God who would later send His Son to the cross: "Whom have I in heaven but You? And earth has nothing I desire besides You. My flesh and my heart may fail, but God is the strength of my heart and my portion forever" (Psalm 73:25–26). Words of encouragement for the unemployed. God will guide you through the difficult period and sustain you. He will help you serve others and will, in His good time, open the doors of opportunity to you.

Prayer: Fear not, I am with you, oh, be not dismayed, For I am your God and will still give you aid; I'll strengthen you, help you, and cause you to stand, Upheld by my righteous, omnipotent hand.

An Autumn Meditation on Sin

I just finished three hours of hard work in our backyard. I raked and bagged more leaves than I care to think about. I mowed the lawn to get any remaining leaves. Now I sit exhausted looking out the window. Already a few leaves dot the backyard. And the front yard, which I cut yesterday, sports a carpet of more leaves. Will the cycle ever end?

I think of Paul's struggle with sin described in Romans 7: "For what I do is not the good I want to do; no, the evil I do not want to do—this I keep on doing" (Romans 7:19). He adds, "What a wretched man I am! Who will rescue me from this body of death?" (Romans 7:24). Will the cycle ever end?

We share Paul's struggle. Our spiritual nature wants to do right and avoid what is wrong, but our sinful flesh leads us astray. We feel helpless. We rake and bag leaves, but they keep coming back like a nightmare. With Paul, helpless on our own, we cry out, "Who will rescue me from this body of death?" Will the cycle ever end?

Paul answers his own question, "Thanks be to God—through Jesus Christ our Lord!" (Romans 7:25a). God's Son has set me free from the cycle of sin and death. The Law could not free me. But Christ paid the full price for the sin of the world. He is our Righteousness. Therefore we are controlled not by our sinful nature but by the Spirit of God. We live by the Lord's power, and so we can defeat sin in our lives.

I know that while the battle with the leaves will last yet for a week or so, I will win the victory because they are almost gone. And I thank God that He likewise has put sin to death and will give me the victory in my daily struggle.

Prayer: Dear Father, help me win daily victories over sin through the victorious power of Your Son, Jesus Christ. Amen.

Really Free

On Reformation Day we celebrate the gift of God to the Church through His servant Martin Luther. Luther reminded us of our freedom from the Law in the Gospel of Jesus Christ.

Jesus told the self-satisfied religious leaders of His time, "Everyone who sins is a slave to sin" (John 8:34). You see, they thought, "I've got it made." They believed that their birth automatically made them free. In the 16th century many religious people felt much the same way. Birth and religious vocation gave a false sense of freedom. Is it possible for lifelong church members with good records to make the same mistake—"I've got it made"?

Another tragically mistaken group says, "I've got to make it." People in Jesus' day followed the Pharisees and tried to keep their religious laws to the finest detail. Paul once lived by those standards: "I've got to make it." In the 16th century many struggled to gain freedom from guilt through prayers, fastings, pilgrimages, and indulgences. Is it possible that today many depend on church attendance, financial contributions, church work, and acts of service to make it before God? A hopeless task!

Then we joyfully realize: The Son makes me free. Jesus Christ took on the slavery of the Law and died to atone for the world's sin. God declares the world righteous for Jesus' sake. "So if the Son sets you free, you will be free indeed" (John 8:36). Luther discovered that freedom through faith in Christ, and the gates of paradise opened to him. We rejoice in our movement from slavery to freedom and live in that freedom.

Prayer: Dear Jesus, thank You for making me really free. Keep me always in that freedom. Amen.

Alive with the Heartbeat of the Reformation

Often taken for granted, we realize how very important the heart is to the body when problems arise.

The heart of the Reformation is the Scriptural teaching of justification by grace for Christ's sake through faith. This vital teaching provides life for the church at all times. When this teaching predominates, a healthy church worships, obeys, serves, and grows. When it is neglected, the church is threatened.

The early church had heart problems. Paul's opponents held up the Law as the means to salvation. This teaching led either to self-righteousness or despair. Paul writes about this in Romans 3. The 16th century also had heart problems. The church recommended doing penance, buying indulgences, and venerating relics to earn salvation. Again people became either self-righteous or despairing. Then Martin Luther spoke out boldly. Today's church faces heart problems too whenever we make the Law a means of justification before God. If we think our giving, serving, witnessing, and church-involvement will justify us, we grow either self-righteous or despairing.

But Paul renews the Church with the ringing affirmation of our text. We stand before the Judge. The evidence of our sins against the Law cries out for a guilty verdict. But God looks to the sacrifice of His sinless Son on Calvary and declares us not guilty. He gives us faith in Christ's death and resurrection, and as a result we are justified by grace. Our spiritual heart beats strong, and we serve Him. The Church's heart beats strong, and the Gospel sounds forth to the world.

Prayer: Lord, keep us alive with the heartbeat of the Reformation. Amen.

Building with the Heart

What a task! Rebuilding the walls of Jerusalem. The city lies in shambles. After years of captivity in Babylon, a small group returns to the scene of former glory. Led by Nehemiah, they begin to rebuild the city. Nearby peoples threaten to attack every day. The Jews have to build with a sword in one hand and a trowel in the other. What obstacles!

But the walls are getting built because the people work with all their heart. Previously Judah's heart strayed from God to idolatry and personal gain. But now, chastened by captivity and repentant, the returning exiles desire with all their heart to restore the sacred city as a monument of praise to God. They are willing to struggle and sacrifice to accomplish the task.

What building does God have in mind for you? A church? A school? Your own family? Whether or not brick and mortar are involved, God calls us to build. What a task! Money seems lacking and relationships may lie in shambles from misunderstanding, hurt, and jealousy. Opposition mounts as other people say it can't be done. What obstacles!

But we can build when we work together with all our heart. When our hearts stray from God, we get wrapped up in selfish desires and seek material gain. But God shatters our self-serving dreams and points us to His heart, a heart willingly broken on the cross in payment for our sins. Chastened, repentant, restored, forgiven, we begin to build. God gives us a heart for the work. The building progresses to the glory of God. God's kingdom comes. His Church is built into a temple of living stones. What a joy to participate with all our heart!

Prayer: Dear Father, fill our hearts with courage for the task of building Your kingdom. Amen.

God's Building Project

Despite constant opposition, Nehemiah completes the city walls. Yes, the people build with all their heart. Yes, Nehemiah is a capable leader. But something far more significant leads to this amazing result.

God is the builder! He wants those walls completed. He wants the faithful remnant to praise Him again in Jerusalem. God's people know who deserves credit. They assemble to hear Ezra read the Law from daybreak to noon (Nehemiah 8:2–3). They then thank and praise God in celebration with Nehemiah's reminder: "The joy of the LORD is your strength" (Nehemiah 8:10c). And even the enemies of the Jews recognize this as God's building project. We are told they lose their self-confidence "because they realized that this work had been done with the help of our God" (Nehemiah 6:16b).

When we build a church or Christian school, we certainly rejoice when it is complete. When we see a Christian fellowship growing in size, depth, and closeness, we feel a sense of accomplishment. Yes, people work together with all their heart. Yes, faithful pastors and lay members provide good leadership. But something far more significant is involved.

God is the builder! He wants His Church to grow and serve Him. He built His Church on the foundation of the apostles and prophets, with Jesus Christ as the Chief Cornerstone. Christ gave His life for the Church. We assemble to hear His life-changing Word and to celebrate God's grace in sacramental worship. Even enemies of the Gospel have to recognize that "this work has been done with the help of our God."

Prayer: Dear Father, thank You for the privilege of participating in Your building project. Amen.

Time of Trouble: The Fowler's Snare

Psalm 91 addresses the believer in time of trouble. The psalmist writes, "Surely He will save you from the fowler's snare" (Psalm 91:3). Unsuspecting birds faced serious trouble when a wooden cage was dropped on top of them. Hopelessly trapped, they could not escape.

We are often trapped by our own troubles. Other people set traps for us, and sometimes we set traps for ourselves. We may choose the wrong kind of friends and so be led into sin. The fowler's snare drops on us. Trapped.

We develop a hectic pace of life. Work takes long hours if we expect to advance in rank and salary. Social engagements crowd our calendar—part of the good life, we think. We encourage the children to participate in sports, music lessons, and school events. We struggle to make our home and yard a showplace. The fowler's snare drops on us. Trapped.

We spend money on necessities and luxuries we call necessities. We borrow money to pay for house, cars, boats, and campers. Then we get additional jobs to pay off our loans. The fowler's snare drops on us. Trapped.

The psalmist talks about God's rescue. "He will cover you with His feathers, and under His wings you will find refuge" (Psalm 91:4a). In this word picture, the mother bird stretches out her wings to protect her young from the snare. God rescues you by sending His Son to break forever the snares of sin and death by His death on the cross. When Satan thought Jesus was trapped, the Son won the victory and burst the bonds of death on the third day. Free from our self-made traps, we gather under the warm protective wings of the Almighty.

Prayer: Lord, keep us from getting trapped! Amen.

Time of Trouble: Terror and Pestilence

The psalmist continues describing times of trouble with the imagery of the terror of night and the pestilence that stalks in the darkness.

We still fear darkness. When a violent storm cuts the electric power supply, we grope for candles. A small child calls out in the night for reassurance.

Dread diseases of mysterious origin strike fear in our hearts. AIDS, with its terminal nature and contagious character, has created panic worldwide. Meningitis, hepatitis, and salmonella outbreaks put the public on alert. Sometimes we feel that nothing is safe to eat, drink, wear, drive, or breathe! Sickness, whether acute or chronic, creates a time of trouble which drains our energies and brings discouragement.

We also face spiritual and supernatural troubles. Satan attacks at every opportunity, including at night when we are alone with our thoughts. He robs us of peace by magnifying our guilt. We cannot handle trouble on our own.

But the psalmist suggests the remedy: "He will call upon me, and I will answer him; I will be with him in trouble, I will deliver him and honor him" (Psalm 91:15). God promises to shelter us from danger. He sent His Son to penetrate the darkness as the Light of the world. Triumphant on the cross in the darkness of Good Friday, Jesus lives with us and in us. He also prepares a heavenly home for us who believe in Him as Savior. Whether endangered by the fowler's snare or attacked by pestilence in the darkness, we have God as our very present Help in time of trouble.

Prayer: Father, thank You for rescuing us in time of trouble through Your Son, Jesus Christ. Amen.

Penetrating the Fog

I just returned from driving my daughter to high school through a thick fog. Heavy, dense fog. Visibility zero. My headlights barely penetrated. Cars crept along. Drivers strained to see a few feet ahead.

Life often seems shrouded in a dense, thick fog. So much confusion in our world. Knotty problems. Moral breakdown. Strident voices. Many conflicting opinions, but no solid answers. Uncertainty regarding the future of the world, our country, our town, and our lives. What can penetrate the fog?

The psalmist suggests, "Your word is a lamp to my feet and a light for my path" (Psalm 119:105). Though afflicted with much suffering and tempted to go astray, the psalmist continues to trust in the promises and guidance of God's unchanging Word.

The apostle John further identifies that Light with the Word made flesh, Jesus Christ: "In Him was life, and that life was the Light of men. The Light shines in the darkness, but the darkness has not understood it" (John 1:4–5). "The true Light that gives light to every man was coming into the world" (John 1:9). Yes, the light of God's Word penetrates the fog of sin and death by revealing Jesus Christ as Savior.

The fog remains. We admit the inadequacy of our feeble efforts to penetrate the sin, confusion, and uncertainty of our world. But we turn to God's Word. In it God shines forth to penetrate the fog with His Son, the crucified and risen Savior. We can see again. We can drive confidently through the fog and even light the way for others.

Prayer: Visit then this soul of mine, Pierce the gloom of sin and grief; Fill me, radiancy divine, Scatter all my unbelief; More and more thyself display, Shining to the perfect day.

Come for the Cleansing!

Scripture contains some beautiful "comes"—God's gracious invitations. Through Isaiah He exposes the rebellion and guilt, the insincere offerings and prayers of His Old Testament people. He pictures them lifting hands in prayer—hands full of blood. Then Isaiah offers the invitation of God, "Come now, let us reason together. Though your sins are like scarlet, they shall be as white as snow" (Isaiah 1:18). Those blood-stained hands will be washed clean by God's forgiving action.

These words strike our hearts. We also rebel against God in many ways, walking from Him to the lure of our selfish goals—money, prestige, power, success. We come to worship piously, only to raise sin-stained hands in prayer. He pleads with us, "Come now, let us reason together. Though your sins be as scarlet, they shall be as white as snow."

We know how God's forgiving action works. We see the bloodstained hands of the Son of God. His nail-pierced hands bore our sins as He died on the cross. We are washed clean in the blood of the Lamb. Through Baptism we experience a daily cleansing of our sins as we live the life of repentance. How precious those promises to our ears: Come for cleansing!

Prayer: Today your mercy calls us To wash away our sin. However great our trespass, Whatever we have been, However long from mercy Our hearts have turned away, Your precious blood can wash us And make us clean today.

Come for Refreshment!

Isaiah describes the plight of a rebellious Israel with wilderness imagery. Because of her sin she wandered in a trackless wasteland with no water to drink. Her captivity in Babylon far from Jerusalem was a spiritual wilderness. Now God issues the beautiful invitation of our text to a hopeless, despairing people. God's overflowing love is freely poured out for sinners. Refreshing water to drink. Food and drink for sustenance. Spiritual refreshment that lasts forever. All without cost!

In the wilderness of our existence, God also issues an invitation to us. "Come, all who are thirsty, come to the waters ..." (Isaiah 55:1a). Having squandered our money on food that doesn't satisfy (Isaiah 55:2) and having rebelled against God, we now come to Jesus Christ for refreshment. He has paid the full price for our sins and offers us spiritual food and drink without cost. The living water of His Word refreshes our parched throats. The solid food of His love and forgiveness nourishes us for daily living. Now we can sound the summons for others to come and drink the water and to eat the food freely offered. Come for refreshment!

Prayer: I heard the voice of Jesus say, "Behold, I freely give The living water, thirsty one; Stoop down and drink and live." I came to Jesus, and I drank Of that life-giving stream; My thirst was quenched, my soul revived, And now I live in him.

Come for Rest!

Jesus places a yoke of discipleship on each of His followers. His own road to Calvary involved many burdens and trials, but He bore them willingly. He candidly told His followers they also would experience crosses in their lives. John the Baptist's imprisonment and death for exposing King Herod's sin witnessed to the cost of discipleship.

But Jesus never asks for anything He does not freely bestow. He offers a most comforting invitation to struggling disciples: "Come to Me, all you who are weary and burdened, and I will give you rest" (Matthew 11:28). "Come to Me." All sins and failures are covered by His sacrificial death. "All you who are weary and burdened." He has already shouldered our burdens. He understands them, and He cares about us. He puts His arms around us and comforts us. "And I will give you rest." We don't deserve rest, but He gives us rest nevertheless. Peace in His forgiveness. Shelter from the storms of life. Quiet meditation on His promises. Rest for today and the promise of that eternal rest which belongs to the people of God.

The discipleship goes on with the yoke of obedience shouldered. But He makes our yoke easy and our burden light (Matthew 11:30), because of His death and resurrection. He gives rest to our souls. Come for rest!

Prayer: I heard the voice of Jesus say, "Come unto me and rest; Lay down, O weary one, lay down Your head upon my breast." I came to Jesus as I was, So weary, worn, and sad; I found in him a resting place, And he has made me glad.

Come to the Banquet

The beautiful word "come" fills Scripture. Come for cleansing. Come for refreshment. Come for rest. In Matthew 22 our attention is directed ahead to the heavenly invitation: Come for the banquet.

In the parable a king prepares a banquet for his son. His servants invite many to come, but they refuse. He tells his servants to invite the guests again with the news that the oxen and fattened cattle have been butchered, and "everything is ready. Come to the wedding banquet" (Matthew 24:4c). They pay no attention but tend to work; some even kill his servants. Swift judgment came upon these ungrateful guests. Now he sends servants into the streets and gathers everyone they can find to the banquet. The king then provides wedding garments for these new guests.

Our King invites us to the heavenly banquet. All things are ready. His Son Jesus Christ, the crucified and risen Lord, attends as guest of honor. We do not deserve to attend because of our sin. But the King searches in the streets and alleys: "Everything is ready. Come to the wedding banquet." He then furnishes us with the wedding garment of Christ's righteousness so we are worthy to enter the banquet hall. Accepting the invitation by God's grace, we also extend the invitation to others as long as we live: Come to the banquet!

Prayer: "And whosoever cometh, I will not cast him out." O patient love of Jesus, Which drives away our doubt, Which, though we be unworthy Of love so great and free, Invites us very sinners To come, dear Lord, to thee!

Baking Blessings

Kitchen delight is baking in process. Sift the flour. Measure and pack down the brown sugar. Stir in the eggs and vanilla. Mix the ingredients. Spoon out the teaspoonfuls on the cookie sheet. Bake. Smell the aroma and eat the finished product. A blessing of God!

As Jesus says, "Give, and it will be given to you. A good measure, pressed down, shaken together and running over, will be poured into your lap" (Luke 6:38). An abundance of grain poured into the fold of the garment for use in preparing the daily meal. The widow of Zarephath discovered that the cruse of oil and flour in the jar never emptied as she continued to bake bread for Elijah and her family. God's bountiful blessing!

Baking blessings. As we prepare good things for others and lovingly use the ingredients He supplies, God's blessings flow in abundance. God spared not His Son but gave Him up for us all. "Freely [we] have received, freely give" (Matthew 10:8). The lesson learned in the kitchen applies to life in the factory, the school, the neighborhood, and the church. "For with the measure you use, it will be measured to you" (Luke 6:38b). All by grace. All from God's love. Shared with others freely, freshly baked cookies are indeed baking blessings!

Prayer: All the plenty summer pours; Autumn's rich, abundant stores, Flocks that whiten all the plain, Yellow sheaves of ripened grain: Lord, for these our souls shall raise Grateful vows and solemn praise.

Cleaning the Refrigerator

Baking may provide blessings, but cleaning the refrigerator, that's another matter. What modern kitchen can survive without a refrigerator to preserve food and keep drinks cold? We fill it with produce, meat, and dairy products. We store leftovers for use later. What a service to the family!

But then comes the time for cleaning. The process begins. Everything removed. Plastic containers emptied of spoiled food. Heavy glass jars discarded. Soap applied inside. Elbow grease on the sponge. At last sparkling clean and plenty of room! The cycle begins again.

How much our life resembles a refrigerator! Shiny on the outside. Potentially useful to others. Constantly taking in words and experiences from the world, stored for future use. But then we have to examine the inside. "All of us have become like one who is unclean, and all our righteous acts are like filthy rags" (Isaiah 64:6a). Within our hearts the world's input quickly sours and molds. We are so cluttered that our ability to help others is hindered. Only God can clean us properly. The sins confessed and removed are covered by the blood of Christ. The waters of Baptism continue to cleanse us daily. Sparkling clean in Christ and useful again for service, we begin again the cycle of God's love as we live for Him. What a lesson from cleaning the refrigerator!

Prayer: Lord, on you I cast my burden. Sink it to the depths below. Let me know your gracious pardon, Wash me, make me white as snow. Let your Spirit leave me never; Make me only yours forever.

Spiritual Dullness

"That knife couldn't cut hot butter." Frustration at trying to cut something with a dull blade. "He doesn't catch on to anything I'm saying." Frustration of a teacher with a dull student. Dull means ineffective and slow.

Micah describes the spiritual dullness of nations gathered against Israel: "But they do not know the thoughts of the Lord; they do not understand His plan" (Micah 4:12a). These people may have been powerful and clever, much to be feared, but spiritually they could neither cut hot butter nor catch on to the simplest teaching. Therefore, as Micah prophesies, they will be broken to pieces (Micah 4:13).

Do we have a problem with spiritual dullness? "Called... out of darkness into His wonderful light" (1 Peter 2:9), we nevertheless at times fail to understand and live effective lives in relation to God's plan for us. Why? Our sinful flesh rebels against God. Micah promised a new day for Judah after the Babylonian captivity and a Ruler to come out of Bethlehem, One who would "shepherd His flock" (Micah 5:2, 4). That Ruler, Jesus, has come to be our Light in darkness, to replace our spiritual dullness with bright understanding and keen-edged living. We turn to His Word for illumination. As a result we know His thoughts, understand His plan, and live joyfully each day. Thank God for His Son, who carried out the Father's plan on Calvary and lives in our hearts forever.

Prayer: Renew me, O eternal Light, And let my heart and soul be bright, Illumined with the light of grace That issues from your holy face.

Spiritual Discernment

The story of Solomon's dream deserves attention. As he began his reign over Israel, God appeared to him during the night and said, "Ask for whatever you want Me to give you" (1 Kings 3:5b). Solomon could have asked for wealth or long life. Instead he prayed, "So give Your servant a discerning heart to govern Your people and to distinguish between right and wrong" (1 Kings 3:9a).

Solomon showed spiritual discernment by his request and asked for a discerning heart as he governed. He recognized the difficulty of his task and the need for dependence on God's wisdom. God granted his request and promised wealth and long life as well. Unfortunately we also know that in later years Solomon grew distracted by his many foreign wives and his wealth, thus dulling his spiritual discernment.

What better request could we make than for a discerning heart—the spiritual discernment to know the difference between right and wrong, to admit our sins and ask forgiveness, to look to God's Son Jesus Christ, "One greater than Solomon" (Matthew 12:42), as our Savior from sin, and to live joyfully according to God's commandments. Though we don't rule a nation, we do have heavy responsibilities in our home, church, and employment. Only God's gift of a discerning heart will enable us to serve Him wisely and lovingly.

Prayer: Give me the strength to do With ready heart and willing Whatever you command, My calling here fulfilling. Help me do what I should With all my might, and bless The outcome for my good, For you must give success.

Fingers in the Cookie Jar

Mother tells Junior, "You can play now until supper. And stay out of the cookie jar." Junior plays with one thought in his mind—those chocolate cookies. Just one cookie can do no harm while Mother works in another room. He sneaks into the kitchen, takes off the lid, and grabs a delicious cookie. With fingers in the cookie jar, Junior hears footsteps and then a voice, "Junior, what did I tell you—no cookies! No dessert for you tonight."

I still love cookies and pass the cookie jar frequently. No penalty awaiting me from a parent, but I rationalize to myself that one or two won't add any pounds. Then I think of the proverb, "He who conceals his sins does not prosper, but whoever confesses and renounces them finds mercy" (Proverbs 28:13). We live with our fingers in the cookie jar. We know what God says in His Word about cheating, stealing, lying, adultery, and gossip. We have freedom to enjoy His creation, yet our minds focus on the forbidden. We decide that one time won't hurt, and no one will know.

But inevitably we get caught, at least by God, who found Adam and Eve hiding in the garden. With fingers in the cookie jar we try to conceal our sin, but to no avail. The better course is openly confessing our sin and asking forgiveness. God sent His Son for us. He defeated those cookie jar temptations and died for our sins. He offers full forgiveness. His mercy is dessert of the best kind. Ahead by grace through faith in Jesus—the heavenly feast. Who needs fingers in the forbidden cookie jar anyway?

Prayer: *Dear Lord, help me to come clean with my misdeeds. Point me to Your forgiveness won on Calvary. Help me to desire Your will only. Amen.*

Songs of Joy or Wails of Brokenness?

Through the prophet Isaiah, God articulates a clear choice for the people of Israel. On the one hand, those who disobey can expect wails in brokenness of spirit. They provoke God, forget His holy mountain, offer sacrifices to idols, and walk in evil ways. God vows to pay them back in full for their sins and the sins of their fathers.

How easily we can forget God in the midst of our selfish pursuits, follow the example of those who pursue modern idols, and say that we are above reproach! Persistent disobedience can lead to anguish of heart and wails of brokenness when we experience God's wrath against our sins.

But God offers us salvation freely by His grace. He sent His Son to pay for our sins by dying on the cross. Chosen by Him in Baptism, we sing out of the joy of our hearts. We treasure our inheritance, thank Him for many blessings, hear the answers to our prayers before we even ask, and anticipate new heavens and a new earth which He will create for us. No wonder we fill the air with songs of joy.

"The Sovereign Lord says: 'My servants will eat, but you will go hungry; My servants will drink, but you will go thirsty; My servants will rejoice, but you will be put to shame' " (Isaiah 65:14). Songs of joy or wails of brokenness? Thank God for the gift of His Son!

Prayer: Oh, grant the consummation Of this our song above In endless adoration And everlasting love; Then shall we praise and bless you Where perfect praises ring And evermore confess you, Our Savior and our King!

A New Thing!

Israel lived in the past. She developed elaborate laws and practiced formalized religion. Her corporate life resembled a desert wasteland. Disobedient and rebellious, she faced destruction.

Today's Church sometimes lives on tradition in the desert of disobedience and rebellion. We often bring God the leftovers and weary Him with our offenses.

Isaiah electrifies the discouraged nation by bringing the Word of the Lord: "See, I am doing a new thing!" (Isaiah 43:19). He refers to God's new covenant of grace initiated by the coming of the Messiah, Jesus Christ. God will make a new way in the desert, where streams of water will flow to quench the thirst of His chosen people. Jesus by His death on the cross would blot out the transgressions of the world.

That new thing continues to bring new life today. Our society falls over itself for the latest fad and the newest discoveries. These fads quickly fade. But in a modern desert of selfishness, materialism, and rebellion against God, He continues to pour forth the streams of life to quench our thirst. Baptized, we drink the clear, cold water of God's Word and sacraments. Refreshed, we participate in God's new thing which is drawing people to Himself from every nation, tribe, and clan. We witness God at work in our own lives and share His goodness with those around us. "See, I am doing a new thing."

Prayer: Let the earth now praise the Lord, Who has truly kept his word And at last to us did send Christ, the sinner's help and friend.

Trivial Pursuit

The board game Trivial Pursuit captured the hearts of millions of Americans a few years ago. The game appeared at many parties and family gatherings. It has difficult questions in a wide variety of categories such as arts and literature, history, and sports and leisure—questions that challenge the most knowledgeable participants. And the questions stress trivia, often obscure and otherwise unimportant facts but tantalizing morsels for game enthusiasts.

Trivial pursuit, unfortunately, describes the lifestyle of many people. We choose unimportant goals, waste time on activities without much value, and fill our heads with useless knowledge. Our world bombards us with glittering goods, exotic travel, promising investments, and get-rich-quick schemes. We often pursue the trivial, forgetting eternal values.

The Teacher in Ecclesiastes points out the trivial nature of most things: "Meaningless! Meaningless! Utterly meaningless! Everything is meaningless" (Ecclesiastes 1:2). While admittedly pessimistic, the Teacher helps us to question values and choices. By contrast, says the same writer, "Wisdom, like an inheritance, is a good thing and benefits those who see the sun" (Ecclesiastes 7:11). In our New Testament understanding, wisdom refers to a right relationship with God. He sent His Son, the Word made flesh (John 1:14) to live and die for our sins. Christ is the Power and Wisdom of God. Because of His faithful pursuit of the cross, we can live with clear goals of service and witness as members of God's family. In the light of eternity, no trivial pursuits for us!

Prayer: Forth in your name, O Lord, I go, My daily labor to pursue, You, only you, resolved to know In all I think or speak or do.

Monopoly

How I used to love the board game Monopoly! I would eagerly purchase all the property I could afford and start placing houses and hotels on it. My excitement grew as I won more and more money and continued amassing property. Of course, sometimes I lost everything I had while someone else grew wealthy. Monopoly has experienced enduring sales over the past 50 years. Obviously a strong appeal to game lovers.

Monopoly mirrors life. The Teacher in Ecclesiastes refers to our insatiable desire for material possessions: "Whoever loves money never has money enough; whoever loves wealth is never satisfied with his income" (Ecclesiastes 5:10). We want more money, clothes, televisions, cars, and the list goes on. We think we can handle income circumspectly, but our sinful nature pushes us to spend or keep it for ourselves. We seek monopoly in the sense that we want to amass wealth, even if it comes at the expense of others. The Teacher cuts us short: "This too is meaningless" (Ecclesiastes 5:10b). We need to admit the fleeting nature of possessions and to repent of our greed.

Enter God. He shares abundantly with the righteous and the unrighteous alike (Matthew 5:45b). He gives everything away. He gave us His Son, who gave His life for us on Calvary. Jesus learned contentment in doing the Father's will. Now in possession of the gift of eternal life, we can spend a lifetime not gaining a monopoly, but giving everything away to others— our life, our Savior, and our material possessions. Such a lifestyle will not be judged "meaningless."

Prayer: All that I am and have, Thy gifts so free, In joy, in grief, through life, Dear Lord, for thee! And when thy face I see, My ransomed soul shall be Through all eternity Something for thee.

Clue

A third popular board game, Clue, engages the players in a who-done-it mystery. A murder has been committed, and the purpose of the game is to identify the murderer, the weapon, and the scene of the crime. Clues lead toward a solution, but usually one clue sheds the most light on the mystery.

How does one make sense out of the game of life? With all the confusing values, philosophies, and lifestyles, how does one choose the right path? What clues can lead to a solution? The Teacher in Ecclesiastes has systematically eliminated one option after another—knowledge, wealth, and pleasure.

But the significant clue comes near the end of the book: "Now all has been heard; here is the conclusion of the matter: Fear God and keep His commandments, for this is the whole duty of man" (Ecclesiastes 12:13). The clue comes from God, not from human beings. God wants us to fear Him and keep His commandments: "Love the Lord your God ... and your neighbor as yourself" (Matthew 22:37, 39). Not selfish living, but selfless living.

The clue points toward the solution. We can't fear God or keep His commandments on our own. That's why God sent His Son to live the life and pay the price. A murder in a sense. They nailed Him to a tree. But in the end He did it Himself. He willingly died for us on Calvary. Now you know the solution for your life. He works faith in your heart. He instills in you a fear of God and obedience to His commandments. Purpose for living. Sure hope in dying. The saving clue—Christ crucified.

Prayer: Not the labors of my hands Can fulfill thy law's demands; Could my zeal no respite know, Could my tears forever flow, All for sin could not atone; Thou must save, and thou alone.

Our Family: Together in Thanksgiving

With Thanksgiving approaching, we think of celebrating with our families, remembering the many blessings of the past. The ideal Thanksgiving dinner is a bountifully laden table with the family gathered around it.

In reality the Thanksgiving meal often serves up bickering and complaining. "Mom, she's taking all the white meat." "Why are there so many onions in the dressing?" "Can I be excused to watch football on television?" "No one thanks me for the meal, all that work and no appreciation!" "Will everyone be quiet? I can't stand all the nagging and the noise. Why can't we relax on a holiday?"

The psalmist, however, describes how family togetherness can be a reality. "Blessed are all who fear the Lord, who walk in His ways" (Psalm 128:3). God sent His Son, Jesus, for us. At the cross He bridged all divisions between God and human beings, including families. God chooses us in our Baptism and brings us to faith in Christ. As we grow in faith, He fills us with reverence and obedience. By His power we reach out to our family at Thanksgiving and throughout the year.

What blessings flow from God to us by His grace! "You will eat the fruit of your labor; blessings and prosperity will be yours. Your wife will be like a fruitful vine within your house; your sons will be like olive shoots around your table" (Psalm 128:2–3). By faith we rejoice in God's Thanksgiving blessings. Our family: together in thanksgiving.

Prayer: With voices united our praises we offer And gladly our songs of thanksgiving we raise. With you, Lord, beside us, your strong arm will guide us. To you, our great redeemer, forever be praise!

Have You Learned to Be Content?

Picture your family around the Thanksgiving table with turkey and all the trimmings. It is a Norman Rockwell moment. The larger question, however: Have you learned to be content?

Leaving the serene tableau, many live in perpetual discontent. Paul writes that, "whether well fed or hungry, whether living in plenty or in want" (Philippians 4:12c), he has learned to be content. For the discontented, circumstances always spell trouble. Never enough. We want more wages, profits, possessions. Perhaps we even want more of the turkey's white meat than the person sitting next to us.

Some seek false contentment. They aim at self-sufficiency and self-satisfaction. The Stoics used the Greek word for "contentment" to describe wanting little and not caring. Desire and feelings were eliminated through willpower. Yet self-imposed contentment robs us of genuine joy and peace.

Paul describes true contentment as Christ-sufficient and Christ-satisfied. "I can do everything through Him who gives me strength" (Philippians 4:13). Jesus Christ was content to do the Father's bidding. He came to earth, with the forces of hell pitted against Him. Yet He could enjoy the lilies of the field, sleep peacefully in a storm-tossed boat, stand silent before His tormentors, and ultimately cry, "It is finished" (John 19:30). "He died for all" (2 Corinthians 5:15a). He forgives sins of both discontent and false contentment.

As you celebrate Thanksgiving and savor the pumpkin pie, learn the meaning of true contentment—doing everything through Christ, who strengthens us.

Prayer: Lord, let me rest content in Your salvation. Amen.

Thanksgiving Confession and Praise

Aware of God's overflowing blessings recorded in Psalm 103 and conscious of being more often like the nine cleansed lepers than the one who returned to give thanks, we confess to God:

O Lord, we come before You as often thankless people—rich in turkey and dressing, but poor in thanks; rich in houses, cars, and TV sets, but poor in thanks. For our thanklessness, forgive us Lord. We often forget to thank You, Lord—for comfortable homes and abundant food, for pardon and forgiveness, for Your suffering and death on the cross, for Your resurrection and ascension, for our Baptism and new life, for togetherness with Your family. For our forgetfulness, forgive us, Lord. Sometimes, Lord, we are thankful for blessings, but not thankful enough to share them with others—our new-found life with the lost, our food with the hungry, our clothes with the ill-clad, our love with the unlovable. For our selfishness, forgive us, Lord. Forgive us, Lord, for our thanklessness, our forgetfulness, and our selfishness.

God forgives us our sin for the sake of His Son, Jesus Christ, and fills our hearts with true thanksgiving as we live for Him and for others. Now we can rejoice and praise Him with all our heart, as our Bible reading and our closing hymn verse do.

Prayer: Sing to the Lord of harvest, Sing songs of love and praise; With joyful hearts and voices Your alleluias raise. By him the rolling seasons In fruitful order move; Sing to the Lord of harvest A joyous song of love.

A Thief in the Night

With the family sleeping, a thief quietly breaks in and enters through a window or door. Armed with knife or gun, he stealthily sneaks around looking for money and valuables. Just thinking about it strikes terror in our hearts.

Paul uses this imagery to describe the day of the Lord at the end of the world. People will be talking about "peace and safety" (1 Thessalonians 5:3) when destruction comes suddenly. We think of the Flood that came without warning.

At the end of the church year Christians contemplate the end of the world. For everyone living in darkness that day spells terror, destruction, punishment. Judgment Day means a day of reckoning, with no escape, no warning.

But Paul has good news for us, "You, brothers, are not in darkness so that this day should surprise you like a thief. You are all sons of the light and sons of the day" (1 Thessalonians 5:4–5a). "God did not appoint us to suffer wrath but to receive salvation through our Lord Jesus Christ" (1 Thessalonians 5:9). In the very darkness of Good Friday, Jesus shone forth on the cross as the Savior of the world. Easter morning light brought proof of His victory.

We live in the light of Easter. The Lord has "called you out of darkness into His wonderful light" (1 Peter 2:9b). Forgiven, we wait for the day of the Lord, when Jesus will appear again to take us to heaven. We don't know the day or the hour when He will return. But as children of the light we will not be surprised but will welcome our salvation with open arms.

Prayer: *Lord, prepare us with Your saving light for Your sudden return. Amen.*

Living in the Daylight

Many discussions about the end of the world focus on the time and other details. Paul, however, emphasizes the implications of Christ's Second Coming for daily living. "Since we belong to the day, let us be self-controlled" (1 Thessalonians 5:8a). He first admonishes us to be awake and sober. Does the world tranquilize us with its pleasures? How easy to get wrapped up in television, sports, shopping, and travel! These activities, fine in themselves, can divert us from God's plan for us. Satan tempts us to succumb to the sins of the night—revelry, drunkenness, and sexual immorality.

Second, Paul encourages us to put on the armor of God. The breastplate of faith enables us to trust God with each day's problems. The breastplate of love flows from faith. Love penetrates the darkness as nothing else can. The helmet of hope equips us to live soberly each day. No matter how dark the day, the hope of Christ's return keeps the light burning.

Third, Paul asks us to "encourage one another and build each other up" (1 Thessalonians 5:11). The world discourages us and tears us down. But we have the precious Gospel message to share with one another. "He [Christ] died for us so that, whether we are awake or asleep, we may live together with Him" (1 Thessalonians 5:10).

Living in the light is possible because God makes us children of the light. By God's grace we stay awake, wear the armor of God, and encourage one another with salvation through Jesus Christ.

Prayer: "I am the light; I light the way, A godly life displaying; I help you walk as in the day; I keep your feet from straying. I am the way, and well I show How you should journey here below."

Ready for the Bridegroom?

The time—7:15 a.m. The place—the MGM Hotel in Las Vegas. Many asleep, unsuspecting. Suddenly the unexpected, a devastating fire sweeps through the hotel. Over 100 lives lost, 500 injured.

The text describes a more joyful event, but readiness remains the issue. Ten maidens await the wedding procession with lamps. Five are wise, with lamps trimmed and well-supplied with oil. Five are foolish, with lamps not supplied with oil. Unexpectedly the Bridegroom comes.

Are you looking forward to the Bridegroom's coming? When you consider Jesus Christ coming again at the end of the world, do you thrill with anticipation or stir uneasily? Are you ready to die and go to heaven? Do these events remind you more of a destructive hotel fire or a joyful wedding feast? Are you prepared for the Bridegroom's coming? Preparation means trusting Jesus Christ alone for salvation. God prepared the way for Him to take on human flesh, to live a perfect life, and to die for the world's sin. God prepares us to meet Jesus through Baptism, the Word of God, and the Lord's Supper.

Lacking motivation and discipline, we often neglect God's grace for us. Like the foolish virgins we may find the lamps of our faith going out. But God is faithful and just to rekindle our faith, to forgive us our sins of poor preparation, and to cleanse us from all unrighteousness. Thus we await His coming.

Prayer: The bridegroom comes, awake! Your lamps with gladness take! Alleluia! With bridal care And faith's bold prayer, To meet the bridegroom, come, prepare!

Thanksgiving before the Throne

Thanksgiving Day and the end of the church year occur around the end of November. They present contrasting scenes. The first conjures up thoughts of the family gathered around a bountiful table. Thanksgiving, yes, but short-lived and often directed more toward material blessings.

The second suggests Judgment Day and then the gathering of the saints around the throne of the Lamb. There the multitudes of the redeemed join with the angels in an endless song of praise. It continues forever and focuses on God—Father, Son, and Holy Spirit—who loves us and chose us as His people. This celebration combines Christmas Eve and Easter worship, infinitely magnified.

How can our thanksgiving each day become less like a short-lived holiday and more like the endless thanksgiving before the throne? We first confess that our old nature, still clinging to us, is indeed thankless. On our own, we cannot participate in endless thanksgiving.

Admitting our failure, we look to the Lamb. His perfect life and death on the cross offered a spotless sacrifice to the Father. God now stands before us with His love and forgiveness 365 days a year. We join the fellowship of God's people gathered around Word and Sacrament. There we join with angels and archangels and all the company of heaven in praising God. Every Sunday a thanksgiving before the throne.

Prayer: All praise and thanks to God The Father now be given, The Son, and him who reigns With them in highest heaven, The one eternal God, Whom earth and heav'n adore; For thus it was, is now, And shall be evermore.

Deliverance on the Interstate

After an enjoyable visit home, our family was headed back to the city where I served as pastor. The car headed west on the interstate into the afternoon sun. My wife and two small children fell asleep. With the monotonous drive and glare of the sun, I found myself getting drowsy. Suddenly I saw the grass rushing up at us. Applying the brakes, we smashed through a barbed wire fence, the front wheels coming to rest in the mud a few feet from a creek. The final landing was gentle. No one was hurt.

We took stock of our situation. The interstate was way up a hillside. Another car had stopped up on the road. The people in that car offered to drive us to a nearby town to contact the police. They also provided us with hot food and shelter. We were so thankful to be safe, although shaken. A few hours later two wreckers pulled our car back to the road. Except for the grillwork, our vehicle had sustained no damage. We were able to continue our journey.

"Call upon Me in the day of trouble; I will deliver you, and you will honor Me" (Psalm 50:15). I had only a moment to call on God, but certainly He delivered us. We concluded that He had a purpose for the remainder of our lives. We rejoiced in that deliverance and in God's love in His Son, Jesus Christ, who had delivered us from eternal death by His death on the cross.

Many years later that deliverance on the interstate still stands out in my mind. God is alive. He has power to save. Thank Him for His unfailing mercy!

Prayer Thought: Discuss days of trouble when God has delivered you. Thank Him.

Two Kinds of Sinners

In Luke 15 two kinds of sinners are mentioned. We could call them "insider" and "outsider" sinners.

Do you feel like an outsider sinner? Perhaps you have lived a lifestyle in the past which you regret. Even now you may not be fitting in with other church members. As an outsider sinner you either have no desire for repentance and say, "I'm outside and I plan to stay that way. I'm a sinner and I can't change now. Stay away from me, Shepherd. I don't want to be rescued." Or God brings you to Jesus repentant as you say, "I'm lost as an outsider. I'm lonely. I'm sinful. I need help. I want a complete change of heart. Thank You, Shepherd."

The text also describes insider sinners, "the Pharisees and the teachers of the law" (Luke 15:2). They consider themselves righteous because they are lifelong sons of Abraham and obey the Law. Are you an insider sinner? You may be a lifelong believer with a well-known family in the church. You may be active in church leadership. But you may also be puffed up with pride or be lacking in love. As an insider sinner you either have no desire for repentance and say, "I'm okay—a sinner yes, but not too bad a sinner. I don't need help right now." Or God brings you to Jesus repentant as you say, "I have the heritage, but I'm missing something. My pride and lovelessness are sinful. I need help from You, Shepherd."

We meet Jesus Christ. He came to die for insider and outsider sinners alike. Shepherd of the lost sheep, Jesus comes to us repentant sinners and fills us with a rejoicing that extends to other sinners everywhere.

Prayer: *Father, forgive my sin for Jesus' sake. Amen.*

Leading Others to Sin

As the word "sex" was once "unmentionable," so has the word "sin" become today. All sorts of milder words flood our language—"mistake," "error," "miscalculation." In Luke 17 Jesus deals bluntly with sin.

Jesus considers the sin of leading others to sin. "Things that cause people to sin are bound to come, but woe to that person through whom they come" (Luke 17:1). He adds that it would be better for such a person to have "a millstone tied around his neck" and "to be thrown into the sea" (Luke 17:2).

Leading others to sin. Parents so easily set wrong examples for their children—materialistic lifestyle, poor church attendance, excessive drinking and smoking, no love between husband and wife. A frightening list when we know our own shortcomings and our influence on our children!

We can also lead others to sin by engaging in gossip. Many times our careless tongue harms the Lord and His Church and leads others to doubt their faith. When we engage in false teaching, we lead others to sin. We deny Christ and raise questions about the reliability of God's Word. We may sound skeptical and cynical about God's power to change lives.

Since many of our sins may lead others to sin, we need to set aside the pervasive sin in our midst. Instead we turn to the great Sin-bearer, Jesus Christ. Sinless in His own life, He went to the cross to defeat the power of sin for us. He offers full forgiveness to us. No millstones for believers in Jesus! "If we confess our sins, He is faithful and just and will forgive us our sins and purify us from all unrighteousness" (1 John 1:9). Instead of leading others to sin, Jesus helps us lead others to Him.

Prayer: *Father, keep us from leading others to sin. Amen.*

Not Rebuking Sin in Others

Second, Jesus addresses the sin of not rebuking sin in others. He says plainly, "If your brother sins, rebuke him" (Luke 17:3b). We would rather overlook sin in others. If we ignore their sin, perhaps they will ignore our sin. We want them to like us, so we remain silent.

But sin threatens to engulf our world. Abortion results in the murder of millions. Pornography corrupts the minds of youth and adults. Sexual perversions profane God's name and destroy lives. Cheating takes place on a wide scale. Exploitation victimizes people on many levels. People slander others with a barrage of rumor and innuendo. Church members evidence a coldness of faith and life that deadens the fellowship of God's people and derails His magnificent plan of taking the Gospel to the ends of the world.

Jesus simply says, "If your brother sins, rebuke him." He intends that we rebuke out of love. We hate the sin because we love the sinner. We speak to the offending brother because we recognize our own sin and need for forgiveness. We believe in the power of daily confession and absolution. And we confess the sin of not rebuking sin in others.

Jesus has the answer for us. He addressed blunt words to the hypocritical Pharisees and drove money-changers out of the temple. But He also asked the Father to forgive His enemies and died for the sins of the whole world. He also lives in us and through us so we can rebuke sin in a loving manner. We "carry each other's burdens, and in this way ... fulfill the law of Christ" (Galatians 6:2).

Prayer: Delay not, delay not! Why longer abuse The love and compassion of Jesus, your God? A fountain is opened; how can you refuse To wash and be cleansed in his pardoning blood?

Failing to Forgive

We have been dealing bluntly with sin by confessing our sins of leading others to sin and not rebuking sin in others. Jesus adds a third sin for our consideration—failing to forgive. He says, "If your brother repents, forgive him" (Luke 17:3). He expands the instructions to forgive. "If he sins against you seven times in a day ... forgive him" (Luke 17:4). We like to set standards and impose limits for forgiveness. We are impatient when someone repeatedly sins against us.

The husband leaves a ring around the tub for the hundredth time. The wife squeezes the toothpaste tube in the middle again. Little Billy lets the dog escape through an open door for the third time this week. Forgiveness? They say they are sorry. But we wonder: Why do they keep repeating their thoughtless conduct? Forgiveness comes hard.

Bluntly Jesus exposes our sin. He knows our tendency to keep score on others. He knows we often hold grudges even after we have spoken a word of forgiveness. We confess our sin of failing to forgive.

Clearly Jesus forgives. He lived in a world which wronged Him. He opposed sin, but constantly offered forgiveness to others. And He died on the cross to pay for the world's sins. He forgave His disciples and gave them the power to forgive sins for His sake. He forgives our failure to forgive, and empowers us to go the extra mile. Dealing bluntly with sin leads to clear forgiveness from the Savior.

Prayer: Today your gate is open, And all who enter in Shall find a Father's welcome And pardon for their sin. The past shall be forgotten, A present joy be giv'n, A future grace be promised, A glorious crown in heav'n.

Waiting for the Morning

When the well-known preacher Peter Marshall had his second heart attack, he said softly to his wife Catherine as he was carried out of the house—on a stretcher, "See you in the morning, Darling." That dark night ended in the morning of eternal life, for Peter Marshall died at the hospital. His wife treasured those words in the days of grief which followed.

Jeremiah writes that the Lord's compassions are new every morning. Precious words of comfort in the gloomiest book in the Bible—Lamentations. Jeremiah in his effort to proclaim God's Word of judgment upon Judah faces ridicule and persecution. He is imprisoned, beaten and thrown in a well. He agonizes, doubts, and turns bitter. The root of his bitterness is self-pity. A dark night of the soul.

We often walk in darkness. We experience illness, family problems, problems on the job. The more we try to be faithful, the more the problems mount. We feel rejected and persecuted. No one seems to understand. At root we are engaging in self-pity. A dark night of the soul.

Jesus understands our dark night of the soul, for He experienced it in Gethsemane and at Calvary, where He cried out, "My God, My God, why have You forsaken Me?" (Matthew 27:46). He waited on the Father and won the victory over the darkness. With Jeremiah, we who have experienced God's love, can say the words of our text and add, as did Jeremiah, "It is good to wait quietly for the salvation of the Lord" (Lamentations 3:26). Whether awaiting a new day of God's mercy or the eternal morning of heaven, we can say with Peter Marshall, "See you in the morning, Darling."

Prayer: *Lord, help us wait for Your morning mercy. Amen.*

Repentance and Joy

Judea, first century. There is excitement in the air, a new stirring of life and hope. A rugged wilderness man appearing to proclaim that Jesus the Messiah has come.

In the middle of a difficult world—perhaps bleak weather, heavy burdens, family problems—we remember "the beginning of the gospel about Jesus Christ, the Son of God" (Mark 1:1). We look to Christmas in its true meaning: Jesus has come as the Babe in Bethlehem, the Man from Galilee, and the Lamb of Calvary. He has come for us.

But John's message starts with repentance. Great crowds came to hear him as the excitement grew. A stern preacher, he exposed their sins, broke through their facade of self-righteousness and religiosity. Confessing their sins, they repented and humbled themselves in a Jordan River baptism. Forgiven, they awaited the appearance of "the Lamb of God, who takes away the sin of the world" (John 1:29).

Christmas often provides a superficial joy of the tinsel, glitter, and wrapping paper variety. We sometimes come to Christ wearing masks, desiring sin and heaven, too. What secrets lurk in the shadows of our hearts—hidden adultery, a serious drinking problem, cheating on the job, bitterness and hatred toward another. John's message pierces the facade, sweeps away the superficial, and penetrates to our hearts. Confessing, we humbly turn to the cross of Jesus for forgiveness and live daily in the humbling but joy-giving waters of our Baptism. True excitement in the air, new life and hope, from the forerunner's message of repentance. Jesus has come—for us!

Prayer: Lord, repentant we seek Your Advent forgiveness and joy. Amen.

Bearing Witness to the Light

The lights of Christmas—Advent candles, decorated street lamps, thousands of outdoor Christmas lights in dazzling colors, Christmas tree light strands, Bethlehem stars everywhere. Temporary joy and comfort in the darkness of our world. But do the lights of Christmas sometimes detract from the one Light shining forever to defeat the dreadful darkness of sin?

John was sent by God into a dark world. He came bearing witness to that one Light, Jesus Christ. Many looked to John as the Light, or at least as Elijah or the Prophet. John could have accepted the praise and pointed to himself as the shining Light. But he refused to identify himself as more than a "voice ... calling in the desert" (John 1:23). As John's gospel says, "He himself was not the light; he came only as a witness to the light" (John 1:8). And how well he served to point to Jesus as the Light of the world!

In the midst of Christmas lights and so many "stars" who draw attention to themselves as famous, important people, we are sorely tempted to seek recognition. We often secretly think that our light does shine rather brightly. But John's example serves to convict us of pride.

On our own, by nature, we live in darkness. God's Son has shined brightly through His birth, life, death, and resurrection. He continues to bring light through His Word and sacraments. By God's grace He shines in our hearts with His light. We now recognize that whatever light we have is reflected only from Him. So we can joyfully bear witness to the Light of the world, at Christmas and all year long.

Prayer: The people that in darkness sat A glorious light have seen; The light has shined on them who long In shades of death have been.

Christmas Shallow or Christmas Deep?

Everywhere, at this time of year, we notice that Christmas is near. The decorations, the bells, the carols all give evidence that the Christmas celebration is already in full swing. But are we celebrating Christmas shallow or Christmas deep?

Too often Americans observe a shallow Christmas complete with tinsel, glitter, holly and ivy, gift buying in crowded department stores, Christmas carols, and, oh yes, silver bells. But these externals, fine in themselves, frequently leave little time for a deep reflection on the true meaning of Christmas.

There by the manger in the still of the night we find Mary looking in wonder at the newborn Christ Child and the visiting shepherds from the fields of Bethlehem. Luke writes, "But Mary treasured up all these things and pondered them in her heart" (Luke 2:19). Mary is celebrating a deep Christmas. Already reflecting for nine months on the visit of the angel and the growing new life within her, she continues to focus on the meaning of this birth for the world. She knows the Savior is born from her womb.

Mary is a model for our celebration of Christmas deep. We enjoy the sights and sounds of the season along with family and friends. But we take time to kneel at the manger and worship the Christ Child who is to die on the cross for our sins. By the Spirit's power, as we worship together during Advent, we treasure up all these things and ponder them in our hearts. Not Christmas shallow, but Christmas deep.

Prayer: *A great and mighty wonder, A full and holy cure: The virgin bears the infant With virgin honor pure!*

Eyes Right!

Military drills sometimes include the command, "Eyes right!" As one unit, the troops turn their eyes and salute. Only the greatest discipline can control our wandering eyes. We enter a large metropolitan area at night and find ourselves captivated by neon lights, lighted billboards, and colorful marquees. We window-shop in crowded malls and can't take our eyes off the fashionable clothing, elegant furniture, and expensive jewelry. When celebrities come to town, we strain for a glimpse and a photograph.

The psalmist writes, "Turn my eyes away from worthless things; preserve my life according to Your word" (Psalm 119:37). The world's glitter distracts our eyes from God and His saving Word. When gazing at Jesus, the One who died for us, we can see the things of the world in the proper perspective, as part of God's gracious creation. But when our eyes wander from Jesus to the glamour of worldly possessions, we lose perspective and our heart follows our eyes to a new love.

Only God through His renewing Word can turn our eyes right. He fixes our eyes on Jesus, on whom our faith depends from beginning to end. We rejoice to see our salvation drawing nigh. We humbly praise and thank Him for life and salvation. We see Him now by faith and will someday see Him face-to-face eternally.

Prayer: Help us, dear Lord Jesus, to turn our eyes away from the tinsel of the world and keep them fixed on You. Amen.

Announcing the New Reign of God

When the president visits, people gather. You strain to see the approaching helicopter or motorcade. An advance speaker talks. Finally, the president steps to the platform to speak.

Similar excitement gripped Israel as the advance man, John the Baptist, emerged from the desert announcing, "Repent, for the kingdom of heaven is near" (Matthew 3:2). With the appearance and authority of a prophet, John clearly communicated that the new reign of God was beginning. Israel, dissatisfied with national and personal conditions, turned out in droves. Waiting in the wings was the King, Jesus of Nazareth.

As we begin a new church year, the announcement of a new reign of God stirs us up as well. With long-standing problems in the world, in our nation, and in our personal lives, we long to hear of the King who brings peace and salvation. Unfortunately, like Israel, we often look for material prosperity and earthly peace in the new reign of God.

But John preaches a strong message of repentance. God wants to rule our hearts and lives. The new reign of God creates obedient servants who are willing to suffer for the King. We are called, not as spectators but as participants in announcing God's reign to the world.

Joyfully, the new reign of God changes hearts. The King, Jesus, arrives on the scene as Suffering Servant and moves from swaddling clothes in a manger, through an Upper Room foot-washing, to a rough-hewn cross for us and our salvation. Forgiven, we rejoice to participate in the new reign of God.

Prayer: On Jordan's bank the Baptist's cry Announces that the Lord is nigh; Awake and hearken, for he brings Glad tidings of the King of kings!

Shall We Look for Another?

John the Baptist, mighty preacher and announcer of the new reign of God, now lies in prison in danger of execution. He hears word of Jesus' ministry. Plagued with doubts, he sends messengers to Jesus asking the question of our text.

He expected another kind of Christ, one who would bring judgment upon King Herod, the Pharisees, and evildoers. He wonders if his ministry has been in vain. How easily we also expect another kind of Christ. We, too, might prefer more judgment on others—drug dealers, prosperous unbelievers, the irresponsible. We also might expect a sugary, sentimental Christ, a superficial Christmas celebration with a cute little baby. That kind of Christ wouldn't affect our lives or ask for commitment or devotion. When faced with the real Christ, we ask with John, "Are You the One who was to come, or should we expect someone else?" (Matthew 11:3)

God helps us to accept Christ as He is. Jesus replied to John that the Good News was being preached and the blind, deaf, and lame healed—a sure sign that the Messiah had come. Judgment comes to the individual when Christ is rejected, but God wants the world to be saved. This good news of salvation must have reassured John.

The same good news of a crucified and risen Christ comes also to us to heal our hurts and fears. The Messiah has come for us. Forgiven for our judgmental attitudes and our anemic view of a meek and mild Christ, we look to the real Christ and receive power to live bravely for Him.

Prayer: Thus, if we have known him, Not ashamed to own him, Nor have spurned him coldly But will trust him boldly, He will then receive us, Heal us, and forgive us.

Accepting Jesus' Birth Announcement

What a momentous occasion when a wife tells her husband, "I'm expecting a child." The months pass. The child grows within—morning sickness, weight gain, movement inside, discomfort, preparation for the arrival. Then the words, "I think it's time to go to the hospital." The rush to the labor room. Breathtaking, exciting, frightening, joyful waiting. Then the words, "It's a boy!" or "It's a girl!"

Mary got the word from an angelic messenger: "You will be with child and give birth to a son" (Luke 1:31a). Overwhelming news. An unmarried virgin giving birth to a child. Mother of the Messiah. Incomprehensible, frightening news. Yet Mary obeys: "I am the Lord's servant." (Luke 1:38a). And Mary trusts: "May it be to me as you have said." (Luke 1:38b).

We hear the news. Jesus Christ is born in us through Baptism. But what implications! He calls us to service and obedience. We get no credit for this new birth, nor do we control what being a follower of Christ will mean for our life. Will we trust like Mary—"May it be to me as you have said"? Will we obey like Mary—"I am the Lord's servant"? Are we able to accept Jesus' birth announcement in our lives?

Mary had help. "Fear not," she was told. Words like "Holy Spirit," "power of the Most High," and "Son of God" penetrated to her heart with Gospel comfort. God helps us, too, with His Gospel. We can radiate the joy of Mary as we again this Christmas announce the birth of Jesus Christ.

Prayer: *O holy Child of Bethlehem, Descend to us, we pray; Cast out our sin, And enter in, Be born in us today. We hear the Christmas angels, The great glad tidings tell; Oh, come to us, Abide with us, Our Lord Immanuel!*

White Christmas?

The Irving Berlin song and movie with Bing Crosby set the stage for preoccupation with snow for Christmas. Children wait expectantly. Adults watch endless weather reports on television. Choruses of glee greet the snowflakes.

Certainly snow doesn't make Christmas. When the Son of God was born in Bethlehem, no snow fell in the Middle Eastern climate. The miracle lay in the Word becoming flesh at God's right time to bring salvation to a sinful world. A white Christmas, while beautiful and part of God's creation, belongs with Christmas trees and store displays as traditions which may actually detract from the Savior's birth.

Or perhaps our white Christmases treasured from childhood could remind us of Isaiah's words, "Though your sins are like scarlet, they shall be as white as snow" (Isaiah 1:18b). Exposing the blatant sins of Jerusalem, Isaiah also brings the hope and comfort of God for repentant sinners. He reminds them that God forgives the worst of sins and makes them as white and clean as snow through the promised Messiah who will go to a cross to pay for those sins.

There is nothing wrong with a white Christmas, particularly when the snow reminds us of the cleansing power of Jesus' death and resurrection for our sins. Nothing wrong either with a Christmas more barren and brown than white, because the Babe of Bethlehem turned Calvary sufferer still cleanses us from our sins. "Though your sins are like scarlet, they shall be as white as snow."

Prayer: Dear Lord, thank You for making this Christmas white with or without snow through Your forgiveness won on Calvary. Amen.

Green Christmas?

A few years ago, satirist Stan Freburg produced a jarring recording, exposing the commercialization of Christmas. He entitled the record "Green Christmas." A group of advertisers gather to find new angles and pitches for tying their products to Christmas. Bob Cratchet, owner of a small spice company in East Orange, New Jersey, objects and simply wants to send a card with the Wise Men bearing gifts to the Savior. Drowned by their protests, he is offered a medley of Christmas tunes which "Deck the Halls with Advertising," ending with the sound of a cash register ringing three times and coins spilling out on the countertop.

Is your Christmas green? How easily we fall prey to centering our Christmas celebration on gift buying and receiving! How often squabbles develop about the checkbook balance and credit card usage. Television and newspaper advertising and the glittering appeal of attractive displays in shopping malls often seduce us into a Christmas celebration far removed from the Bethlehem manger.

St. Paul in our text points us to the true meaning of Christmas. The eternal Son of God, wealthy beyond imagination, came to earth as a humble baby, in poverty. He grew up to walk the dusty roads of Palestine with nowhere to lay His head, and ended up with all clothing stripped away on a shameful cross. But through His death He offers us forgiveness and the endless treasures of heaven. We don't need a green Christmas. We worship the Babe of Bethlehem, our Savior, and give Him our costliest treasures.

Prayer: *We are rich, for he was poor; Is not this a wonder? Therefore praise God evermore Here on earth and yonder.*

Anger on Trial

Many spectacular murders have filled the media. We gasp at the brutal, premeditated slaughter. But Jesus, while upholding the commandment against murder, probes deeper into the emotions and places anger on trial: "Anyone who is angry with his brother will be subject to judgment" (Matthew 5:22).

How often we have been angry! Sometimes we explode and lash out. Sometimes we maintain outward control but burn inside and find ways to get even. Other times we internalize anger and find ourselves gripped with depression or experiencing peptic ulcers and migraines. But anger affects all of us and too often leads to direct sin against the brother or sister. Who can forget Cain, angry with his brother and ignoring God's warning about sin crouching at his door, murdering his brother?

Recognizing anger as a valid emotion, we nevertheless confess our mishandling of it, leading to sin against brother and sister. We turn to Jesus. Angry at the sin of the Pharisees and money changers in the temple, He nevertheless loves every sinner. He stood trial for our anger and for the world's hatred and murder. He was convicted of our sin and paid the full price on the cross.

Forgiven and free, we rely on His power to manage our anger. We recognize our anger, don't let the sun go down on it (Ephesians 4:26), confess our sin to God and the offended person, and receive His daily forgiveness. God can help us control our anger in constructive ways.

Prayer: Dear Father, forgive us for uncontrolled anger, which harms others and ourselves. Help us to deal with it on the basis of Your Son's death and resurrection. Amen.

The Angel's Message to Joseph

Joseph needed convincing. Mary, his betrothed, was pregnant. Shocking news. God acts unexpectedly—the miraculous birth of the Messiah to a virgin, a poor, humble Galilean girl. Joseph assumed the worst, that Mary had been unfaithful to him. He could not see the uniqueness of this birth nor its cosmic significance. Yes, Joseph needed help.

And so do we. God still acts to carry out His plan for the world in the midst of nuclear armaments, terrorist attacks, school shootings. We tend to think the worst. Obviously someone is at fault! We think of immediate concerns: Christmas preparations, gifts, and eating the next meal. We cannot see God's great plan for the world through Jesus Christ with its Great Commission challenge. Yes, we need help too.

God helps Joseph through an angel appearing in a dream: "Joseph ... do not be afraid to take Mary home as your wife, because what is conceived in her is from the Holy Spirit. She will give birth to a Son, and you are to give Him the name Jesus, because He will save His people from their sins" (Matthew 1:20b–21). Joseph, believing the message, obeys and gladly plays his role in God's saving plan.

God helps us through His powerful Word. As we worship together and immerse ourselves in study of the Bible, God points us to His Son, Jesus, who has saved His people from their sins. Believing God's saving message of the crucified and risen Christ, we take our place in His worldwide plan and live for Him in the midst of a wicked world.

Prayer: Dear Father, open our doubting hearts to Your clarifying message of Jesus the Savior, so that we may participate in Your plan for the world. Amen.

Advent Preparation: Quiet or Haughty?

Christmas is a great festival occasion, the celebration of Christ's birthday, but it often poses a dilemma. On the one hand, we need to get ready for the family celebration, which means crowded stores, gift-buying, and decorating. The Christmas rush. On the other hand, we desire to prepare our hearts for meaningful worship. Advent quiet. How does one reconcile Advent quiet with the Christmas rush?

The psalm contrasts quiet with haughty. Perhaps Advent quiet and the Christmas rush present false alternatives. The question: Are we haughty in both rush and quietness? Haughty when rushing: "I must make sure my family has a nice Christmas. Everything depends on me!" Haughty when quiet: "I will go to all the special services during Advent and Christmas. We will have daily devotions during Advent and religious ornaments on our tree. I will find quiet time with God if it kills me!"

If we can be haughty during Advent either while rushing or seeking quiet, then what does Advent quiet mean? Psalm 131 suggests a quiet dependence on the Lord for everything. Admitting our pride and confessing it, we look outside of ourselves for a solution to the Christmas dilemma. God sent His Son for us, to be fed at His mother's breast. He lived for us and died for us so our sins could be forgiven.

Whether we head for the shopping mall or attend a midweek Advent service, we need to depend on Him. He can then bring His Advent quiet into our rushing and our quiet times. Begone, haughtiness! Enter, quiet dependence on the Babe of Bethlehem!

Prayer: As your coming was in peace, Quiet, full of gentleness, Let the same mind dwell in me Which is yours eternally.

Advent Preparation: Strength in Quietness

Every year we wrestle with Advent preparation because of the Christmas rush. Meanwhile, problems of the world and our personal lives continue. How can we cope?

Judah had problems. The northern kingdom had been destroyed, and Judah was subjugated to the Assyrians. There were opportunities to make alliances with Egypt and Babylon that might allow Judah to throw off the Assyrian yoke. Isaiah warns against such folly.

How often do we seek strength in alliances, military armaments, or new economic proposals! Just around the corner, we think, lies a solution to our problems if we use clever tactics. We even turn to the magic of the Christmas season and hope that our frantic activity will somehow solve our problems. Such folly to rely on our own strength!

Isaiah points to the only solution: strength in quietness. Isaiah told Hezekiah that Assyria would be destroyed by God, and alliances should be shunned. When Sennacherib's army threatened Jerusalem, the angel of the Lord destroyed the army. Trusting quietly in God, Hezekiah saw a marvelous victory.

Repentant, we quietly kneel at the manger and trust God. He used Caesar Augustus' decree to bring about the Savior's birth in Bethlehem, foiled Herod's plot against the infant, and arranged for Jesus to be crucified under Pontius Pilate. Jesus Christ has won the victory over sin and death. He rules the world. In this Advent season the key to world and personal problems lies in the same words of Isaiah, "In quietness and trust is your strength" (Isaiah 30:15).

Prayer: Dear Advent Lord, come to our hearts with Your strength as we wait in quietness. Amen.

The Art of Rejoicing

"Rejoice … always" (Philippians 4:4). Really? How? Rejoice sometimes. That's plausible—on the wedding day, at the birth of a child, because of the new job or the promotion, during the thrilling festival worship service, when a loved one comes to believe in Christ. But rejoice always? Impossible—when the car accident occurs, when the tornado rips through the neighborhood, when divorce shatters a family, when the factory closes its doors, when a teenager runs away from home. Surely Paul doesn't mean what he says!

But Paul's words stand. The whole Letter to the Philippians overflows with rejoicing. Paul writes from prison. He may soon lose his life. He knows he lives in evil times. He realizes there is feuding in the Philippian church. Yet he writes, "Rejoice … always." How? What secret does Paul possess?

He explains, "Rejoice in the Lord always" (Philippians 4:4). He treasures the surpassing greatness of knowing Christ Jesus as his Lord. He knows Christ's servant death and the power of His resurrection. He rejoices that Christ lives in the Philippian Christians as they reach out to him and others. He awaits the return of the Savior, who has already given him citizenship in heaven. He receives strength from Christ to do everything. Paul rejoices in the Lord always.

We, too, can rejoice in the Lord always—in His cross and resurrection power, His presence in the love of the Christian fellowship, His daily strength, His promised return. Deeply rooted in the Gospel, dependent upon Christ's power in every situation, we learn the art of rejoicing in the Lord always.

Prayer: Rejoice, my heart, be glad and sing, A cheerful trust maintain; For God, the source of ev'rything, Your portion shall remain.

Waiting for the Lord

Waiting is not an American virtue. Impatient motorists change lanes to gain a car-length advantage. Shoppers race for the checkout line. Travelers claw for a final seat on a departing plane. Waiting patiently seems to imply weakness, lack of assertiveness. We live impatiently. College graduates want a top-paying job immediately without starting at the bottom. Newlyweds want a fashionable home with all the conveniences. When obstacles arise, we want them removed at once and at any cost.

The psalmist is learning a lesson in patience. He is surrounded by evil men. His enemies attack. False witnesses accuse. Perhaps his own parents forsake him. Certainly these circumstances could describe David on the run from an angry, jealous Saul, in physical danger, fearful for his life. But David also makes a beautiful confession of faith in a God who will keep him safe, permit him to worship in the house of the Lord, and enable him to see the Lord's goodness.

God pierces our impatience with enemies, roadblocks, uncertainties, and failures. He brings us to our knees, helpless and hopeless. Then through David He asks us to wait for Him. But He also bestows what He asks. In the fullness of time after centuries of waiting, God sent His Son to be born of a virgin. Jesus waited for the right time to begin His public ministry. He willingly endured the cross, drinking the cup of suffering. Risen from the dead, Jesus asked the disciples to wait for power from on high. Our fast-paced society only serves as a foil to build patience in our lives.

Prayer: Enter now my waiting heart, Glorious King and Lord most holy.

Not Worthy to Untie His Sandals

"Who are you?" (John 1:22) the messengers from Jerusalem asked John the Baptizer. A rising religious leader, someone to take seriously, he was cut in the mold of the great Old Testament prophets. Who is he: Christ, Elijah, or one of the prophets? Important company.

"Who are you?" today's messengers ask. Apparently our Christian life is showing. We seem to be effective, successful, caring people. An opportunity for witnessing.

Our answer: "A good church member, regular in attendance. Even serve on a board." Pride. Self-righteousness.

John's answer: "I am the voice of one calling in the desert ... I am not worthy to untie [His sandals]" (John 1:27). Pointing to Jesus Christ as everything, John points to himself as nothing. Only slaves did the work of carrying a man's shoes or taking them off his feet. And a Hebrew slave was not even obliged to perform such a menial task. John the Baptizer, therefore, places himself even lower than a slave. Why? He knows himself as a sinner. He knows the Messiah as true God and the Savior of the world. There is no pride in John's answer, only humble dependence on Jesus Christ.

The question again: "Who are you?" Humbled by our pride in the presence of the Christ who took on the form of a servant and became obedient even to death on a cross (Philippians 2:7–8), we answer with John, "I am not worthy to untie [His sandals]." We rejoice that the Lamb makes us worthy by His death to stand before God and to receive His body and blood in Holy Communion, a foretaste of the feast to come. This royal gift empowers us to live as humble servants, pointing to the Christ at Christmastime and throughout the year.

Prayer: Lord, I humbly bow at Your feet. Amen.

Mary's Visit

Mary accepted the angel's word that she would give birth to the Messiah. But as the period of waiting stretched on, God used a visit to Elizabeth as a faith strengthener.

Mary's faith was, first, confirmed by a friend. Suspect in Nazareth for being pregnant out of wedlock, she greatly needed her three-month stay with Elizabeth, who welcomed and affirmed her. We also need our faith confirmed by Christian friends. When faced with problems, we find strength and comfort from Christian friends who listen and understand.

Mary's faith was, second, confirmed by a sign. The baby leaped in Elizabeth's womb. Although a normal occurrence, Elizabeth saw the timing as a definite indication that Mary was to be the mother of the Messiah. While our faith is not based on signs, God often uses events in our lives to confirm His loving care and plan. Again Christian friends help each other.

Mary's faith was, third, confirmed by the Word of God. Elizabeth told her by the Spirit's power that she was blessed and would give birth to the Savior. Mary was strengthened and she rejoiced, praising God with the Magnificat.

We also need to have our faith confirmed by the Word of God—spoken by a friend, preached in a sermon, sung in a hymn, taught in a Bible class. That Word points us to the Christ Child who came to save us from our sins. That Word assures us of God's promises for us.

Mary's visit to Elizabeth strengthened her faith in God's promises. We also are strengthened through the Word of God working in our Christian friends and the events of our lives.

Prayer: Lord Jesus, visit our home with Your love through friends, events, and especially Your saving Word. Amen.

Come to the Manger!

Picture yourself with the shepherds and hear the message of the angel—incredible message of good news. It was far beyond the shepherds' routine and understanding.

What if the shepherds had decided to stay with their flocks? They could have absorbed all of the glory and been dazzled—brilliant light, angel message, angel choirs, a great story to tell their grandchildren. But without a visit to the manger that glorious hillside experience would have been empty.

What if we decide to stay in the Christmas glow? Visions of sugar plums. Warm family times. Christmas Eve services, almost like angel choirs with carols and candlelight. A great story, then a fading memory. Without a visit to the manger that glorious Christmas experience is empty.

But the shepherds did not stay. They said, "Let's go to Bethlehem and see this thing that has happened, which the Lord has told us about" (Luke 2:15). They came with haste and found the babe, their lives were changed. They "spread the word" about what they had seen and "returned, glorifying and praising God" (Luke 2:17, 20). No fading memory, the manger visit continued to motivate them.

The Spirit works in our Christmas celebration so we want to go and see what the Lord has done. We come to the manger and see the Christ Child. Our lives are changed. Through His birth, death, and resurrection Jesus has won salvation for us. Sins forgiven, we spread the Good News and glorify and praise God. No fading memory, the manger visit continues to motivate us for witness, service, and praise. Changed lives change the world, for we have come to the manger!

Prayer: Lord, bring us to Your manger again. Amen.

No Room for Them in the Inn

Last-minute shoppers, pushing to find a place in line for a final purchase. We know the feeling of waiting in line and being passed by someone bolder and pushier.

The holy couple comes to Bethlehem. Mary needs a place to rest and deliver her baby. But Luke tells us "there was no room for them in the inn" (Luke 2:7). Conditions were crowded and accommodations inadequate. No room in the inn for a pregnant woman, for the mother of the Messiah, the Son of God.

The humble birth of the Savior symbolizes His ministry. Mary and Joseph soon had to flee Bethlehem for Egypt. Herod had no room for Him in Israel. When Jesus began His public ministry, He was not welcome in His hometown. In our Bible reading Jesus says that "the Son of Man has no place to lay His head" (Matthew 8:20b). He would even be crucified outside the city walls and be buried in a borrowed tomb.

Is there room for Jesus in our hearts and homes? Sometimes our crowded celebration leaves no room for the Savior who makes Christmas possible. We may give Jesus room in the corner but not at the center of our lives.

Yet God has room for all in His heart and home. He desires all people to be saved. The angel brings good news for all, including common shepherds and foreign Wise Men. Jesus died even for the innkeeper, Herod, and the Roman soldiers. The Word made flesh dwells among us (John 1:14). He who died and rose is truly present in Holy Communion. He welcomes us as His forgiven children. There is room for Him in our hearts and homes, because He has room for us always.

Prayer: Enter now my waiting heart, Glorious King and Lord most holy.

A Shepherd's Tale: Hearing the Good News

Amidst the sights and sounds of Christmas, is the Good News penetrating to your heart? For the next three devotions, remove yourself from the blur of preparations, return to the fields near Bethlehem, and listen to the tale of a shepherd:

"I am a shepherd from the hills of Bethlehem. I have come to tell you about the birth of the Christ Child. Behold, I have seen, and I believe. One evening we were resting by our campfire as we watched the sheep nibble the closely cropped grass of the hillside. Suddenly a great light appeared, and as we cringed in the shadows a radiant figure clothed in white stood before us and said, 'Do not be afraid. I bring you good news of great joy that will be for all the people. Today in the town of David a Savior has been born to you; He is Christ the Lord' (Luke 2:10). And suddenly thousands of other figures clad in white appeared before our eyes and began to sing a beautiful song. The words they sang were unforgettable: 'Glory to God in the highest, and on earth peace to men ...' (Luke 2:14). They were trying to prepare us for a visit to the Baby who was born in Bethlehem."

What an impact on the shepherd! How unexpected the angelic visit and the joyful news of Christ born in the city of David! Does not the shepherd's tale move us to joy and expectation in these days before Christmas? Does not the quiet of the hillside after the angels' visit give pause for a simple focus on the Babe in the manger, our Savior from sin? The shepherd's tale continues tomorrow.

Prayer: Angels we have heard on high, Sweetly singing o'er the plains, And the mountains in reply, Echoing their joyous strains. Gloria in excelsis Deo.

A Shepherd's Tale: Hurrying to the Manger

The tale of the shepherd continues: "That was the most glorious thing I have ever seen. When the angels left the skies, darkness filled the air again. Almost immediately we all said, 'Let's go to Bethlehem and see this thing that has happened' (Luke 2:15). We went as fast as we could and found Mary and Joseph and the Baby just as the angel said we would. I don't think any of us thought much about what would happen to the sheep. We just wanted to hurry to Bethlehem. Preparation? We didn't have time to prepare. God spoke to us, and we wanted to move as fast as we could.

"When we reached Bethlehem, none of us knew what to do or say. We entered quietly and saw the man and the woman and the manger cradling the little Babe. I fumbled for words. I shuffled my feet. Finally, I knelt awkwardly at the manger and gave thanks in my heart for the wonderful Child, the Savior."

How would you describe the unfolding story of your Christmas celebration this year? Dazzled by the angelic glory or overexposed to Christmas glitter? Deeply moved by the Messianic message or exhausted by hectic preparations? Hurrying expectantly to the manger or continually sidetracked by baking and shopping and decorating and partying?

Hear the shepherd's tale. God has come to our world in Christ. This Savior went to the cross to pay for our sins. He lives and will return again. We enter His presence again this Christmas, and His love forgives us, quiets us, and fills us with joy and thanksgiving.

Prayer: Come to Bethlehem and see Him whose birth the angels sing; Come, adore on bended knee Christ the Lord, the newborn king. Gloria in excelsis Deo.

A Shepherd's Tale: Sharing the Savior's Birth

The tale of the shepherd concludes: "I rose and pressed the hands of Mary and Joseph in my own. I felt like a helpless child in the presence of this Child who I knew was the true Son of God. But still I felt perfectly secure and happy in His presence. I left the stable a different person. My friends and I scarcely spoke a word to each other for quite a while. But we shared the same thoughts. We realized that we had seen a great sight and that we had experienced true joy. Then, all of a sudden, we began to talk at the same time. Gradually our words began to fit together into one story, a story of peace, of joy, of love, of the birth of the Son of God.

"We told this story to everyone we met along the way— the local carpenter, the man who sold fresh fish, the beggar on a doorstep, the rich noble with the gold ring and the long robes. Why don't you rejoice with me, my friend, and help me spread the Good News?"

What an agenda for our Christmas celebration! We hear again the angel tidings. We journey with the shepherds to the manger. Transformed by the Christ, we arise to share the Good News with our family and friends, our neighbors, our co-workers. Like the shepherds, we speak only because God has spoken to us in Christ and through His Word empowers us to share with others. And the telling further strengthens us to share more of the Good News.

Thank you, shepherd, for your tale of Christmas tidings. We will help you spread the message.

Prayer: Shepherds, why this jubilee? Why your joyous strains prolong? What the gladsome tidings be Which inspire your heavenly song? Gloria in excelsis Deo.

The Slavery of Christmas

Could Christmas for us at times be a form of slavery? We set up standards to evaluate the success of our celebration—managing to buy just the right gifts for our children, preparing just the right dinner, attending all the church services.

Galatians describes a type of slavery that is close to the heart of the problem. Paul preached the freeing Gospel to the Galatians. Later false teachers came, insisting on again observing Jewish rites. "It's fine to believe in Christ," they said, "but you must also be circumcised as the Law says and obey Sabbath regulations. Then you will be saved."

In the white heat of anger Paul writes against such ideas. He knows that the Galatians are in danger of exchanging their new Gospel freedom for the old slavery of the Law. They are losing Christ.

As Christians we easily become slaves to the Law. Despite the Christmas Gospel we, like the Galatian Christians, tend to put ourselves back under the Law. But, as our text reminds us, the whole purpose of Christmas is to free us from slavery to the Law. Christ became a slave to make us sons and daughters of the King. He was born under the Law, lived in the world as an outcast, and died as a common criminal. This slavery of Christ was the price God paid in order to make us His free children.

God's Spirit can free us from Christmas slavery by reminding us again through the Christmas story that we are free children of God through Christ.

Prayer: *From the bondage that oppressed us, From sin's fetters that possessed us, From the grief that sore distressed us, We, the captives, now are free.*

A Sign: Cloths and a Manger

Signs of Christmas are all around. Santa, silver bells, candlelight, and carols. But the only sign that counts was given to the shepherds in the Judean hills—cloths and a manger.

The shepherds, you see, lived in a rough world with daily hard work and a struggle for survival. There was very little tinsel and glitter in their lives! Yet God came to them with His realistic sign, "You will find a baby wrapped in cloths and lying in a manger" (Luke 2:12). Swaddling cloths—a square of cloth with a long bandagelike strip coming diagonally off from one corner. The Child was first wrapped in the square and then the long strip was wound round and round about Him. Manger—smelly feed trough for animals. What a sign! The Messiah was born in a down-to-earth place of humble origin, very much in the real world. The wood of the manger prefigured the wood of the cross on which Jesus was to die for real sins. Strengthened by their visit to the manger, the shepherds returned to their real world to live for Jesus.

We also live in a rough, wicked world filled with major problems, drudgery, hard work, and sins. To us also comes God's enduring sign—swaddling cloths and a manger. The manger lies in the shadow of the cross. God's Son joined Himself to our flesh, lived and died in our real world, and triumphed over death and sin. Like the shepherds, we kneel at the manger, receive strength from the Lord, and return to our real world to serve Him and those in need.

Prayer: To you in David's town this day Is born of David's line A Savior, who is Christ the Lord; And this shall be the sign: The heav'nly Babe you there shall find To human view displayed, All meanly wrapped in swaddling clothes And in a manger laid.

Why a Partridge in a Pear Tree?

"Four calling birds, three French hens, two turtle doves, and a partridge in a pear tree." The 12 days of Christmas. Who observes them anymore? December 25 ends the celebration. Everyone returns to work and begins thinking about the New Year's Eve party. Decorations are taken down. The live tree, already brittle after three weeks in the house, is consigned to the garbage heap. Gifts are put away.

This somewhat somber dismantling may be delayed for two or three days, or perhaps (for some faithful souls) until January 6 when we celebrate Epiphany and the journey of the Magi to Bethlehem. The 12 days of Christmas provide us opportunity to continue celebrating the Savior's birth. Still fresh are the visit to the manger, the message of the angels to the shepherds, the joy of Mary and Joseph. After weeks of Advent preparation with repentance and hopeful anticipation, the church bursts forth in a sustained chorus of praise that is just getting started on Christmas Day.

Whether or not we formally celebrate Christmas for 12 days, or how long the Christmas tree remains decorated, does not really matter. But the idea of celebrating Christmas continually has considerable merit. One thing is certain: The joy of Christmas continues; the angel songs continue to ring out in our world. Jesus is right beside us on the job, on the highway, in our home. He offers forgiveness, strength, and joy.

Yes, we can sustain the joy of Christmas, even without leaping lords, waiting ladies, golden rings, and a partridge in a pear tree.

Prayer: Dear Lord, help me to continue celebrating Your saving presence. Amen.

The Ironies of Christmas

A baby born—Jesus the Savior of the world! Angel messages, running shepherds, adoring Wise Men, and a jealous, furious, vindictive King Herod. There are many ironies about Christmas.

One year on Christmas Eve, vandals stole a plaque and wreath from the door of a Midwestern church. The plaque, a gift from the daughter of the former pastor, pictured the three Wise Men bearing gifts to the Savior. Ironic.

But are there not also ironies in your own home during the Christmas season? Children squabble about who gets to use the new toys. Tempers flare about picking up the discarded wrapping paper. These little irritations are ironies because they don't seem to fit a season of peace and goodwill.

These examples are reflections of worldwide evil. Nothing really changes much over the holidays. Nations that hated our country still hate it. Politicians still undercut one another. Crime continues. In the face of these ironies, should we abandon the celebration of Christmas next year?

No, indeed. The presence of evil explains why God chose to send His Son in the first place. Only the birth, death, and resurrection of Jesus Christ could bring forgiveness into a fractured and broken world. And the message of Christmas takes on deeper meaning against the background of a stolen church plaque, squabbles over Christmas toys, and global bitterness and hatred. This year once again we perceive a real need for God's Son. And God continues to love us in Christ.

Prayer: Oh, the joy beyond expressing When by faith we grasp this blessing And to you we come confessing Your great love has set us free.

Simeon's Christmas

How did your Christmas celebration go? St. Luke helps us evaluate by describing Simeon's Christmas—his preparation, his perception of the Christ Child, and his praise.

Simeon was prepared for the Messiah's birth. He was righteous, righteous in God's eyes by faith. He was devout, that is, conscientious about his worship. "He was waiting for the consolation of Israel" (Luke 2:25b), even though many years had passed since God's original promise.

Our preparation, as we know only too well, usually leaves much to be desired. May God help us learn from Simeon!

Simeon's perception of the Christ Child was shaped by his patience. The Spirit revealed that he would not die before seeing the Christ. Led into the temple when Mary and Joseph arrived, Simeon, recognized Jesus as the Messiah. Later Simeon described Jesus to the parents as "a light for ... the Gentiles" (Luke 2:32) and "a sign that will be spoken against" (Luke 2:34). He perceived Jesus both as the Savior of the world and as the Messiah who would have to suffer and die.

How clear is our perception of the Christ Child? So often we don't see Him as the Savior, but as a sentimental child, not as the One who was crucified for our sins.

Simeon's praise filled the temple. Based on God's faithfulness to His promise of the Messiah, Simeon overflowed with witness to Him.

How was our praise for the Christ Child this Christmas? Despite our poor preparation and narrow perceptions. God remains faithful to us. Christ's forgiveness, won on the cross, helps us to praise Him fervently.

Prayer: Dear Father, help us learn much from Simeon. Amen.

Purified for Love

Another year draws to a close. Time for reflection on the old year and anticipation of the new year. Think of our reading with the theme: *Purified for love.*

The verse gives the standard: "Love one another deeply, from the heart" (1 Peter 1:22). Love is described as "sincere" and as "deep." Has your love held steady or fluctuated erratically during the past year? Think of your relationships at home, on the job, in church, in your social contacts. I fear that my "love thermometer" registers lovelessness, inconstancy, selfishness.

Enter God's purifying process for the new year. We are purified by the blood of Christ (1 Peter 1:18–19). He came as the Father's love incarnate. He consistently loved friends and enemies alike, even to His death on a cross for us. His "love thermometer" registers warmth, sincerity, and depth at all times. He purifies us in our Baptism. That process continues in our lives as new creatures. His Word cleanses us. The Holy Meal cleanses us. He then purifies us in our obedience to the truth through trials and suffering (1 Peter 1:3–7). In short, God, who forgives our lovelessness of the past year, promises to purify us for love in the new year as we look to His loving Son.

Prayer: Love divine, all love excelling, Joy of heav'n, to earth come down! Fix in us thy humble dwelling, All thy faithful mercies crown. Jesus, thou art all compassion, Pure, unbounded love thou art; Visit us with thy salvation, Enter ev'ry trembling heart.